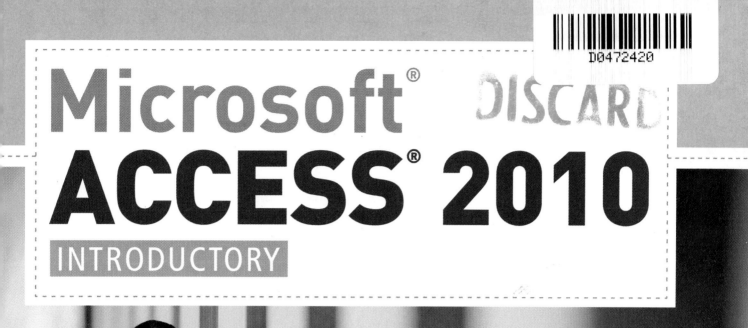

Microsoft® ACCESS® 2010
INTRODUCTORY

Gary B. Shelly
Philip J. Pratt
Mary Z. Last

COURSE TECHNOLOGY
CENGAGE Learning™

Australia • Brazil • Japan • Korea • Mexico • Singapore • Spain • United Kingdom • United States

SHELLY CASHMAN SERIES®

COURSE TECHNOLOGY
CENGAGE Learning™

Microsoft® Access® 2010: Introductory
Gary B. Shelly, Philip J. Pratt, Mary Z. Last

Vice President, Publisher: Nicole Pinard

Executive Editor: Kathleen McMahon

Product Manager: Jon Farnham

Associate Product Manager: Aimee Poirier

Editorial Assistant: Lauren Brody

Director of Marketing: Cheryl Costantini

Marketing Manager: Tristen Kendall

Marketing Coordinator: Stacey Leasca

Print Buyer: Julio Esperas

Director of Production: Patty Stephan

Content Project Manager: Jennifer Feltri

Development Editor: Amanda Brodkin

Copyeditor: Troy Lilly

Proofreader: Karen Annett

Indexer: Rich Carlson

QA Manuscript Reviewers: Chris Scriver,
  John Freitas, Serge Palladino, Susan Pedicini,
  Danielle Shaw

Art Director: Marissa Falco

Cover Designer: Lisa Kuhn, Curio Press, LLC

Cover Photo: Tom Kates Photography

Text Design: Joel Sadagursky

Compositor: PreMediaGlobal

For product information and technology assistance, contact us at
Cengage Learning Customer & Sales Support, 1-800-354-9706

For permission to use material from this text or product,
submit all requests online at **cengage.com/permissions**
Further permissions questions can be emailed to
permissionrequest@cengage.com

Library of Congress Control Number: 2010929407

ISBN-13: 978-1-4390-7847-1

ISBN-10: 1-4390-7847-5

Course Technology
20 Channel Center Street
Boston, MA 02210
USA

Cengage Learning is a leading provider of customized learning solutions with office locations around the globe, including Singapore, the United Kingdom, Australia, Mexico, Brazil, and Japan. Locate your local office at:
international.cengage.com/region

Cengage Learning products are represented in Canada by Nelson Education, Ltd.

Visit our Web site **www.cengage.com/ct/shellycashman** to share and gain ideas on our textbooks!

To learn more about Course Technology,
visit **www.cengage.com/coursetechnology**

Purchase any of our products at your local college bookstore or at our preferred online store at **www.cengagebrain.com**

We dedicate this book to the memory of James S. Quasney (1940 – 2009), who for 18 years co-authored numerous books with Tom Cashman and Gary Shelly and provided extraordinary leadership to the Shelly Cashman Series editorial team. As series editor, Jim skillfully coordinated, organized, and managed the many aspects of our editorial development processes and provided unending direction, guidance, inspiration, support, and advice to the Shelly Cashman Series authors and support team members. He was a trusted, dependable, loyal, and well-respected leader, mentor, and friend. We are forever grateful to Jim for his faithful devotion to our team and eternal contributions to our series.

The Shelly Cashman Series Team

Printed in the United States of America
1 2 3 4 5 6 7 13 12 11 10

Microsoft ACCESS® 2010 INTRODUCTORY

Contents

Microsoft Office 2010 and Windows 7

Microsoft **Access 2010**

CHAPTER ONE
Databases and Database Objects:
An Introduction

CHAPTER TWO
Querying a Database

Appendices

Preface

The Shelly Cashman Series® offers the finest textbooks in computer education. We are proud that since Mircosoft Office 4.3, our series of Microsoft Office textbooks have been the most widely used books in education. With each new edition of our Office books, we make significant improvements based on the software and comments made by instructors and students. For this Microsoft Access 2010 text, the Shelly Cashman Series development team carefully reviewed our pedagogy and analyzed its effectiveness in teaching today's Office student. Students today read less, but need to retain more. They need not only to be able to perform skills, but to retain those skills and know how to apply them to different settings. Today's students need to be continually engaged and challenged to retain what they're learning.

With this Microsoft Access 2010 text, we continue our commitment to focusing on the user and how they learn best.

Objectives of This Textbook

Microsoft Access 2010: Introductory is intended for a first course on Access 2010. No experience with a computer is assumed, and no mathematics beyond the high school freshman level is required. The objectives of this book are:

- To offer an introduction to Microsoft Access 2010

- To expose students to practical examples of the computer as a useful tool

- To acquaint students with the proper procedures to create databases suitable for coursework, professional purposes, and personal use

- To help students discover the underlying functionality of Access 2010 so they can become more productive

- To develop an exercise-oriented approach that allows learning by doing

New to This Edition

Microsoft Access 2010: Introductory offers a number of new features and approaches, which improve student understanding, retention, transference, and skill in using Access 2010. The following enhancements will enrich the learning experience:

- Office 2010 and Windows 7: Essential Concepts and Skills chapter presents basic Office 2010 and Windows 7 skills.

- Streamlined first chapter allows the ability to cover more advanced skills earlier.

- Chapter topic redistribution offers concise chapters that ensure complete skill coverage.

- New pedagogical elements enrich material creating an accessible and user-friendly approach.

  - Break Points, a new boxed element, identify logical stopping points and give students instructions regarding what they should do before taking a break.

  - Within step instructions, Tab | Group Identifiers, such as (Home tab | Bold button), help students more easily locate elements in the groups and on the tabs on the Ribbon.

  - Modified step-by-step instructions tell the student what to do and provide the generic reason why they are completing a specific task, which helps students easily transfer given skills to different settings.

The Shelly Cashman Approach

A Proven Pedagogy with an Emphasis on Project Planning

Each chapter presents a practical problem to be solved, within a project planning framework. The project orientation is strengthened by the use of Plan Ahead boxes, which encourage critical thinking about how to proceed at various points in the project. Step-by-step instructions with supporting screens guide students through the steps. Instructional steps are supported by the Q&A, Experimental Step, and BTW features.

A Visually Engaging Book that Maintains Student Interest

The step-by-step tasks, with supporting figures, provide a rich visual experience for the student. Call-outs on the screens that present both explanatory and navigational information provide students with information they need when they need to know it.

Supporting Reference Materials (Appendices and Quick Reference)

The appendices provide additional information about the Application at hand and include such topics as project planning guidelines and certification. With the Quick Reference, students can quickly look up information about a single task, such as keyboard shortcuts, and find page references of where in the book the task is illustrated.

Integration of the World Wide Web

The World Wide Web is integrated into the Access 2010 learning experience by (1) BTW annotations; (2) BTW, Q&A, and Quick Reference Summary Web pages; and (3) the Learn It Online section for each chapter.

End-of-Chapter Student Activities
Extensive end-of-chapter activities provide a variety of reinforcement opportunities for students where they can apply and expand their skills.

Instructor Resources

The Instructor Resources include both teaching and testing aids and can be accessed via CD-ROM or at www.cengage.com/login.

Instructor's Manual Includes lecture notes summarizing the chapter sections, figures and boxed elements found in every chapter, teacher tips, classroom activities, lab activities, and quick quizzes in Microsoft Word files.

Syllabus Easily customizable sample syllabi that cover policies, assignments, exams, and other course information.

Figure Files Illustrations for every figure in the textbook in electronic form.

BOOK RESOURCES
Blackboard Testbank
Instructor's Manual
Lecture Success System
PowerPoint Presentations
Solutions to Exercises (Windows)
Syllabus
Test Bank and Test Engine
WebCT Testbank

PowerPoint Presentations A multimedia lecture presentation system that provides slides for each chapter. Presentations are based on chapter objectives.

Solutions To Exercises Includes solutions for all end-of-chapter and chapter reinforcement exercises.

Test Bank & Test Engine Test Banks include 112 questions for every chapter, featuring objective-based and critical thinking question types, and including page number references and figure references, when appropriate. Also included is the test engine, ExamView, the ultimate tool for your objective-based testing needs.

Data Files For Students Includes all the files that are required by students to complete the exercises.

Additional Activities For Students Consists of Chapter Reinforcement Exercises, which are true/false, multiple-choice, and short answer questions that help students gain confidence in the material learned.

SAM: Skills Assessment Manager

SAM 2010 is designed to help bring students from the classroom to the real world. It allows students to train on and test important computer skills in an active, hands-on environment.

SAM's easy-to-use system includes powerful interactive exams, training, and projects on the most commonly used Microsoft Office applications. SAM simulates the Microsoft Office 2010 application environment, allowing students to demonstrate their knowledge and think through the skills by performing real-world tasks such as bolding word text or setting up slide transitions. Add in live-in-the-application projects, and students are on their way to truly learning and applying skills to business-centric documents.

Designed to be used with the Shelly Cashman Series, SAM includes handy page references so that students can print helpful study guides that match the Shelly Cashman textbooks used in class. For instructors, SAM also includes robust scheduling and reporting features.

Content for Online Learning

Course Technology has partnered with the leading distance learning solution providers and class-management platforms today. To access this material, instructors will visit our password-protected instructor resources available at www.cengage.com/coursetechnology. Instructor resources include the following: additional case projects, sample syllabi, PowerPoint presentations per chapter, and more. For additional information or for an instructor user name and password, please contact your sales representative. For students to access this material, they must have purchased a WebTutor PIN-code specific to this title and your campus platform. The resources for students may include (based on instructor preferences), but are not limited to: topic review, review questions, and practice tests.

CourseNotes

Course Technology's CourseNotes are six-panel quick reference cards that reinforce the most important and widely used features of a software application in a visual and user-

course|notes™
quick reference guide

friendly format. CourseNotes serve as a great reference tool during and after the student completes the course. CourseNotes are available for software applications such as Microsoft Office 2010, Word 2010, Excel 2010, Access 2010, PowerPoint 2010, and Windows 7. Topic-based CourseNotes are available for Best Practices in Social Networking, Hot Topics in Technology, and Web 2.0. Visit www.cengage.com/ct/coursenotes to learn more!

A GuidedTour

Add excitement and interactivity to your classroom with "*A Guided Tour*" product line. Play one of the brief mini-movies to spice up your lecture and spark classroom discussion. Or, assign a movie for homework and ask students to complete the correlated assignment that accompanies each topic. "*A Guided Tour*" product line takes the prep work out of providing your students with information about new technologies and applications and helps keep students engaged with content relevant to their lives; all in under an hour!

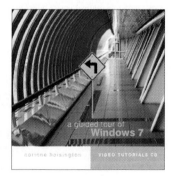

About Our Covers

The Shelly Cashman Series is continually updating our approach and content to reflect the way today's students learn and experience new technology. This focus on student success is reflected on our covers, which feature real students from the University of Rhode Island using the Shelly Cashman Series in their courses, and reflect the varied ages and backgrounds of the students learning with our books. When you use the Shelly Cashman Series, you can be assured that you are learning computer skills using the most effective courseware available.

Textbook Walk-Through

The Shelly Cashman Series Pedagogy: Project-Based — Step-by-Step — Variety of Assessments

Plan Ahead boxes prepare students to create successful projects by encouraging them to think strategically about what they are trying to accomplish before they begin working.

Step-by-step instructions now provide a context beyond the point-and-click. Each step provides information on why students are performing each task, or what will occur as a result.

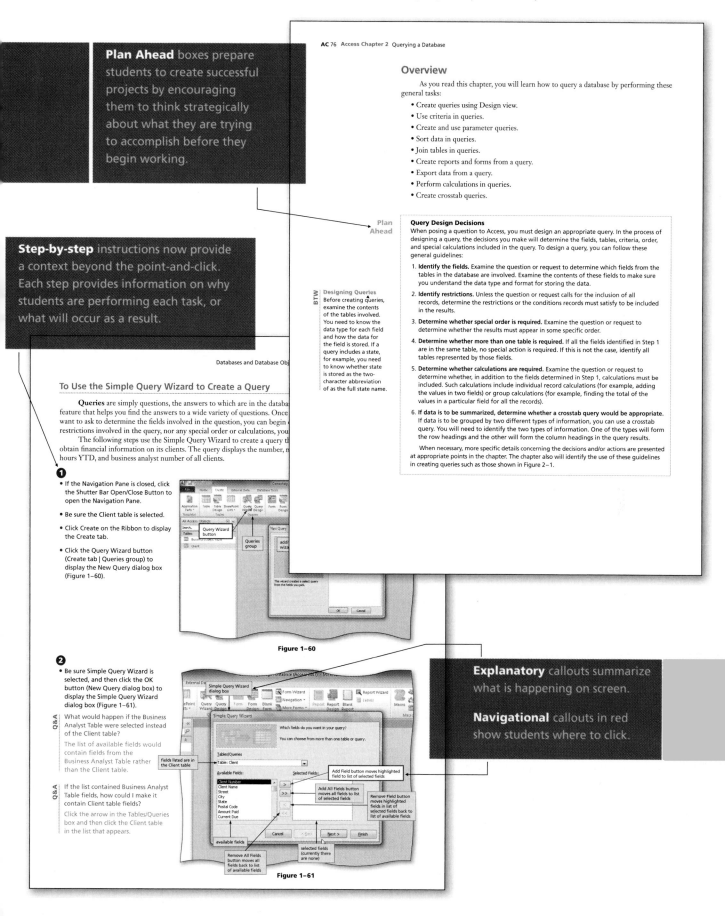

Overview

As you read this chapter, you will learn how to query a database by performing these general tasks:

- Create queries using Design view.
- Use criteria in queries.
- Create and use parameter queries.
- Sort data in queries.
- Join tables in queries.
- Create reports and forms from a query.
- Export data from a query.
- Perform calculations in queries.
- Create crosstab queries.

Plan Ahead

Query Design Decisions

When posing a question to Access, you must design an appropriate query. In the process of designing a query, the decisions you make will determine the fields, tables, criteria, order, and special calculations included in the query. To design a query, you can follow these general guidelines:

1. **Identify the fields.** Examine the question or request to determine which fields from the tables in the database are involved. Examine the contents of these fields to make sure you understand the data type and format for storing the data.

2. **Identify restrictions.** Unless the question or request calls for the inclusion of all records, determine the restrictions or the conditions records must satisfy to be included in the results.

3. **Determine whether special order is required.** Examine the question or request to determine whether the results must appear in some specific order.

4. **Determine whether more than one table is required.** If all the fields identified in Step 1 are in the same table, no special action is required. If this is not the case, identify all tables represented by those fields.

5. **Determine whether calculations are required.** Examine the question or request to determine whether, in addition to the fields determined in Step 1, calculations must be included. Such calculations include individual record calculations (for example, adding the values in two fields) or group calculations (for example, finding the total of the values in a particular field for all the records).

6. **If data is to be summarized, determine whether a crosstab query would be appropriate.** If data is to be grouped by two different types of information, you can use a crosstab query. You will need to identify the two types of information. One of the types will form the row headings and the other will form the column headings in the query results.

When necessary, more specific details concerning the decisions and/or actions are presented at appropriate points in the chapter. The chapter also will identify the use of these guidelines in creating queries such as those shown in Figure 2–1.

BTW

Designing Queries
Before creating queries, examine the contents of the tables involved. You need to know the data type for each field and how the data for the field is stored. If a query includes a state, for example, you need to know whether state is stored as the two-character abbreviation of as the full state name.

Databases and Database Obj

To Use the Simple Query Wizard to Create a Query

Queries are simply questions, the answers to which are in the databa[...] feature that helps you find the answers to a wide variety of questions. Once [...] want to ask to determine the fields involved in the question, you can begin [...] restrictions involved in the query, nor any special order or calculations, you [...]

The following steps use the Simple Query Wizard to create a query t[...] obtain financial information on its clients. The query displays the number, n[...] hours YTD, and business analyst number of all clients.

❶
- If the Navigation Pane is closed, click the Shutter Bar Open/Close Button to open the Navigation Pane.
- Be sure the Client table is selected.
- Click Create on the Ribbon to display the Create tab.
- Click the Query Wizard button (Create tab | Queries group) to display the New Query dialog box (Figure 1–60).

Query Wizard button

Queries group

Figure 1–60

❷
- Be sure Simple Query Wizard is selected, and then click the OK button (New Query dialog box) to display the Simple Query Wizard dialog box (Figure 1–61).

Q&A
What would happen if the Business Analyst Table were selected instead of the Client table?

The list of available fields would contain fields from the Business Analyst Table rather than the Client table.

Q&A
If the list contained Business Analyst Table fields, how could I make it contain Client table fields?

Click the arrow in the Tables/Queries box and then click the Client table in the list that appears.

Explanatory callouts summarize what is happening on screen.

Navigational callouts in red show students where to click.

Simple Query Wizard dialog box

Which fields do you want in your query?

You can choose from more than one table or query.

Tables/Queries

Table: Client

fields listed are in the Client table

Available Fields:

Client Number
Client Name
Street
City
State
Postal Code
Amount Paid
Current Due

Selected Fields:

Add Field button moves highlighted field to list of selected fields

Add All Fields button moves all fields to list of selected fields

Remove Field button moves highlighted fields in list of selected fields back to list of available fields

available fields

selected fields (currently there are none)

Remove All Fields button moves all fields back to list of available fields

Figure 1–61

Textbook Walk-Through

Q&A boxes offer questions students may have when working through the steps and provide additional information about what they are doing right where they need it.

Experiment Steps within our step-by-step instructions, encourage students to explore, experiment, and take advantage of the features of the Access 2010 user interface. These steps are not necessary to complete the projects, but are designed to increase the confidence with the software and build problem-solving skills.

6
- Click the Next button to move to the next Import Spreadsheet Wizard screen (Figure 1–57).

Q&A What happens if I later realize I have selected the wrong table?

If you have not yet clicked the Finish button, you can click the Back button to return to the screen where you selected the table, and then select the correct table.

name of table that will receive the records

Finish button

Figure 1–57

7
- Because the table name is correct, click the Finish button to import the data (Figure 1–58).

Q&A I got an error message that stated that a particular field did not exist in the Client

message indicates that the import process is complete

Close button

Figure 1–58

5
- Press the TAB key to complete the entry for the field.
- Type **3 4 5 0** in the Incentive YTD field, and then press the TAB key to complete the entry of the first record (Figure 1–25).

Q&A How and when do I save the record?

As soon as you have entered or modified a record and moved to another record, the original record is saved. This is different from other applications. The rows entered in an Excel worksheet, for example, are not saved until the entire worksheet is saved.

Business Analyst Number field selected

position to enter business analyst number on second record

first record entered and saved

currently positioned on record 2 out of 2

Figure 1–25

6
- Use the techniques shown in Steps 3 through 5 to enter the data for the second record (Figure 1–26).

Experiment
- Click the Salary YTD field on either of the records. Be sure the Table Tools Fields tab is selected. Click the Format box arrow and then click each of the formats in the Format box menu to see the effect on the values in the Salary YTD field. When finished, click Currency in the Format box menu.

record selector

second record entered and saved

Close button for Business Analyst Table

Figure 1–26

Other Ways
1. Right-click table in Navigation Pane, click Import on shortcut menu.

Making Changes to the Data

As you enter data, check your entries carefully to ensure they are correct. If you make a mistake and discover it before you press the TAB key, correct it by pressing the BACKSPACE key until the incorrect characters are removed, and then type the correct characters. If you do not discover a mistake until later, you can use the following techniques to make the necessary corrections to the data:

- To undo your most recent change, click the Undo button on the Quick Access Toolbar. If there is nothing that Access can undo, this button will be dimmed, and clicking it will have no effect.
- To add a record, click the New (blank) record button, click the position for the Business Analyst Number field on the first open record, and then add the record. Do not worry about it being in the correct position in the table. Access will reposition the record based on the primary key, in this case, the Business Analyst Number.

BTW
Adding Records
You can add records in any order. When you close a table and re-open it, the records will be in order by primary key.

Break Points identify logical breaks in the chapter if students need to stop before completing the project.

Break Point: If you wish to take a break, this is a good place to do so. You can quit Access now. To resume at a later time, start Access, open the database called Camashaly Design, and continue following the steps from this location forward.

Creating and Printing Reports

Camashaly Design wants to create the Client Financial Report shown in

Chapter Summary

Chapter Summary A concluding paragraph, followed by a listing of the tasks completed within a chapter together with the pages on which the step-by-step, screen-by-screen explanations appear.

In this chapter you have learned to design a database, create an Access database, create tables and add records to them, print the contents of tables, create queries, create forms, and create reports. You also have learned how to change database properties. The items listed below include all the new Access skills you have learned in this chapter.

1. Start Access (AC 12)
2. Create a Database (AC 13)
3. Create a Database Using a Template (AC 14)
4. Modify the Primary Key (AC 16)
5. Define the Remaining Fields in a Table (AC 19)
6. Save a Table (AC 21)
7. View the Table in Design View (AC 21)
8. Close the Table (AC 23)
9. Add Records to a Table (AC 23)
10. Quit Access (AC 26)
11. Open a Database from Access (AC 27)
12. Add Additional Records to a Table (AC 28)
13. Resize Columns in a Datasheet (AC 29)
14. Preview and Print the Contents of a Table (AC 31)
15. Create a Table in Design View (AC 33)
16. Import an Excel Worksheet (AC 38)
17. Use the Simple Query Wizard to Create a Query (AC 43)
18. Use a Criterion in a Query (AC 46)
19. Print the Results of a Query (AC 48)
20. Create a Form (AC 48)
21. Create a Report (AC 52)
22. Modify Column Headings and Resize Columns (AC 54)
23. Add Totals to a Report (AC 57)
24. Change Database Properties (AC 59)
25. Back Up a Database (AC 61)
26. Compact and Repair a Database (AC 61)
27. Open Another Database (AC 62)
28. Close a Database without Exiting Access (AC 62)
29. Save a Database with Another Name (AC 62)
30. Delete a Table or Other Object in the Database (AC 62)
31. Rename an Object in the Database (AC 62)

If you have a SAM 2010 user profile, your instructor may have assigned an autogradable version of this assignment. If so, log into the SAM 2010 Web site at www.cengage.com/sam2010 to download the instruction and start files.

Learn It Online

Learn It Online Every chapter features a Learn It Online section that is comprised of six exercises. These exercises include True/False, Multiple Choice, Short Answer, Flash Cards, Practice Test, and Learning Games.

Test your knowledge of chapter content and key terms.

Instructions: To complete the Learn It Online exercises, start your browser, click the Address bar, and then enter the Web address **scsite.com/ac2010/learn**. When the Access 2010 Learn It Online page is displayed, click the link for the exercise you want to complete and then read the instructions.

Chapter Reinforcement TF, MC, and SA
A series of true/false, multiple choice, and short answer questions that test your knowledge of the chapter content.

Flash Cards
An interactive learning environment where you identify chapter key terms associated with displayed definitions.

Who Wants To Be a Computer Genius?
An interactive game that challenges your knowledge of chapter content in the style of a television quiz show.

Wheel of Terms
An interactive game that challenges your knowledge of chapter key terms in the style of the television show *Wheel of Fortune*.

Crossword Puzzle Challenge
A crossword puzzle that challenges your knowledge of key terms presented in the chapter.

Apply Your Knowledge

Reinforce the skills and apply the concepts you learned in this chapter.

Adding a Caption, Creating a Query, Creating a Form, and Creating a Report
Instructions: Start Access. Open the Babbage CPA Firm database. See the inside back cover of this book for instructions for downloading the Data Files for Students, or see your instructor for information on accessing the files required in this book.

The Babbage CPA Firm employs bookkeepers who maintain the books for those clients who need bookkeeping services. The Babbage CPA Firm has a database that keeps track of its bookkeepers and clients. Each client is assigned to a single bookkeeper, but each bookkeeper may be assigned many clients. The database has two tables. The Client table contains data on the clients who use the bookkeeping services of the Babbage CPA Firm. The Bookkeeper table contains data on the bookkeepers employed by Babbage CPA Firm.

Perform the following tasks:
1. Open the Bookkeeper table in Design view and add BKR # as the caption for Bookkeeper Number. Save the changes to the table.
2. Open the Bookkeeper table in Datasheet view and resize all columns to best fit the data. Save the changes to the layout of the table.
3. Use the Simple Query Wizard to create a query for the Client table that contains the Client Number, Client Name, Amount Paid, and Balance Due. Use the name, Client Query, for the query.
4. Create a simple form for the Bookkeeper table. Use the name, Bookkeeper, for the form.
5. Close the Bookkeeper form.

Apply Your Knowledge This exercise usually requires students to open and manipulate a file from the Data Files that parallels the activities learned in the chapter. To obtain a copy of the Data Files for Students, follow the instructions on the inside back cover of this text.

Textbook Walk-Through

Extend Your Knowledge

Extend the skills you learned in this chapter and experiment with new skills. You may need to use Help to complete the assignment.

Using a Database Template to Create a Students Database

Instructions: Access includes a number of templates that you can use to create a beginning database that can be modified to meet your specific needs. You will create a Students database using the Students template. The database includes sample tables, queries, forms, and reports. You will change the database and create the Student Birthdays Query, shown in Figure 1–91.

Figure 1–91

Perform the following tasks:
1. Start Access.
2. With a USB flash drive connected to one of the computer's USB po[...] selected in the Backstage view and select Sample templates in the N[...]
3. Select the Students template and create a new database on your USB d[...]
4. Close the Student List form and change the organization of the Nav[...] Related Views .
5. Delete the Student Details form.
6. Use the Query Wizard to create the query shown in Figure 1–91. S[...] Birthdays Query.
7. Open the Student Phone List in Layout view and use the tools on th[...] Student Phone List title bold and change the font size to 24. Delete [...]
8. Save your changes to the report.
9. Compact the database.
10. Change the database properties, as specified by your instructor. Sub[...] format specified by your instructor.

Extend Your Knowledge projects at the end of each chapter allow students to extend and expand on the skills learned within the chapter. Students use critical thinking to experiment with new skills to complete each project.

Make It Right projects call on students to analyze a file, discover errors in it, and fix them using the skills they learned in the chapter.

Make It Right

Analyze a database and correct all errors and/or improve the design.

Correcting Errors in the Table Structure

Instructions: Start Access. Open the Beach Rentals database. See the inside back cover of this book for instructions for downloading the Data Files for Students, or see your instructor for information on accessing the files required in this book.

Beach Rentals is a database containing information on rental properties available at a beach resort. The Rentals table shown in Figure 1–92 contains a number of errors in the table structure. You are to correct these errors before any additional records can be added to the table. The Rental Code field is a Text field that contains a maximum of three characters. The field Address was omitted from the table. The Address field is a Text field with a maximum of 20 characters. It should appear after Rental Code. Only whole numbers should be allowed in the Bedrooms and Bathrooms fields. The column heading Weakly Rental is misspelled, and the field should contain monetary values. The Distance field represents the walking distance from the beach; the field should display two decimal places. The table name should be Rental Units, not Rentals.

Change the database properties, as specified by your instructor. Submit the revised database in the format specified by your instructor.

Figure 1–92

In the Lab

Design, create, modify, and/or use a database using the guidelines, concepts, and skills presented in this chapter. Labs are listed in order of increasing difficulty.

Lab 1: Creating Objects for the ECO Clothesline Database

Problem: ECO Clothesline is a local company that designs and manufactures eco-friendly casual wear, yoga clothing, and fitness apparel. All clothes are made from earth-friendly fabrics, such as bamboo, hemp, organic cotton, and natural silk. The company recently decided to store its customer and sales rep data in a database. Each customer is assigned to a single sales rep, but each sales rep may be assigned many customers. The database and the Customer table have been created, but there is no data in the Customer table. The Sales Rep table has not been created. The company plans to import the Customer data from an Excel workbook, shown in Figure 1–93a. The other Excel workbook (Figure 1–93b) contains information on the sales representatives that ECO employs. ECO would like to finish storing this data in a database and has asked for your help.

Instructions: Perform the following tasks: Start Access and open the ECO Clothesline database. See the inside back cover of this book for instructions for downloading the Data Files for Students, or see your instructor for information on accessing the files required in this book.
1. Import the Lab 1-1 Customer Data workbook into the Customer table.
2. Add the captions Cust # to the Customer Number field and SR # to the Sales Rep Number field in the Customer table and save the changes.
3. Open the Customer table in Datasheet view and resize the columns to best fit the data. Save the changes to the layout of the table.
4. Use Datasheet view to create a table in which to store the data related to sales reps. Use the name Sales Rep for the table. The fields and the data for the Sales Rep table are shown in Figure 1–93b.

In the Lab

Lab 2: Creating the Walburg Energy Alternatives Database

Problem: Walburg Energy Alternatives is a nonprofit organization that promotes the use of energy alternatives such as solar power and wind power. The organization provides a variety of services and funds itself through donations. Recently, the organization decided to sell a small number of items in its education center to help fund programs. The store purchases the items from vendors that deal in energy-saving products. Currently, the information about the items and vendors is stored in the Excel workbook shown in Figure 1–95. Each item is assigned to a single vendor, but each vendor may be assigned many items. You volunteer part-time at the store, and the store manager has asked you to create a database that will store the item and vendor information. You have already determined that you need two tables in which to store the information: an Item table and a Vendor table.

Instructions: Perform the following tasks:

1. Design a new database in which to store all the objects related to the items for sale. Call the database Walburg Energy Alternatives.

2. Use the information shown in the Excel workbook in Figure 1–95 to determine the primary keys and determine additional fields. Then, determine the relationships between tables, the data types, and the field sizes.

3. Create the Item table using the information shown in Figure 1–95.

4. Create the Vendor table using the information shown in Figure 1–95. Be sure that the field size for the Vendor Code in the Item table is identical to the field size for the Vendor Code in the Vendor table. Add the caption, Phone, for the Telephone Number field.

Figure 1–95

In the Lab Three all new in-depth assignments per chapter require students to utilize the chapter concepts and techniques to solve problems on a computer.

Cases and Places

Apply your creative thinking and problem solving skills to design and implement a solution.

See the inside back cover of this book for instructions for downloading the Data Files for Students, or see your instructor for information on accessing the files required in this book.

1: Design and Create an Advertising Database

Academic

You are a Marketing major currently doing an internship with the Chamber of Commerce in a local city. The Chamber publishes a Newcomer's Guide that contains advertisements from local businesses. Ad reps contact the businesses to arrange for advertising. Each advertiser is assigned to a single ad rep, but each ad rep may be assigned many advertisers. The Chamber would like your help in creating a database of advertisers and advertising representatives.

Based on the information in the Case 1-1 Chamber of Commerce workbook, use the concepts and techniques presented in this chapter to design and create a database to store the data that the Chamber needs. Submit your assignment in the format specified by your instructor.

2: Design and Create a Consignment Database

Personal

You are involved in a volunteer organization that provides clothing and school supplies to needy children. Recently, the Board of Directors decided to open a consignment shop as a way to raise additional funds. In a consignment shop, individuals bring in unwanted items, and the shop sells the items. Proceeds are split between the seller and the shop. The database must keep track of the items for sale in the shop as well as maintain data on the sellers. Each item is assigned to a single seller, but each seller may be assigned many items. The Board has asked you to create a database to store information about the consignment items.

Use the concepts and techniques presented in this chapter to design and create a database to store the consignment data. Then create the necessary tables and enter the data from the Case 1-2 Consignment workbook. Create an Available Items Report that lists the item number, description, price, and seller code. Submit your assignment in the format specified by your instructor.

3: Design and Create a Senior Care Database

Professional

You are co-owner of a company, Senior Care, that provides nonmedical services to older adults who need assistance with daily living. Helpers will drive individuals to appointments, do the grocery shopping, fill prescriptions, help with personal care, and provide companionship. Each client is assigned to a single helper, but each helper may be assigned many clients. The other owners have asked you to create a database of clients and helpers. Use the concepts and techniques presented in this chapter to design and create a database to meet Senior Care needs. Then create the necessary tables and enter the data from the Case 1-3 Senior Care workbook. Create a Client Report that lists each client's client number, client last name, client first name, balance, and helper number. Submit your assignment in the format specified by your instructor.

Cases & Places exercises call on students to create open-ended projects that reflect academic, personal, and business settings.

Office 2010 and Windows 7: Essential Concepts and Skills

Objectives

You will have mastered the material in this chapter when you can:

- Perform basic mouse operations
- Start Windows and log on to the computer
- Identify the objects on the Windows 7 desktop
- Identify the programs in and versions of Microsoft Office
- Start a program
- Identify the components of the Microsoft Office Ribbon

- Create folders
- Save files
- Change screen resolution
- Perform basic tasks in Microsoft Office programs
- Manage files
- Use Microsoft Office Help and Windows Help

Office 2010 and Windows 7: Essential Concepts and Skills

Office 2010 and Windows 7

This introductory chapter covers features and functions common to Office 2010 programs, as well as the basics of Windows 7.

Overview

As you read this chapter, you will learn how to perform basic tasks in Windows and Office programs by performing these general activities:

- Start programs using Windows.
- Use features common across Office programs.
- Organize files and folders.
- Change screen resolution.
- Quit Office programs.

Introduction to the Windows 7 Operating System

Windows 7 is the newest version of Microsoft Windows, which is the most popular and widely used operating system. An **operating system** is a computer program (set of computer instructions) that coordinates all the activities of computer hardware such as memory, storage devices, and printers, and provides the capability for you to communicate with the computer.

The Windows 7 operating system simplifies the process of working with documents and programs by organizing the manner in which you interact with the computer. Windows 7 is used to run **application software**, which consists of programs designed to make users more productive and/or assist them with personal tasks, such as word processing.

Windows 7 has two interface variations, Windows 7 Basic and Windows 7 Aero. Computers with up to 1 GB of RAM display the Windows 7 Basic interface (Figure 1a). Computers with more than 1 GB of RAM also can display the Windows Aero interface (Figure 1b), which provides an enhanced visual appearance. The Windows 7 Professional, Windows 7 Enterprise, Windows 7 Home Premium, and Windows 7 Ultimate editions have the capability to use Windows Aero.

Using a Mouse

Windows users work with a mouse that has at least two buttons. For a right-handed user, the left button usually is the primary mouse button, and the right mouse button is the secondary mouse button. Left-handed people, however, can reverse the function of these buttons.

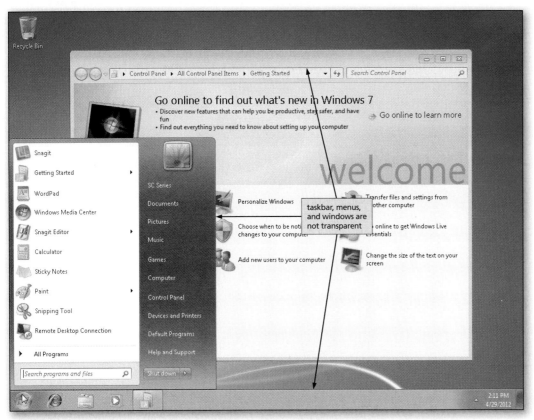

Figure 1(a) Windows 7 Basic interface

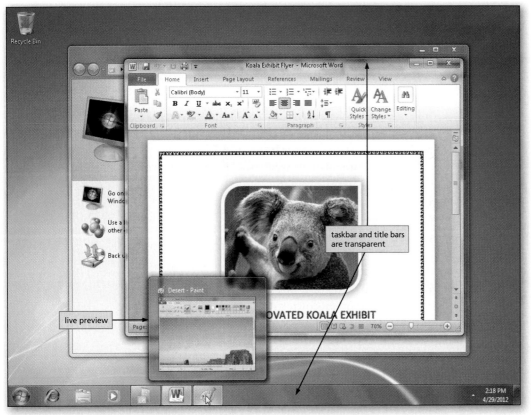

Figure 1(b) Windows 7 Aero interface

Table 1 explains how to perform a variety of mouse operations. Some programs also use keys in combination with the mouse to perform certain actions. For example, when you hold down the CTRL key while rolling the mouse wheel, text on the screen becomes larger or smaller based on the direction you roll the wheel. The function of the mouse buttons and the wheel varies depending on the program.

Table 1 Mouse Operations

Operation	Mouse Action	Example*
Point	Move the mouse until the pointer on the desktop is positioned on the item of choice.	Position the pointer on the screen.
Click	Press and release the primary mouse button, which usually is the left mouse button.	Select or deselect items on the screen or start a program or program feature.
Right-click	Press and release the secondary mouse button, which usually is the right mouse button.	Display a shortcut menu.
Double-click	Quickly press and release the left mouse button twice without moving the mouse.	Start a program or program feature.
Triple-click	Quickly press and release the left mouse button three times without moving the mouse.	Select a paragraph.
Drag	Point to an item, hold down the left mouse button, move the item to the desired location on the screen, and then release the left mouse button.	Move an object from one location to another or draw pictures.
Right-drag	Point to an item, hold down the right mouse button, move the item to the desired location on the screen, and then release the right mouse button.	Display a shortcut menu after moving an object from one location to another.
Rotate wheel	Roll the wheel forward or backward.	Scroll vertically (up and down).
Free-spin wheel	Whirl the wheel forward or backward so that it spins freely on its own.	Scroll through many pages in seconds.
Press wheel	Press the wheel button while moving the mouse.	Scroll continuously.
Tilt wheel	Press the wheel toward the right or left.	Scroll horizontally (left and right).
Press thumb button	Press the button on the side of the mouse with your thumb.	Move forward or backward through Web pages and/or control media, games, etc.

*Note: the examples presented in this column are discussed as they are demonstrated in this chapter.

Scrolling

A **scroll bar** is a horizontal or vertical bar that appears when the contents of an area may not be visible completely on the screen (Figure 2). A scroll bar contains **scroll arrows** and a **scroll box** that enable you to view areas that currently cannot be seen. Clicking the up and down scroll arrows moves the screen content up or down one line. You also can click above or below the scroll box to move up or down a section, or drag the scroll box up or down to move up or down to move to a specific location.

Shortcut Keys

In many cases, you can use the keyboard instead of the mouse to accomplish a task. To perform tasks using the keyboard, you press one or more keyboard keys, sometimes identified as

BTW

Minimize Wrist Injury
Computer users frequently switch between the keyboard and the mouse during a word processing session; such switching strains the wrist. To help prevent wrist injury, minimize switching. For instance, if your fingers already are on the keyboard, use keyboard keys to scroll. If your hand already is on the mouse, use the mouse to scroll.

Figure 2

a **shortcut key** or **keyboard shortcut**. Some shortcut keys consist of a single key, such as the F1 key. For example, to obtain help about Windows 7, you can press the F1 key. Other shortcut keys consist of multiple keys, in which case a plus sign separates the key names, such as CTRL+ESC. This notation means to press and hold down the first key listed, press one or more additional keys, and then release all keys. For example, to display the Start menu, press CTRL+ESC, that is, hold down the CTRL key, press the ESC key, and then release both keys.

Starting Windows 7

It is not unusual for multiple people to use the same computer in a work, educational, recreational, or home setting. Windows 7 enables each user to establish a **user account**, which identifies to Windows 7 the resources, such as programs and storage locations, a user can access when working with a computer.

Each user account has a user name and may have a password and an icon, as well. A **user name** is a unique combination of letters or numbers that identifies a specific user to Windows 7. A **password** is a private combination of letters, numbers, and special characters associated with the user name that allows access to a user's account resources. A **user icon** is a picture associated with a user name.

When you turn on a computer, an introductory screen consisting of the Windows logo and copyright messages is displayed. The Windows logo is animated and glows as the Windows 7 operating system is loaded. After the Windows logo appears, depending on your computer's settings, you may or may not be required to log on to the computer. **Logging on** to a computer opens your user account and makes the computer available for use. If you are required to log on to the computer, the **Welcome screen** is displayed, which shows the user names of users on the computer (Figure 3). Clicking the user name or picture begins the process of logging on to the computer.

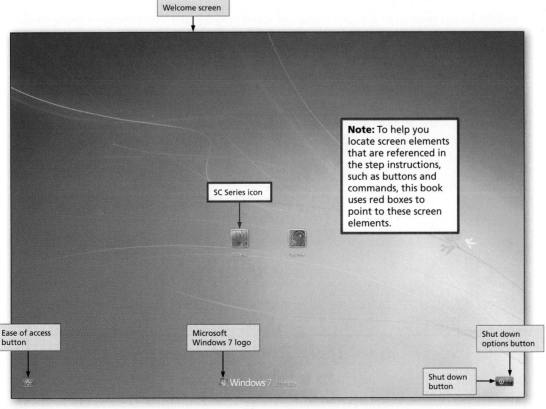

Note: To help you locate screen elements that are referenced in the step instructions, such as buttons and commands, this book uses red boxes to point to these screen elements.

Figure 3

At the bottom of the Welcome screen is the 'Ease of access' button, Windows 7 logo, a Shut down button, and a 'Shut down options' button. The following list identifies the functions of the buttons and commands that typically appear on the Welcome screen:

- Clicking the 'Ease of access' button displays the Ease of Access Center, which provides tools to optimize your computer to accommodate the needs of the mobility, hearing, and vision impaired users.
- Clicking the Shut down button shuts down Windows 7 and the computer.
- Clicking the 'Shut down options' button, located to the right of the Shut down button, provides access to a menu containing commands that perform actions such as restarting the computer, putting the computer in a low-powered state, and shutting down the computer. The commands available on your computer may differ.
  - The **Restart command** closes open programs, shuts down Windows 7, and then restarts Windows 7 and displays the Welcome screen.
  - The **Sleep command** waits for Windows 7 to save your work and then turns off the computer fans and hard disk. To wake the computer from the Sleep state, press the power button or lift a notebook computer's cover, and log on to the computer.
  - The **Shut down command** shuts down and turns off the computer.

To Log On to the Computer

After starting Windows 7, you might need to log on to the computer. The following steps log on to the computer based on a typical installation. You may need to ask your instructor how to log on to your computer. This set of steps uses SC Series as the user name. The list of user names on your computer will be different.

1

- Click the user icon (SC Series, in this case) on the Welcome screen (shown in Figure 3 on the previous page); depending on settings, this either will display a password text box (Figure 4) or will log on to the computer and display the Windows 7 desktop.

Q&A Why do I not see a user icon?

Your computer may require you to type a user name instead of clicking an icon.

Q&A What is a text box?

A text box is a rectangular box in which you type text.

Q&A Why does my screen not show a password text box?

Your account does not require a password.

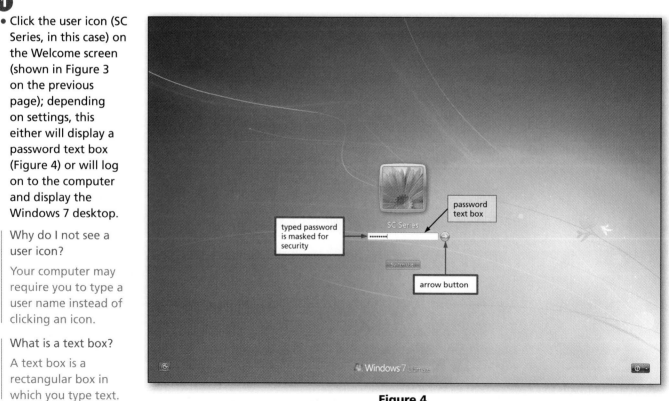

Figure 4

2

- If Windows 7 displays a password text box, type your password in the text box and then click the arrow button to log on to the computer and display the Windows 7 desktop (Figure 5).

Why does my desktop look different from the one in Figure 5?

The Windows 7 desktop is customizable, and your school or employer may have modified the desktop to meet its needs. Also, your screen resolution, which affects the size of the elements on the screen, may differ from the screen resolution used in this book. Later in this chapter, you learn how to change screen resolution.

Figure 5

The Windows 7 Desktop

The Windows 7 desktop (Figure 5) and the objects on the desktop emulate a work area in an office. Think of the Windows desktop as an electronic version of the top of your desk. You can perform tasks such as placing objects on the desktop, moving the objects around the desktop, and removing items from the desktop.

When you start a program in Windows 7, it appears on the desktop. Some icons also may be displayed on the desktop. For instance, the icon for the **Recycle Bin**, the location of files that have been deleted, appears on the desktop by default. A **file** is a named unit of storage. Files can contain text, images, audio, and video. You can customize your desktop so that icons representing programs and files you use often appear on your desktop.

Introduction to Microsoft Office 2010

Microsoft Office 2010 is the newest version of Microsoft Office, offering features that provide users with better functionality and easier ways to work with the various files they create. These features include enhanced design tools, such as improved picture formatting tools and new themes, shared notebooks for working in groups, mobile versions of Office programs, broadcast presentation for the Web, and a digital notebook for managing and sharing multimedia information.

Microsoft Office 2010 Programs

Microsoft Office 2010 includes a wide variety of programs such as Word, PowerPoint, Excel, Access, Outlook, Publisher, OneNote, InfoPath, SharePoint Workspace, Communicator, and Web Apps:

- **Microsoft Word 2010**, or Word, is a full-featured word processing program that allows you to create professional-looking documents and revise them easily.
- **Microsoft PowerPoint 2010**, or PowerPoint, is a complete presentation program that allows you to produce professional-looking presentations.
- **Microsoft Excel 2010**, or Excel, is a powerful spreadsheet program that allows you to organize data, complete calculations, make decisions, graph data, develop professional-looking reports, publish organized data to the Web, and access real-time data from Web sites.
- **Microsoft Access 2010**, or Access, is a database management system that allows you to create a database; add, change, and delete data in the database; ask questions concerning the data in the database; and create forms and reports using the data in the database.
- **Microsoft Outlook 2010**, or Outlook, is a communications and scheduling program that allows you to manage e-mail accounts, calendars, contacts, and access to other Internet content.
- **Microsoft Publisher 2010**, or Publisher, is a desktop publishing program that helps you create professional-quality publications and marketing materials that can be shared easily.
- **Microsoft OneNote 2010**, or OneNote, is a note taking program that allows you to store and share information in notebooks with other people.
- **Microsoft InfoPath 2010**, or InfoPath, is a form development program that helps you create forms for use on the Web and gather data from these forms.
- **Microsoft SharePoint Workspace 2010**, or SharePoint, is collaboration software that allows you access and revise files stored on your computer from other locations.
- **Microsoft Communicator** is communications software that allows you to use different modes of communications such as instant messaging, video conferencing, and sharing files and programs.
- **Microsoft Web Apps** is a Web application that allows you to edit and share files on the Web using the familiar Office interface.

Microsoft Office 2010 Suites

A **suite** is a collection of individual programs available together as a unit. Microsoft offers a variety of Office suites. Table 2 lists the Office 2010 suites and their components.

Programs in a suite, such as Microsoft Office, typically use a similar interface and share features. In addition, Microsoft Office programs use **common dialog boxes** for performing actions such as opening and saving files. Once you are comfortable working with these elements and this interface and performing tasks in one program, the similarity can help you apply the knowledge and skills you have learned to another Office program(s). For example, the process for saving a file in Word is the same in PowerPoint, Excel, and the other Office programs. While briefly showing how to use several Office programs, this chapter illustrates some of the common functions across the programs and also identifies the characteristics unique to these programs.

Table 2 Microsoft Office 2010 Suites

	Microsoft Office Professional Plus 2010	Microsoft Office Professional 2010	Microsoft Office Home and Business 2010	Microsoft Office Standard 2010	Microsoft Office Home and Student 2010
Microsoft Word 2010	✔	✔	✔	✔	✔
Microsoft PowerPoint 2010	✔	✔	✔	✔	✔
Microsoft Excel 2010	✔	✔	✔	✔	✔
Microsoft Access 2010	✔	✔	✗	✗	✗
Microsoft Outlook 2010	✔	✔	✔	✔	✗
Microsoft Publisher 2010	✔	✔	✗	✔	✗
Microsoft OneNote 2010	✔	✔	✔	✔	✔
Microsoft InfoPath 2010	✔	✗	✗	✗	✗
Microsoft SharePoint Workspace 2010	✔	✗	✗	✗	✗
Microsoft Communicator	✔	✗	✗	✗	✗

Starting and Using a Program

To use a program, you must instruct the operating system to start the program. Windows 7 provides many different ways to start a program, one of which is presented in this section (other ways to start a program are presented throughout this chapter). After starting a program, you can use it to perform a variety of tasks. The following pages use Word to discuss some elements of the Office interface and to perform tasks that are common to other Office programs.

Word

Word is a full-featured word processing program that allows you to create many types of personal and business documents, including flyers, letters, memos, resumes, reports, fax cover sheets, mailing labels, and newsletters. Word also provides tools that enable you to create Web pages and save these Web pages directly on a Web server. Word has many features designed to simplify the production of documents and add visual appeal. Using Word, you easily can change the shape, size, and color of text. You also can include borders, shading, tables, images, pictures, charts, and Web addresses in documents.

To Start a Program Using the Start Menu

Across the bottom of the Windows 7 desktop is the taskbar. The taskbar contains the **Start button**, which you use to access programs, files, folders, and settings on a computer. A **folder** is a named location on a storage medium that usually contains related documents. The taskbar also displays a button for each program currently running on a computer.

Clicking the Start button displays the Start menu. The **Start menu** allows you to access programs, folders, and files on the computer and contains commands that allow you to start programs, store and search for documents, customize the computer, and obtain help about thousands of topics. A **menu** is a list of related items, including folders, programs, and commands. Each **command** on a menu performs a specific action, such as saving a file or obtaining help.

The following steps, which assume Windows 7 is running, use the Start menu to start an Office program based on a typical installation. You may need to ask your instructor how to start Office programs for your computer. Although the steps illustrate starting the Word program, the steps to start any Office program are similar.

1

- Click the Start button on the Windows 7 taskbar to display the Start menu (Figure 6).

Q&A Why does my Start menu look different?

It may look different depending on your computer's configuration. The Start menu may be customized for several reasons, such as usage requirements or security restrictions.

Figure 6

2

- Click All Programs at the bottom of the left pane on the Start menu to display the All Programs list (Figure 7).

Q&A What is a pane?

A **pane** is an area of a window that displays related content. For example, the left pane on the Start menu contains a list of frequently used programs, as well as the All Programs command.

Q&A Why might my All Programs list look different?

Most likely, the programs installed on your computer will differ from those shown in Figure 7. Your All Programs list will show the programs that are installed on your computer.

Figure 7

3

• If the program you wish to start is located in a folder, click or scroll to and then click the folder (Microsoft Office, in this case) in the All Programs list to display a list of the folder's contents (Figure 8).

Q&A Why is the Microsoft Office folder on my computer?

During installation of Microsoft Office 2010, the Microsoft Office folder was added to the All Programs list.

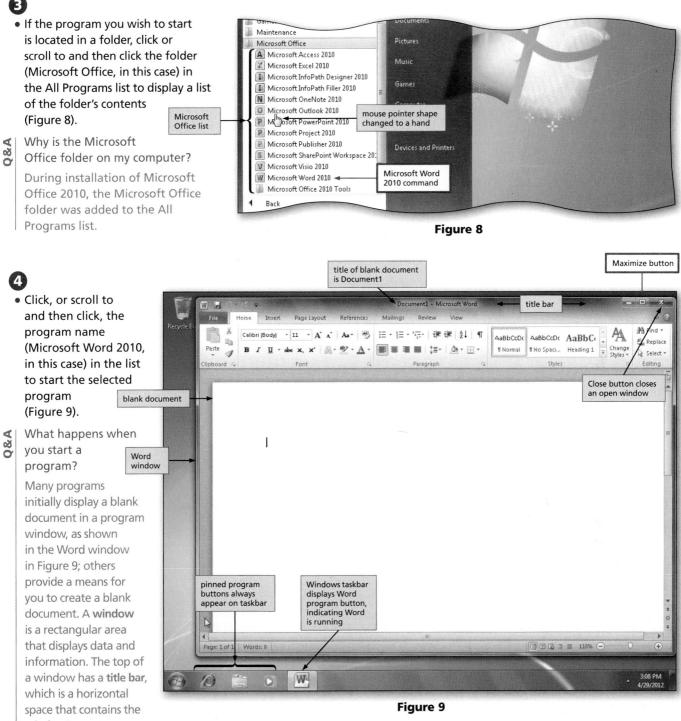

Figure 8

Figure 9

4

• Click, or scroll to and then click, the program name (Microsoft Word 2010, in this case) in the list to start the selected program (Figure 9).

Q&A What happens when you start a program?

Many programs initially display a blank document in a program window, as shown in the Word window in Figure 9; others provide a means for you to create a blank document. A **window** is a rectangular area that displays data and information. The top of a window has a **title bar**, which is a horizontal space that contains the window's name.

Q&A Why is my program window a different size?

The Word window shown in Figure 9 is not maximized. Your Word window already may be maximized. The next steps maximize a window.

Other Ways	
1. Double-click program icon on desktop, if one is present	3. Display Start menu, type program name in search box, click program name
2. Click program name in left pane of Start menu, if present	4. Double-click file created using program you want to start

To Maximize a Window

Sometimes content is not visible completely in a window. One method of displaying the entire contents of a window is to **maximize** it, or enlarge the window so that it fills the entire screen. The following step maximizes the Word window; however, any Office program's window can be maximized using this step.

1

• If the program window is not maximized already, click the Maximize button (shown in Figure 9 on the previous page) next to the Close button on the window's title bar (the Word window title bar, in this case) to maximize the window (Figure 10).

Q&A What happened to the Maximize button?

It changed to a Restore Down button, which you can use to return a window to its size and location before you maximized it.

Q&A How do I know whether a window is maximized?

A window is maximized if it fills the entire display area and the Restore Down button is displayed on the title bar.

Close button

Maximize button changed to Restore Down button

Figure 10

Other Ways

1. Double-click title bar
2. Drag title bar to top of screen

The Word Document Window, Ribbon, and Elements Common to Office Programs

The Word window consists of a variety of components to make your work more efficient and documents more professional. These include the document window, Ribbon, Mini toolbar, shortcut menus, and Quick Access Toolbar. Most of these components are common to other Microsoft Office 2010 programs; others are unique to Word.

You view a portion of a document on the screen through a **document window** (Figure 11). The default (preset) view is **Print Layout view**, which shows the document on a mock sheet of paper in the document window.

Scroll Bars You use a scroll bar to display different portions of a document in the document window. At the right edge of the document window is a vertical scroll bar. If a document is too wide to fit in the document window, a horizontal scroll bar also appears at the bottom of the document window. On a scroll bar, the position of the scroll box reflects the location of the portion of the document that is displayed in the document window.

Figure 11

Status Bar The **status bar**, located at the bottom of the document window above the Windows 7 taskbar, presents information about the document, the progress of current tasks, and the status of certain commands and keys; it also provides controls for viewing the document. As you type text or perform certain tasks, various indicators and buttons may appear on the status bar.

The left side of the status bar in Figure 11 shows the current page followed by the total number of pages in the document, the number of words in the document, and an icon to check spelling and grammar. The right side of the status bar includes buttons and controls you can use to change the view of a document and adjust the size of the displayed document.

Ribbon   The Ribbon, located near the top of the window below the title bar, is the control center in Word and other Office programs (Figure 12). The Ribbon provides easy, central access to the tasks you perform while creating a document. The Ribbon consists of tabs, groups, and commands. Each **tab** contains a collection of groups, and each **group** contains related functions. When you start an Office program, such as Word, it initially displays several main tabs, also called default tabs. All Office programs have a **Home tab**, which contains the more frequently used commands.

In addition to the main tabs, Office programs display **tool tabs**, also called contextual tabs (Figure 13), when you perform certain tasks or work with objects such as pictures or tables. If you insert a picture in a Word document, for example, the Picture Tools tab and its related subordinate Format tab appear, collectively referred to as the Picture Tools Format tab. When you are finished working with the picture, the Picture Tools Format tab disappears from the Ribbon. Word and other Office programs determine when tool tabs should appear and disappear based on tasks you perform. Some tool tabs, such as the Table Tools tab, have more than one related subordinate tab.

Items on the Ribbon include buttons, boxes (text boxes, check boxes, etc.), and galleries (Figure 12). A **gallery** is a set of choices, often graphical, arranged in a grid or in a list. You can scroll through choices in an in-Ribbon gallery by clicking the gallery's scroll arrows. Or, you can click a gallery's More button to view more gallery options on the screen at a time.

Figure 12

Some buttons and boxes have arrows that, when clicked, also display a gallery; others always cause a gallery to be displayed when clicked. Most galleries support **live preview**, which is a feature that allows you to point to a gallery choice and see its effect in the document — without actually selecting the choice (Figure 13).

Figure 13

Some commands on the Ribbon display an image to help you remember their function. When you point to a command on the Ribbon, all or part of the command glows in shades of yellow and orange, and an Enhanced ScreenTip appears on the screen. An **Enhanced ScreenTip** is an on-screen note that provides the name of the command, available keyboard shortcut(s), a description of the command, and sometimes instructions for how to obtain help about the command (Figure 14). Enhanced ScreenTips are more detailed than a typical ScreenTip, which usually displays only the name of the command.

Some groups on the Ribbon have a small arrow in the lower-right corner, called a **Dialog Box Launcher**, that when clicked, displays a dialog box or a task pane with additional options for the group (Figure 15). When presented with a dialog box, you make selections and must close the dialog box before returning to the document. A **task pane**, in contrast to a dialog box, is a window that can remain open and visible while you work in the document.

Figure 14

Mini Toolbar   The **Mini toolbar**, which appears automatically based on tasks you perform, contains commands related to changing the appearance of text in a document. All commands on the Mini toolbar also exist on the Ribbon. The purpose of the Mini toolbar is to minimize mouse movement.

When the Mini toolbar appears, it initially is transparent (Figure 16a). If you do not use the transparent Mini toolbar, it disappears from the screen. To use the Mini toolbar, move the mouse pointer into the toolbar, which causes the Mini toolbar to change from a transparent to bright appearance (Figure 16b). If you right-click an item in the document window, Word displays both the Mini toolbar and a shortcut menu, which is discussed in a later section in this chapter.

Figure 15

(a) transparent Mini toolbar   **(b) bright Mini toolbar**

Figure 16

BTW

Turning Off the Mini Toolbar
If you do not want the Mini toolbar to appear, click File on the Ribbon to open the Backstage view, click Options in the Backstage view, click General (Options dialog box), remove the check mark from the Show Mini Toolbar on selection check box, and then click the OK button.

Quick Access Toolbar The **Quick Access Toolbar**, located initially (by default) above the Ribbon at the left edge of the title bar, provides convenient, one-click access to frequently used commands (Figure 14 on the previous page). The commands on the Quick Access Toolbar always are available, regardless of the task you are performing. The Quick Access Toolbar is discussed in more depth later in the chapter.

KeyTips If you prefer using the keyboard instead of the mouse, you can press the ALT key on the keyboard to display **KeyTips**, or keyboard code icons, for certain commands (Figure 17). To select a command using the keyboard, press the letter or number displayed in the KeyTip, which may cause additional KeyTips related to the selected command to appear. To remove KeyTips from the screen, press the ALT key or the ESC key until all KeyTips disappear, or click the mouse anywhere in the program window.

Figure 17

To Display a Different Tab on the Ribbon

When you start Word, the Ribbon displays eight main tabs: File, Home, Insert, Page Layout, References, Mailings, Review, and View. The tab currently displayed is called the **active tab**.

The following step displays the Insert tab, that is, makes it the active tab.

1

• Click Insert on the Ribbon to display the Insert tab (Figure 18).

🔍 **Experiment**

• Click the other tabs on the Ribbon to view their contents. When you are finished, click the Insert tab to redisplay the Insert tab.

Q&A If I am working in a different Office program, such as PowerPoint or Access, how do I display a different tab on the Ribbon?

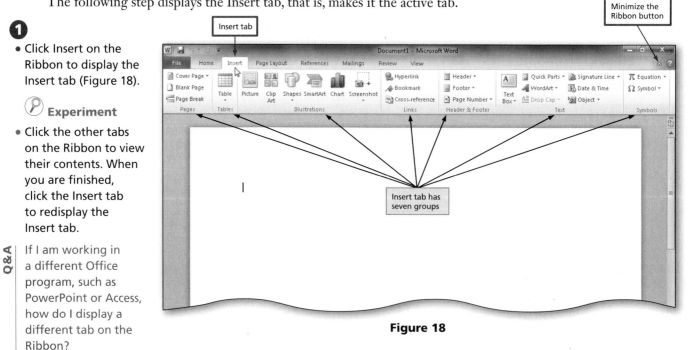

Figure 18

Follow this same procedure; that is, click the desired tab on the Ribbon.

To Minimize, Display, and Restore the Ribbon

To display more of a document or other item in the window of an Office program, some users prefer to minimize the Ribbon, which hides the groups on the Ribbon and displays only the main tabs. Each time you start an Office program, the Ribbon appears the same way it did the last time you used that Office program. The chapters in this book, however, begin with the Ribbon appearing as it did at the initial installation of the software.

The following steps minimize, display, and restore the Ribbon in an Office program.

 1

• Click the Minimize the Ribbon button on the Ribbon (shown in Figure 18) to minimize the Ribbon (Figure 19).

Q&A What happened to the groups on the Ribbon?

When you minimize the Ribbon, the groups disappear so that the Ribbon does not take up as much space on the screen.

Ribbon has been minimized

Expand the Ribbon button replaces Minimize the Ribbon button

Figure 19

Q&A What happened to the Minimize the Ribbon button?

The Expand the Ribbon button replaces the Minimize the Ribbon button when the Ribbon is minimized.

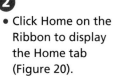 **2**

• Click Home on the Ribbon to display the Home tab (Figure 20).

Home tab

Q&A Why would I click the Home tab?

If you want to use a command on a minimized Ribbon, click the main tab to display the groups for that tab. After you select a command on the Ribbon, the groups will be hidden once again. If you decide not to use a command on the Ribbon, you can hide the groups by clicking the same main tab or clicking in the program window.

Figure 20

3

• Click Home on the Ribbon to hide the groups again (shown in Figure 19).

• Click the Expand the Ribbon button on the Ribbon (shown in Figure 19) to restore the Ribbon.

Other Ways

1. Double-click Home on the Ribbon
2. Press CTRL+F1

To Display and Use a Shortcut Menu

When you right-click certain areas of the Word and other program windows, a shortcut menu will appear. A **shortcut menu** is a list of frequently used commands that relate to the right-clicked object. When you right-click a scroll bar, for example, a shortcut menu appears with commands related to the scroll bar. When you right-click the Quick Access Toolbar, a shortcut menu appears with commands related to the Quick Access Toolbar. You can use shortcut menus to access common commands quickly. The following steps use a shortcut menu to move the Quick Access Toolbar, which by default is located on the title bar.

1

• Right-click the Quick Access Toolbar to display a shortcut menu that presents a list of commands related to the Quick Access Toolbar (Figure 21).

Figure 21

2

• Click Show Quick Access Toolbar Below the Ribbon on the shortcut menu to display the Quick Access Toolbar below the Ribbon (Figure 22).

Figure 22

3

• Right-click the Quick Access Toolbar to display a shortcut menu (Figure 23).

4

• Click Show Quick Access Toolbar Above the Ribbon on the shortcut menu to return the Quick Access Toolbar to its original position (shown in Figure 21).

Figure 23

To Customize the Quick Access Toolbar

The Quick Access Toolbar provides easy access to some of the more frequently used commands in Office programs. By default, the Quick Access Toolbar contains buttons for the Save, Undo, and Redo commands. You can customize the Quick Access Toolbar by changing its location in the window, as shown in the previous steps, and by adding more buttons to reflect commands you would like to access easily. The following steps add the Quick Print button to the Quick Access Toolbar.

1

- Click the Customize Quick Access Toolbar button to display the Customize Quick Access Toolbar menu (Figure 24).

Q&A Which commands are listed on the Customize Quick Access Toolbar menu?

It lists commands that commonly are added to the Quick Access Toolbar.

Q&A What do the check marks next to some commands signify?

Check marks appear next to commands that already are on the Quick Access Toolbar. When you add a button to the Quick Access Toolbar, a check mark will be displayed next to its command name.

Figure 24

2

- Click Quick Print on the Customize Quick Access Toolbar menu to add the Quick Print button to the Quick Access Toolbar (Figure 25).

Q&A How would I remove a button from the Quick Access Toolbar?

You would right-click the button you wish to remove and then click Remove from Quick Access Toolbar on the shortcut menu.

Figure 25

To Enter Text in a Document

The first step in creating a document is to enter its text by typing on the keyboard. By default, Word positions text at the left margin as you type. To begin creating a flyer, for example, you type the headline in the document window. The following steps type this first line of text, a headline, in a document.

1

- Type **SEE THE RENOVATED KOALA EXHIBIT** as the text (Figure 26).

Q&A What is the blinking vertical bar to the right of the text?

The insertion point. It indicates where text, graphics, and other items will be inserted in the document. As you type, the insertion point moves to the right, and when you reach the end of a line, it moves downward to the beginning of the next line.

Q&A What if I make an error while typing?

You can press the BACKSPACE key until you have deleted the text in error and then retype the text correctly.

Figure 26

2

- Press the ENTER key to move the insertion point to the beginning of the next line (Figure 27).

Q&A Why did blank space appear between the entered text and the insertion point?

Each time you press the ENTER key, Word creates a new paragraph and inserts blank space between the two paragraphs.

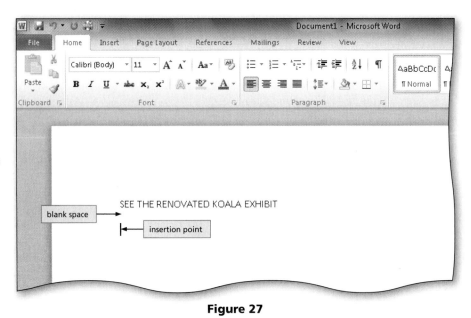

Figure 27

Saving and Organizing Files

While you are creating a document, the computer stores it in memory. When you save a document, the computer places it on a storage medium such as a hard disk, USB flash drive, or optical disc. A saved document is referred to as a file. A **file name** is the name assigned to a file when it is saved. It is important to save a document frequently for the following reasons:

- The document in memory might be lost if the computer is turned off or you lose electrical power while a program is running.
- If you run out of time before completing a project, you may finish it at a future time without starting over.

When saving files, you should organize them so that you easily can find them later. Windows 7 provides tools to help you organize files.

Organizing Files and Folders

A file contains data. This data can range from a research paper to an accounting spreadsheet to an electronic math quiz. You should organize and store these files in folders to avoid misplacing a file and to help you find a file quickly.

If you are a freshman taking an introductory computer class (CIS 101, for example), you may want to design a series of folders for the different subjects covered in the class. To accomplish this, you can arrange the folders in a hierarchy for the class, as shown in Figure 28.

Figure 28

The hierarchy contains three levels. The first level contains the storage device, in this case a USB flash drive. Windows 7 identifies the storage device with a letter, and, in some cases, a name. In Figure 28, the USB flash drive is identified as REMOVABLE (E:). The second level contains the class folder (CIS 101, in this case), and the third level contains seven folders, one each for a different Office program that will be covered in the class (Word, PowerPoint, Excel, Access, Outlook, Publisher, and OneNote).

When the hierarchy in Figure 28 is created, the USB flash drive is said to contain the CIS 101 folder, and the CIS 101 folder is said to contain the separate Office folders (i.e., Word, PowerPoint, Excel, etc.). In addition, this hierarchy easily can be expanded to include folders from other classes taken during additional semesters.

The vertical and horizontal lines in Figure 28 form a pathway that allows you to navigate to a drive or folder on a computer or network. A **path** consists of a drive letter (preceded by a drive name when necessary) and colon, to identify the storage device, and one or more folder names. Each drive or folder in the hierarchy has a corresponding path.

BTW

File Type
Depending on your Windows 7 settings, the file type .docx may be displayed immediately to the right of the file name after you save the file. The file type .docx is a Word 2010 document.

BTW

Saving Online
Instead of saving files on a USB flash drive, some people prefer to save them online so that they can access the files from any computer with an Internet connection. For more information, read Appendix C.

Table 3 shows examples of paths and their corresponding drives and folders.

Table 3 Paths and Corresponding Drives and Folders	
Path	**Drive and Folder**
Computer ▶ REMOVABLE (E:)	Drive E (REMOVABLE (E:))
Computer ▶ REMOVABLE (E:) ▶ CIS 101	CIS 101 folder on drive E
Computer ▶ REMOVABLE (E:) ▶ CIS 101 ▶ Word	Word folder in CIS 101 folder on drive E

The following pages illustrate the steps to organize the folders for this class and save a file in one of those folders:

1. Create the folder identifying your class.
2. Create the Word folder in the folder identifying your class.
3. Create the remaining folders in the folder identifying your class (one each for PowerPoint, Excel, Access, Outlook, Publisher, and OneNote).
4. Save a file in the Word folder.
5. Verify the location of the saved file.

To Create a Folder

When you create a folder, such as the CIS 101 folder shown in Figure 28 on the previous page, you must name the folder. A folder name should describe the folder and its contents. A folder name can contain spaces and any uppercase or lowercase characters, except a backslash (\), slash (/), colon (:), asterisk (*), question mark (?), quotation marks ("), less than symbol (<), greater than symbol (>), or vertical bar (|). Folder names cannot be CON, AUX, COM1, COM2, COM3, COM4, LPT1, LPT2, LPT3, PRN, or NUL. The same rules for naming folders also apply to naming files.

To store files and folders on a USB flash drive, you must connect the USB flash drive to an available USB port on a computer. The following steps create your class folder (CIS 101, in this case) on a USB flash drive.

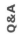

- Connect the USB flash drive to an available USB port on the computer to open the AutoPlay window (Figure 29).

Q&A Why does the AutoPlay window not open?

Some computers are not configured to open an AutoPlay window. Instead, they might display the contents of the USB flash drive automatically, or you might need to access contents of the USB flash drive using the Computer window. To use the Computer window to display the USB flash drive's contents, click the Start button, click Computer on the Start menu, and then click the icon representing the USB flash drive.

Figure 29

Q&A Why does the AutoPlay window look different from the one in Figure 29?

The AutoPlay window that opens on your computer might display different options. The type of USB flash drive, its contents, and the next available drive letter on your computer all will determine which options are displayed in the AutoPlay window.

2

- Click the 'Open folder to view files' link in the AutoPlay window to open the USB flash drive window (Figure 30).

Q&A Why does Figure 30 show REMOVABLE (E:) for the USB flash drive?

REMOVABLE is the name of the USB flash drive used to illustrate these steps. The (E:) refers to the drive letter assigned by Windows 7 to the USB flash drive. The name and drive letter of your USB flash drive probably will be different.

Figure 30

3

- Click the New folder button on the toolbar to display a new folder icon with the name, New folder, selected in a text box.

- Type **CIS 101** (or your class code) in the text box to name the folder.

- Press the ENTER key to create a folder identifying your class on the selected drive (Figure 31). If the CIS 101 folder does not appear in the navigation pane, double-click REMOVABLE (E:) in the navigation pane to display the folder just added.

Q&A What happens when I press the ENTER key?

The class folder (CIS 101, in this case) is displayed in the File list, which contains the folder name, date modified, type, and size.

Q&A Why is the folder icon displayed differently on my computer?

Windows might be configured to display contents differently on your computer.

Figure 31

Folder Windows

The USB flash drive window (shown in Figure 31 on the previous page) is called a folder window. Recall that a folder is a specific named location on a storage medium that contains related files. Most users rely on **folder windows** for finding, viewing, and managing information on their computer. Folder windows have common design elements, including the following (Figure 31).

- The **Address bar** provides quick navigation options. The arrows on the Address bar allow you to visit different locations on the computer.
- The buttons to the left of the Address bar allow you to navigate the contents of the left pane and view recent pages. Other buttons allow you to specify the size of the window.
- The **Previous Locations button** saves the locations you have visited and displays the locations when clicked.
- The **Refresh button** on the right side of the Address bar refreshes the contents of the right pane of the folder window.
- The **search box** to the right of the Address bar contains the dimmed word, Search. You can type a term in the search box for a list of files, folders, shortcuts, and elements containing that term within the location you are searching. A **shortcut** is an icon on the desktop that provides a user with immediate access to a program or file.
- The **Command bar** contains five buttons used to accomplish various tasks on the computer related to organizing and managing the contents of the open window.
- The **navigation pane** on the left contains the Favorites area, Libraries area, Computer area, and Network area.
- The **Favorites area** contains links to your favorite locations. By default, this list contains only links to your Desktop, Downloads, and Recent Places.
- The **Libraries area** shows links to files and folders that have been included in a library.

A **library** helps you manage multiple folders and files stored in various locations on a computer. It does not store the files and folders; rather, it displays links to them so that you can access them quickly. For example, you can save pictures from a digital camera in any folder on any storage location on a computer. Normally, this would make organizing the different folders difficult; however, if you add the folders to a library, you can access all the pictures from one location regardless of where they are stored.

To Create a Folder within a Folder

With the class folder created, you can create folders that will store the files you create using each Office program. The following steps create a Word folder in the CIS 101 folder (or the folder identifying your class).

1

- Double-click the icon or folder name for the CIS 101 folder (or the folder identifying your class) in the File list to open the folder (Figure 32).

Figure 32

2

- Click the New folder button on the toolbar to display a new folder icon and text box for the folder.

- Type **Word** in the text box to name the folder.

- Press the ENTER key to create the folder (Figure 33).

Figure 33

To Create the Remaining Folders

The following steps create the remaining folders in the folder identifying your class (in this case, CIS 101).

1 Click the New folder button on the toolbar to display a new folder icon and text box.

2 Type **PowerPoint** in the text box to name the folder.

3 Repeat Steps 1 and 2 to create each of the remaining folders, using the names Excel, Access, Outlook, Publisher, and OneNote as the folder names (Figure 34).

Figure 34

To Expand a Folder, Scroll through Folder Contents, and Collapse a Folder

Folder windows display the hierarchy of items and the contents of drives and folders in the right pane. You might want to expand a drive in the navigation pane to view its contents, scroll through its contents, and collapse it when you are finished viewing its contents. When a folder is expanded, it lists all the folders it contains. By contrast, a collapsed folder does not list the folders it contains. The following steps expand, scroll through, and then collapse the folder identifying your class (CIS 101, in this case).

1

• Double-click the folder identifying your class (CIS 101, in this case), which expands the folder to display its contents and displays a black arrow to the left of the folder icon (Figure 35).

Q&A Why are the subject folders indented below the CIS 101 folder in the navigation pane?

It shows that the folders are contained within the CIS 101 folder.

Q&A Why did a scroll bar appear in the navigation pane?

When all contents cannot fit in a window or pane, a scroll bar appears. As described earlier, you can view areas currently not visible by (1) clicking the scroll arrows, (2) clicking above or below the scroll bar, and (3) dragging the scroll box.

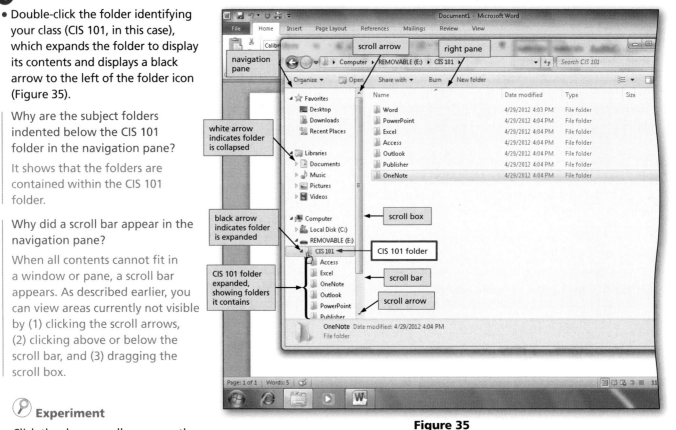

Figure 35

Experiment

• Click the down scroll arrow on the vertical scroll bar to display additional folders at the bottom of the navigation pane.

• Click the scroll bar above the scroll box to move the scroll box to the top of the navigation pane.

• Drag the scroll box down the scroll bar until the scroll box is halfway down the scroll bar.

2

• Double-click the folder identifying your class (CIS 101, in this case) to collapse the folder (Figure 36).

Other Ways

1. Point in navigation pane to display arrows, click white arrow to expand or click black arrow to collapse

2. Select folder to expand or collapse using arrow keys, press RIGHT ARROW to expand; press LEFT ARROW to collapse.

Figure 36

To Switch from One Program to Another

The next step is to save the Word file containing the headline you typed earlier. Word, however, currently is not the active window. You can use the program button on the taskbar and live preview to switch to Word and then save the document in the Word document window.

If Windows Aero is active on your computer, Windows displays a live preview window whenever you move your mouse on a button or click a button on the taskbar. If Aero is not supported or enabled on your computer, you will see a window title instead of a live preview. The steps below use the Word program; however, the steps are the same for any active Office program currently displayed as a program button on the taskbar.

The following steps switch to the Word window.

1

- Point to the Word program button on the taskbar to see a live preview of the open document(s) or the window title(s) of the open document(s), depending on your computer's configuration (Figure 37).

2

- Click the program button or the live preview to make the program associated with the program button the active window (shown in Figure 27 on page OFF 20).

Figure 37

Q&A What if multiple documents are open in a program?

If Aero is enabled on your computer, click the desired live preview. If Aero is not supported or not enabled, click the window title.

To Save a File in a Folder

Now that you have created the folders for storing files, you can save the Word document. The following steps save a file on a USB flash drive in the Word folder contained in your class folder (CIS 101, in this case) using the file name, Koala Exhibit.

1

- With a USB flash drive connected to one of the computer's USB ports, click the Save button on the Quick Access Toolbar to display the Save As dialog box (Figure 38).

Q&A Why does a file name already appear in the File name text box?

Word automatically suggests a file name the first time you save a document. The file name normally consists of the first few words contained in the document. Because the suggested file name is selected, you do not need to delete it; as soon as you begin typing, the new file name replaces the selected text.

Figure 38

2

- Type **Koala Exhibit** in the File name text box (Save As dialog box) to change the file name. Do not press the ENTER key after typing the file name because you do not want to close the dialog box at this time (Figure 39).

Q&A

What characters can I use in a file name?

The only invalid characters are the backslash (\), slash (/), colon (:), asterisk (*), question mark (?), quotation mark ("), less than symbol (<), greater than symbol (>), and vertical bar (|).

Figure 39

3

- Navigate to the desired save location (in this case, the Word folder in the CIS 101 folder [or your class folder] on the USB flash drive) by performing the tasks in Steps 3a, 3b, and 3c.

3a

- If the navigation pane is not displayed in the dialog box, click the Browse Folders button to expand the dialog box.

- If Computer is not displayed in the navigation pane, drag the navigation pane scroll bar until Computer appears.

- If Computer is not expanded in the navigation pane, double-click Computer to display a list of available storage devices in the navigation pane.

- If necessary, scroll through the dialog box until your USB flash drive appears in the list of available storage devices in the navigation pane (Figure 40).

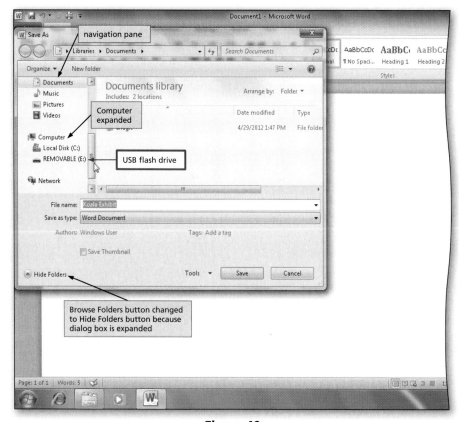

Figure 40

3b

- If your USB flash drive is not expanded, double-click the USB flash drive in the list of available storage devices in the navigation pane to select that drive as the new save location and display its contents in the right pane.

3c

- If your class folder (CIS 101, in this case) is not expanded, double-click the CIS 101 folder to select the folder and display its contents in the right pane.

Q&A What if I do not want to save in a folder?

Although storing files in folders is an effective technique for organizing files, some users prefer not to store files in folders. If you prefer not to save this file in a folder, skip all instructions in Step 3c and proceed to Step 4.

Figure 41

- Click the Word folder to select the folder and display its contents in the right pane (Figure 41).

4

- Click the Save button (Save As dialog box) to save the document in the selected folder on the selected drive with the entered file name (Figure 42).

Q&A How do I know that the file is saved?

While an Office program is saving a file, it briefly displays a message on the status bar indicating the amount of the file saved. In addition, the USB flash drive may have a light that flashes during the save process.

Figure 42

Other Ways	
1. Click File on Ribbon, click Save, type file name, navigate to desired save location, click Save button	2. Press CTRL+S or press SHIFT+F12, type file name, navigate to desired save location, click Save button

Navigating in Dialog Boxes

Navigating is the process of finding a location on a storage device. While saving the Koala Exhibit file, for example, Steps 3a – 3c in the previous set of steps navigated to the Word folder located in the CIS 101 folder. When performing certain functions in Windows programs, such as saving a file, opening a file, or inserting a picture in an existing document, you most likely will have to navigate to the location where you want to save the file or to the folder containing the file you want to open or insert. Most dialog boxes in Windows programs requiring navigation follow a similar procedure; that is, the way you navigate to a folder in one dialog box, such as the Save As dialog box, is similar to how you might navigate in another dialog box, such as the Open dialog box. If you chose to navigate to a specific location in a dialog box, you would follow the instructions in Steps 3a – 3c on pages OFF 28 and OFF 29.

To Minimize and Restore a Window

Before continuing, you can verify that the Word file was saved properly. To do this, you will minimize the Word window and then open the USB flash drive window so that you can verify the file is stored on the USB flash drive. A **minimized window** is an open window hidden from view but that can be displayed quickly by clicking the window's program button on the taskbar.

In the following example, Word is used to illustrate minimizing and restoring windows; however, you would follow the same steps regardless of the Office program you are using.

The following steps minimize the Word window, verify that the file is saved, and then restore the minimized window.

1

- Click the Minimize button on the program's title bar (shown in Figure 42 on the previous page) to minimize the window (Figure 43).

Q&A

Is the minimized window still available?

The minimized window, Word in this case, remains available but no longer is the active window. It is minimized as a program button on the taskbar.

- If necessary, click the Windows Explorer program button on the taskbar to open the USB flash drive window.

Figure 43

2

- Double-click the Word folder to select the folder and display its contents (Figure 44).

Figure 44

Q&A

Why does the Windows Explorer button on the taskbar change?

The button changes to reflect the status of the folder window (in this case, the USB flash drive window). A selected button indicates that the folder window is active on the screen. When the button is not selected, the window is open but not active.

3

- After viewing the contents of the selected folder, click the Word program button on the taskbar to restore the minimized window (as shown in Figure 42 on page OFF 29).

Other Ways
1. Right-click title bar, click Minimize on shortcut menu, click taskbar button in taskbar button area   2. Press WINDOWS+M, press WINDOWS+SHIFT+M

Screen Resolution

Screen resolution indicates the number of pixels (dots) that the computer uses to display the letters, numbers, graphics, and background you see on the screen. When you increase the screen resolution, Windows displays more information on the screen, but the information decreases in size. The reverse also is true: as you decrease the screen resolution, Windows displays less information on the screen, but the information increases in size.

Screen resolution usually is stated as the product of two numbers, such as 1024 × 768 (pronounced "ten twenty-four by seven sixty-eight"). A 1024 × 768 screen resolution results in a display of 1,024 distinct pixels on each of 768 lines, or about

786,432 pixels. Changing the screen resolution affects how the Ribbon appears in Office programs. Figure 45 shows the Word Ribbon at screen resolutions of 1024×768 and 1280×800. All of the same commands are available regardless of screen resolution. Word, however, makes changes to the groups and the buttons within the groups to accommodate the various screen resolutions. The result is that certain commands may need to be accessed differently depending on the resolution chosen. A command that is visible on the Ribbon and available by clicking a button at one resolution may not be visible and may need to be accessed using its Dialog Box Launcher at a different resolution.

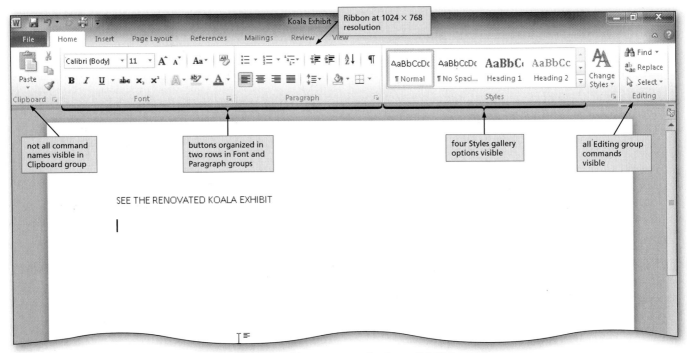

Figure 45 (a) Ribbon at Resolution of 1024 x 768

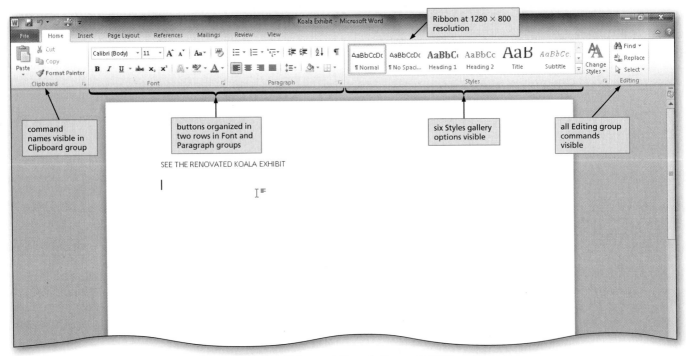

Figure 45 (b) Ribbon at Resolution of 1280 x 800

Comparing the two Ribbons in Figure 45, notice the changes in content and layout of the groups and galleries. In some cases, the content of a group is the same in each resolution, but the layout of the group differs. For example, the same gallery and buttons appear in the Styles groups in the two resolutions, but the layouts differ. In other cases, the content and layout are the same across the resolution, but the level of detail differs with the resolution. In the Clipboard group, when the resolution increases to 1280×800, the names of all the buttons in the group appear in addition to the buttons themselves. At the lower resolution, only the buttons appear.

To Change the Screen Resolution

If you are using a computer to step through the chapters in this book and you want your screen to match the figures, you may need to change your screen's resolution. The figures in this book use a screen resolution of 1024×768. The following steps change the screen resolution to 1024×768. Your computer already may be set to 1024×768 or some other resolution. Keep in mind that many computer labs prevent users from changing the screen resolution; in that case, read the following steps for illustration purposes.

1

- Click the Show desktop button on the taskbar to display the Windows 7 desktop.

- Right-click an empty area on the Windows 7 desktop to display a shortcut menu that displays a list of commands related to the desktop (Figure 46).

Q&A Why does my shortcut menu display different commands?

Depending on your computer's hardware and configuration, different commands might appear on the shortcut menu.

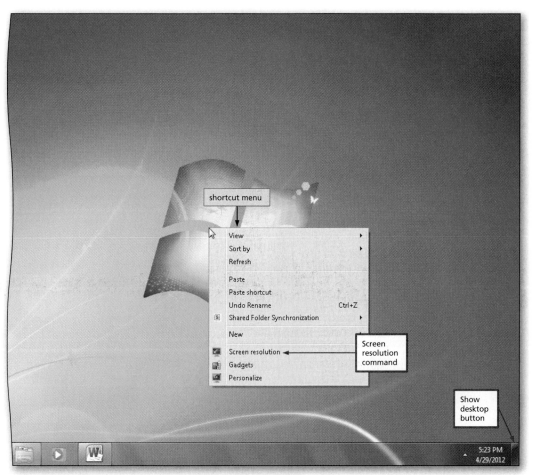

Figure 46

2
- Click Screen resolution on the shortcut menu to open the Screen Resolution window (Figure 47).

Figure 47

3
- Click the Resolution button in the Screen Resolution window to display the resolution slider.

Q&A What is a slider?

A **slider** is an object that allows users to choose from multiple predetermined options. In most cases, these options represent some type of numeric value. In most cases, one end of the slider (usually the left or bottom) represents the lowest of available values, and the opposite end (usually the right or top) represents the highest available value.

4
- If necessary, drag the resolution slider until the desired screen resolution (in this case, 1024 × 768) is selected (Figure 48).

Q&A What if my computer does not support the 1024 × 768 resolution?

Some computers do not support the 1024 × 768 resolution. In this case, select a resolution that is close to the 1024 × 768 resolution.

Figure 48

5

- Click an empty area of the Screen Resolution window to close the resolution slider.

- Click the OK button to change the screen resolution and display the Display Settings dialog box (Figure 49).

- Click the Keep changes button (Display Settings dialog box) to accept the new screen resolution.

Q&A Why does a message display stating that the image quality can be improved?

Some computer monitors are designed to display contents better at a certain screen resolution, sometimes referred to as an optimal resolution.

Figure 49

To Quit an Office Program with One Document Open

When you quit an Office program, such as Word, if you have made changes to a file since the last time the file was saved, the Office program displays a dialog box asking if you want save the changes you made to the file before it closes the program window. The dialog box contains three buttons with these resulting actions: the Save button saves the changes and then quits the Office program, the Don't Save button quits the Office program without saving changes, and the Cancel button closes the dialog box and redisplays the file without saving the changes.

If no changes have been made to an open document since the last time the file was saved, the Office program will close the window without displaying a dialog box.

The following steps quit an Office program. In the following example, Word is used to illustrate quitting an Office program; however, you would follow the same steps regardless of the Office program you were using.

1

- If necessary, click the Word program button on the taskbar to display the Word window on the desktop.

- Point to the Close button on the right side of the program's title bar, Word in this case (Figure 50).

Figure 50

2

- Click the Close button to close the document and quit Word.

Q&A What if I have more than one document open in an Office program?

You would click the Close button for each open document. When you click the last open document's Close button, the Office program also quits. As an alternative, you could click File on the Ribbon to open the Backstage view and then click Exit in the Backstage view to close all open documents and quit the Office program.

Q&A What is the Backstage view?

The **Backstage view** contains a set of commands that enable you to manage documents and data about the documents. The Backstage view is discussed in more depth later in this chapter.

3

- If a Microsoft Word dialog box appears, click the Save button to save any changes made to the document since the last save.

Other Ways

1. Right-click the Office program button on Windows 7 taskbar, click Close window or 'Close all windows' on shortcut menu
2. Press ALT+F4

Break Point: If you wish to take a break, this is a good place to do so. To resume at a later time, continue to follow the steps from this location forward.

Additional Microsoft Office Programs

The previous section used Word to illustrate common features of Office and some basic elements unique to Word. The following sections present elements unique to PowerPoint, Excel, and Access, as well as illustrate additional common features of Office.

In the following pages, you will learn how to do the following:

1. Start an Office program (PowerPoint) using the search box.
2. Create two small documents in the same Office program (PowerPoint).
3. Close one of the documents.
4. Reopen the document just closed.
5. Create a document in a different Office program (Excel).
6. Save the document with a new file name.
7. Create a file in a different Office program (Access).
8. Close the file and then open the file.

PowerPoint

PowerPoint is a complete presentation program that allows you to produce professional-looking presentations (Figure 51). A PowerPoint **presentation** also is called a **slide show**. PowerPoint contains several features to simplify creating a slide show. To make presentations more impressive, you can add diagrams, tables, pictures, video, sound, and animation effects. Additional PowerPoint features include the following:

- **Word processing** — Create bulleted lists, combine words and images, find and replace text, and use multiple fonts and font sizes.
- **Outlining** — Develop a presentation using an outline format. You also can import outlines from Microsoft Word or other word processing programs, including single-level and multilevel lists.
- **Charting** — Create and insert charts into presentations and then add effects and chart elements.
- **Drawing** — Create and modify diagrams using shapes such as arcs, arrows, cubes, rectangles, stars, and triangles. Then, customize and add effects to the diagrams, and arrange these objects by sizing, scaling, and rotating them.
- **Inserting multimedia** — Insert artwork and multimedia effects into a slide show. The Microsoft Clip Organizer, included with Office programs, contains hundreds of media files, including pictures, sounds, and movies.
- **Saving to the Web** — Save presentations or parts of a presentation so that they can be viewed in a Web browser. You can publish your slide show to the Internet or to an intranet.
- **E-mailing** — Send an entire slide show as an attachment to an e-mail message.
- **Collaborating** — Share a presentation with friends and coworkers. Ask them to review the slides and then insert comments that offer suggestions to enhance the presentation.
- **Preparing delivery** — Rehearse integrating PowerPoint slides into your speech by setting timings, using presentation tools, showing only selected slides in a presentation, and packaging the presentation for an optical disc.

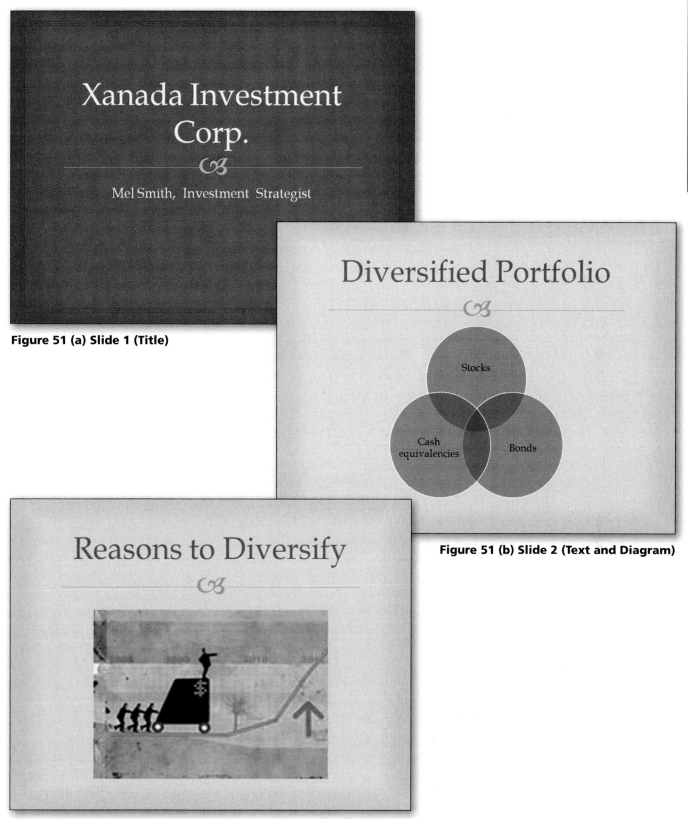

Figure 51 (a) Slide 1 (Title)

Figure 51 (b) Slide 2 (Text and Diagram)

Figure 51 (c) Slide 3 (Text and Picture)

To Start a Program Using the Search Box

The steps on the next page, which assume Windows 7 is running, use the search box to start the PowerPoint Office program based on a typical installation; however, you would follow similar steps to start any Office program. You may need to ask your instructor how to start programs for your computer.

1

- Click the Start button on the Windows 7 taskbar to display the Start menu.

2

- Type **Microsoft PowerPoint** as the search text in the 'Search programs and files' text box and watch the search results appear on the Start menu (Figure 52).

Q&A

Do I need to type the complete program name or correct capitalization?

No, just enough of it for the program name to appear on the Start menu. For example, you may be able to type PowerPoint or powerpoint, instead of Microsoft PowerPoint.

Figure 52

3

- Click the program name, Microsoft PowerPoint 2010 in this case, in the search results on the Start menu to start PowerPoint and display a new blank presentation in the PowerPoint window.

- If the program window is not maximized, click the Maximize button on its title bar to maximize the window (Figure 53).

Figure 53

The PowerPoint Window and Ribbon

The PowerPoint window consists of a variety of components to make your work more efficient and documents more professional: the window, Ribbon, Mini toolbar, shortcut menus, and Quick Access Toolbar. Many of these components are common to other Office programs and have been discussed earlier in this chapter. Other components, discussed in the following paragraphs and later in subsequent chapters, are unique to PowerPoint.

The basic unit of a PowerPoint presentation is a **slide**. A slide may contain text and objects, such as graphics, tables, charts, and drawings. **Layouts** are used to position this content on the slide. When you create a new presentation, the default **Title Slide** layout appears (Figure 54). The purpose of this layout is to introduce the presentation to the audience. PowerPoint includes eight other built-in standard layouts.

The default slide layouts are set up in **landscape orientation**, where the slide width is greater than its height. In landscape orientation, the slide size is preset to 10 inches wide and 7.5 inches high when printed on a standard sheet of paper measuring 11 inches wide and 8.5 inches high.

BTW

Portrait Orientation
If your slide content is dominantly vertical, such as a skyscraper or a person, consider changing the slide layout to a portrait orientation. To change the orientation to portrait, click the Slide Orientation button (Design tab | Page Setup group) and then click Portrait. You can use both landscape and portrait orientation in the same slide show.

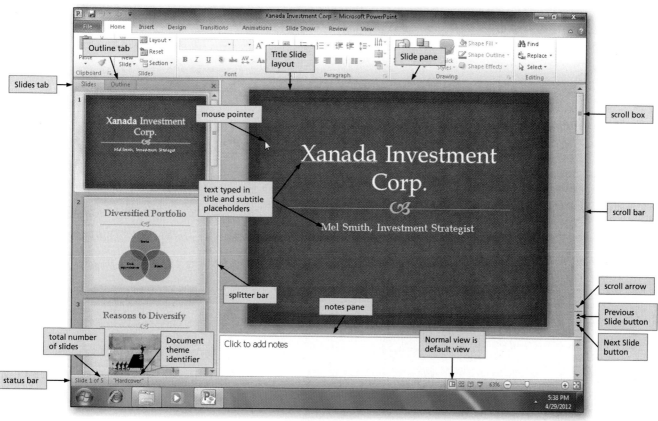

Figure 54

Placeholders **Placeholders** are boxes with dotted or hatch-marked borders that are displayed when you create a new slide. All layouts except the Blank slide layout contain placeholders. Depending on the particular slide layout selected, title and subtitle placeholders are displayed for the slide title and subtitle; a content text placeholder is displayed for text, art, or a table, chart, picture, graphic, or movie. The title slide in Figure 53 has two text placeholders for the main heading, or title, of a new slide and the subtitle.

Ribbon The Ribbon in PowerPoint is similar to the one in Word and the other Microsoft Office programs. When you start PowerPoint, the Ribbon displays nine main tabs: File, Home, Insert, Design, Transitions, Animations, Slide Show, Review, and View.

To Enter Content in a Title Slide

With the exception of a blank slide and a slide with a picture and caption, PowerPoint assumes every new slide has a title. Many of PowerPoint's layouts have both a title text placeholder and at least one content placeholder. To make creating a presentation easier, any text you type after a new slide appears becomes title text in the title text placeholder. As you begin typing text in the title text placeholder, the title text also is displayed in the Slide 1 thumbnail in the Slides tab. The presentation title for this presentation is Xanada Investments. The following steps enter a presentation title on the title slide.

1

- Click the label 'Click to add title' located inside the title text placeholder (shown in Figure 53 on page OFF 38) to select the placeholder (Figure 55).

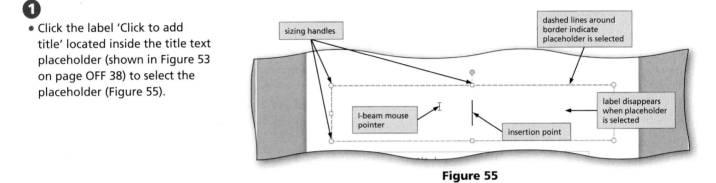

Figure 55

2

- Type **Xanada Investments** in the title text placeholder. Do not press the ENTER key because you do not want to create a new line of text (Figure 56).

 What are the white squares and circles that appear around the title text placeholder as I type the presentation title?

The white squares and circles are sizing handles, which you can drag to change the size of the title text placeholder. Sizing handles also can be found around other placeholders and objects within a presentation.

Figure 56

To Save a File in a Folder

The following steps save the presentation in the PowerPoint folder in the class folder (CIS 101, in this case) on a USB flash drive using the file name, Xanada Investments.

1 With a USB flash drive connected to one of the computer's USB ports, click the Save button on the Quick Access Toolbar to display the Save As dialog box.

2 If necessary, type **Xanada Investments** in the File name text box to change the file name. Do not press the ENTER key after typing the file name because you do not want to close the dialog box at this time.

3 Navigate to the desired save location (in this case, the PowerPoint folder in the CIS 101 folder [or your class folder] on the USB flash drive). For specific instructions, perform the tasks in Steps 3a through 3g.

3a If a navigation pane is not displayed in the Save As dialog box, click the Browse Folders button to expand the dialog box.

3b If Computer is not displayed in the navigation pane, drag the navigation pane scroll bar (Save As dialog box) until Computer appears.

3c If Computer is not expanded in the navigation pane, double-click Computer to display a list of available storage devices in the navigation pane.

3d If necessary, scroll through the Save As dialog box until your USB flash drive appears in the list of available storage devices in the navigation pane.

3e If your USB flash drive is not expanded, double-click the USB flash drive in the list of available storage devices in the navigation pane to select that drive as the new save location and display its contents in the right pane.

3f If your class folder (CIS 101, in this case) is not expanded, double-click the CIS 101 folder to select the folder and display its contents.

3g Click the PowerPoint folder to select it as the new save location and display its contents in the right pane.

4 Click the Save button (Save As dialog box) to save the presentation in the selected folder on the selected drive with the entered file name.

To Create a New Office Document from the Backstage View

As discussed earlier, the Backstage view contains a set of commands that enable you to manage documents and data about the documents. From the Backstage view in PowerPoint, for example, you can create, open, print, and save presentations. You also can share documents, manage versions, set permissions, and modify document properties. In other Office 2010 programs, the Backstage view may contain features specific to those programs. The steps on the following pages create a file, a blank presentation in this case, from the Backstage view.

1

- Click File on the Ribbon to open the Backstage view (Figure 57).

Q&A

What is the purpose of the File tab?

The **File** tab is used to display the Backstage view for each Office program.

Figure 57

2

- Click the New tab in the Backstage view to display the New gallery (Figure 58).

Q&A

Can I create documents through the Backstage view in other Office programs?

Yes. If the Office program has a New tab in the Backstage view, the New gallery displays various options for creating a new file.

Figure 58

3
• Click the Create button in the New gallery to create a new presentation (Figure 59).

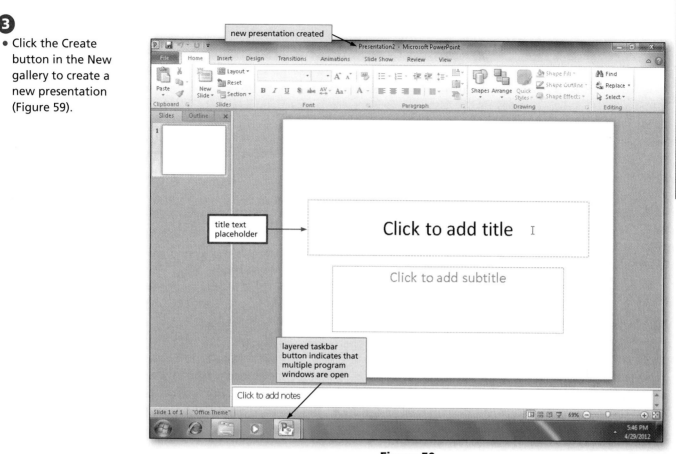

Figure 59

Other Ways
1. Press CTRL+N

To Enter Content in a Title Slide of a Second PowerPoint Presentation

The presentation title for this presentation is Koala Exhibit Gala. The following steps enter a presentation title on the title slide.

1 Click the title text placeholder (shown in Figure 59) to select it.

2 Type **Koala Exhibit Gala** in the title text placeholder. Do not press the ENTER key (Figure 60).

Figure 60

To Save a File in a Folder

The following steps save the second presentation in the PowerPoint folder in the class folder (CIS 101, in this case) on a USB flash drive using the file name, Koala Exhibit Gala.

1 With a USB flash drive connected to one of the computer's USB ports, click the Save button on the Quick Access Toolbar to display the Save As dialog box.

2 If necessary, type **Koala Exhibit Gala** in the File name text box to change the file name. Do not press the ENTER key after typing the file name because you do not want to close the dialog box at this time.

3 If necessary, navigate to the desired save location (in this case, the PowerPoint folder in the CIS 101 folder [or your class folder] on the USB flash drive).

4 Click the Save button (Save As dialog box) to save the presentation in the selected folder on the selected drive with the entered file name.

To Close an Office File Using the Backstage View

Sometimes, you may want to close an Office file, such as a PowerPoint presentation, entirely and start over with a new file. You also may want to close a file when you are finished working with it so that you can begin a new file. The following steps close the current active Office file, that is, the Koala Exhibit Gala presentation, without quitting the active program (PowerPoint in this case).

1
• Click File on the Ribbon to open the Backstage view (Figure 61).

2
• Click Close in the Backstage view to close the open file (Koala Exhibit Gala, in this case) without quitting the active program.

Q&A What if the Office program displays a dialog box about saving?

Click the Save button if you want to save the changes, click the Don't Save button if you want to ignore the changes since the last time you saved, and click the Cancel button if you do not want to close the document.

Q&A Can I use the Backstage view to close an open file in other Office programs, such as Word and Excel?

Yes.

Figure 61

To Open a Recent Office File Using the Backstage View

You sometimes need to open a file that you recently modified. You may have more changes to make such as adding more content or correcting errors. The Backstage view allows you to access recent files easily. The following steps reopen the Koala Exhibit Gala file just closed.

1

- Click File on the Ribbon to open the Backstage view.

- Click the Recent tab in the Backstage view to display the Recent gallery (Figure 62).

2

- Click the desired file name in the Recent gallery, Koala Exhibit Gala in this case, to open the file (shown in Figure 60 on page OFF 43).

Q&A

Can I use the Backstage view to open a recent file in other Office programs, such as Word and Excel?

Yes, as long as the file name appears in the list of recent files in the Recent gallery.

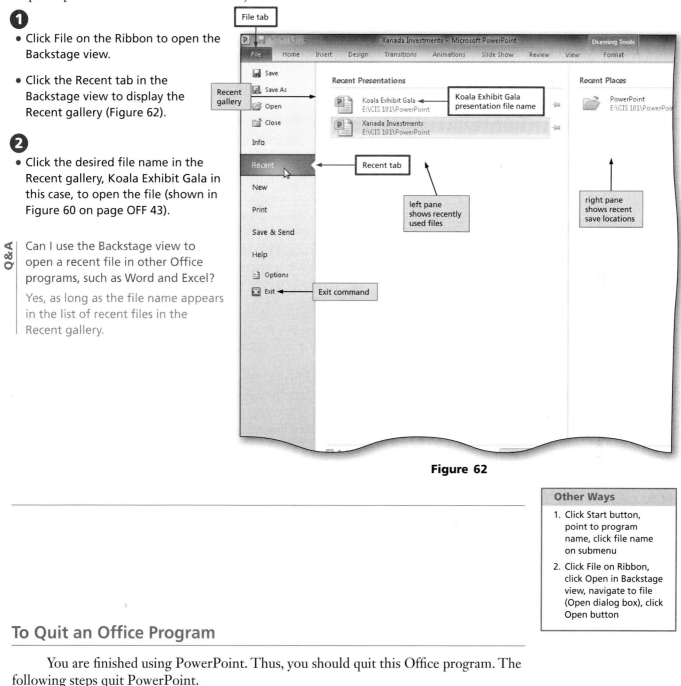

Figure 62

Other Ways

1. Click Start button, point to program name, click file name on submenu
2. Click File on Ribbon, click Open in Backstage view, navigate to file (Open dialog box), click Open button

To Quit an Office Program

You are finished using PowerPoint. Thus, you should quit this Office program. The following steps quit PowerPoint.

1 If you have one Office document open, click the Close button on the right side of the title bar to close the document and quit the Office program; or if you have multiple Office documents open, click File on the Ribbon to open the Backstage view and then click Exit in the Backstage view to close all open documents and quit the Office program.

2 If a dialog box appears, click the Save button to save any changes made to the document since the last save.

Excel

Excel is a powerful spreadsheet program that allows users to organize data, complete calculations, make decisions, graph data, develop professional-looking reports (Figure 63), publish organized data to the Web, and access real-time data from Web sites. The four major parts of Excel are:

- **Workbooks and Worksheets** - A **workbook** is like a notebook. Inside the workbook are sheets, each of which is called a **worksheet**. In other words, a workbook is a collection of worksheets. Worksheets allow users to enter, calculate, manipulate, and analyze data such as numbers and text. The terms worksheet and spreadsheet are interchangeable.

- **Charts** - Excel can draw a variety of charts.

- **Tables** - Tables organize and store data within worksheets. For example, once a user enters data into a worksheet, an Excel table can sort the data, search for specific data, and select data that satisfies defined criteria.

- **Web Support -** Web support allows users to save Excel worksheets or parts of a worksheet in HTML format, so that a user can view and manipulate the worksheet using a browser. Excel Web support also provides access to real-time data, such as stock quotes, using Web queries.

Figure 63

To Create a New Blank Office Document from Windows Explorer

Windows Explorer provides a means to create a blank Office document without ever starting an Office program. The following steps use Windows Explorer to create a blank Excel document.

1

- If necessary, click the Windows Explorer program button on the taskbar to make the folder window the active window in Windows Explorer.

- Double-click your class folder (CIS 101, in this case) in the navigation pane to display the contents of the selected folder.

- Double-click the Excel folder to display its contents in the right pane.

- With the Excel folder selected, right-click an open area in the right pane to display a shortcut menu.

- Point to New on the shortcut menu to display the New submenu (Figure 64).

Figure 64

2

- Click Microsoft Excel Worksheet on the New submenu to display an icon and text box for a new file in the current folder window (Figure 65).

Figure 65

3

- Type **Brain Busters** in the text box and then press the ENTER key to assign a name to the new file in the current folder (Figure 66).

Figure 66

To Start a Program from Windows Explorer and Open a File

Previously, you learned how to start an Office program using the Start menu and the search box. Another way start an Office program is to open an existing file from Windows Explorer, which causes the program in which the file was created to start and then open the selected file. The following steps, which assume Windows 7 is running, use Windows Explorer to start the Excel Office program based on a typical installation. You may need to ask your instructor how to start Office programs for your computer.

1

- If necessary, display the file to open in the folder window in Windows Explorer (shown in Figure 66 on the previous page).

- Right-click the file icon or file name (Brain Busters, in this case) to display a shortcut menu (Figure 67).

2

- Click Open on the shortcut menu to open the selected file in the program used to create the file, Microsoft Excel in this case (Figure 68).

- If the program window is not maximized, click the Maximize button on the title bar to maximize the window.

- For Excel users, if the worksheet window in Excel is not maximized, click the worksheet window Maximize button to maximize the worksheet window within Excel.

Figure 67

Figure 68

Instead of using Windows Explorer, can I start Excel using the same method shown previously for Word and PowerPoint?

Yes, you can use any method of starting an Office program to start Excel.

Unique Features of Excel

The Excel window consists of a variety of components to make your work more efficient and worksheets more professional. These include the document window, Ribbon, Mini toolbar and shortcut menus, Quick Access Toolbar, and the Backstage view. Some of these components are common to other Microsoft Office 2010 programs; others are unique to Excel.

Excel opens a new workbook with three worksheets. If necessary, you can add additional worksheets as long as your computer has enough memory to accommodate them.

Each worksheet has a sheet name that appears on a **sheet tab** at the bottom of the workbook. For example, Sheet1 is the name of the active worksheet displayed in the Brain Busters workbook. If you click the sheet tab labeled Sheet2, Excel displays the Sheet2 worksheet.

The Worksheet   The worksheet is organized into a rectangular grid containing vertical columns and horizontal rows. A column letter above the grid, also called the **column heading**, identifies each column. A row number on the left side of the grid, also called the **row heading**, identifies each row. With the screen resolution set to 1024 × 768 and the Excel window maximized, Excel displays 15 columns (A through O) and 25 rows (1 through 25) of the worksheet on the screen, as shown in Figure 68.

The intersection of each column and row is a cell. A **cell** is the basic unit of a worksheet into which you enter data. Each worksheet in a workbook has 16,384 columns and 1,048,576 rows for a total of 17,179,869,180 cells. Only a small fraction of the active worksheet appears on the screen at one time.

A cell is referred to by its unique address, or **cell reference**, which is the coordinates of the intersection of a column and a row. To identify a cell, specify the column letter first, followed by the row number. For example, cell reference E2 refers to the cell located at the intersection of column E and row 2 (Figure 68).

One cell on the worksheet, designated the **active cell**, is the one into which you can enter data. The active cell in Figure 68 is A1. The active cell is identified in three ways. First, a heavy border surrounds the cell; second, the active cell reference shows immediately above column A in the Name box; and third, the column heading A and row heading 1 are highlighted so it is easy to see which cell is active (Figure 68).

The horizontal and vertical lines on the worksheet itself are called **gridlines**. Gridlines make it easier to see and identify each cell in the worksheet. If desired, you can turn the gridlines off so that they do not show on the worksheet, but it is recommended that you leave them on for now.

The mouse pointer in Figure 68 has the shape of a block plus sign. The mouse pointer appears as a block plus sign whenever it is located in a cell on the worksheet. Another common shape of the mouse pointer is the block arrow. The mouse pointer turns into the block arrow when you move it outside the worksheet or when you drag cell contents between rows or columns. The other mouse pointer shapes are described when they appear on the screen.

Ribbon   When you start Excel, the Ribbon displays eight main tabs: File, Home, Insert, Page Layout, Formulas, Data, Review, and View. The Formulas and Data tabs are specific to Excel. The Formulas tab allows you to work with Excel formulas, and the Data tab allows you to work with data processing features such as importing and sorting data.

BTW

The Worksheet Size and Window
The 16,384 columns and 1,048,576 rows in Excel make for a huge worksheet that – if you could imagine – takes up the entire side of a building to display in its entirety. Your computer screen, by comparison, is a small window that allows you to view only a minute area of the worksheet at one time. While you cannot see the entire worksheet, you can move the window over the worksheet to view any part of it.

BTW

Customizing the Ribbon
In addition to customizing the Quick Access Toolbar, you can add items to and remove items from the Ribbon. To customize the Ribbon, click File on the Ribbon to open the Backstage view, click Options in the Backstage view, and then click Customize Ribbon in the left pane of the Options dialog box. More information about customizing the Ribbon is presented in a later chapter.

Formula Bar   The formula bar appears below the Ribbon (Figure 69). As you type, Excel displays the entry in the **formula bar**. You can make the formula bar larger by dragging the sizing handle at the bottom of the formula bar or clicking the expand button to the right of the formula bar. Excel also displays the active cell reference in the **Name box** on the left side of the formula bar.

Figure 69

To Enter a Worksheet Title

To enter data into a cell, you first must select it. The easiest way to select a cell (make it active) is to use the mouse to move the block plus sign mouse pointer to the cell and then click. An alternative method is to use the arrow keys that are located just to the right of the typewriter keys on the keyboard. An arrow key selects the cell adjacent to the active cell in the direction of the arrow on the key.

In Excel, any set of characters containing a letter, hyphen (as in a telephone number), or space is considered text. **Text** is used to place titles, such as worksheet titles, column titles, and row titles, on the worksheet. The following steps enter the worksheet title in cell A1.

1

- If it is not already the active cell, click cell A1 to make it the active cell (Figure 70).

Figure 70

2

- Type **Brain Buster Book Rentals** in cell A1 (Figure 71).

Q&A

Why did the appearance of the formula bar change?

Excel displays the title in the formula bar and in cell A1. When you begin typing a cell entry, Excel displays two additional boxes in the formula bar: the Cancel box and the Enter box. Clicking the Enter box completes an entry. Clicking the Cancel box cancels an entry.

Figure 71

3

- Click the Enter box to complete the entry and enter the worksheet title in cell A1 (Figure 72).

Figure 72

Other Ways		
1. To complete entry, click any cell other than active cell	2. To complete entry, press ENTER, HOME, PAGE UP, PAGE DOWN, END,	UP, DOWN, LEFT ARROW, or RIGHT ARROW

To Save an Existing Office Document with the Same File Name

Saving frequently cannot be overemphasized. You have made modifications to the file (spreadsheet) since you created it. Thus, you should save again. Similarly, you should continue saving files frequently so that you do not lose your changes since the time you last saved the file. You can use the same file name, such as Brain Busters, to save the changes made to the document. The following step saves a file again.

1

- Click the Save button on the Quick Access Toolbar to overwrite the previously saved file (Brain Busters, in this case) on the USB flash drive (Figure 73).

Q&A

Why did the Save As dialog box not appear?

Office programs, including Excel, overwrite the document using the setting specified the first time you saved the document.

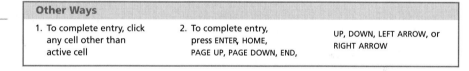

Figure 73

Other Ways
1. Press CTRL+S or press SHIFT+F12

To Use Save As to Change the Name of a File

You might want to save a file with a different name and even to a different location. For example, you might start a homework assignment with a data file and then save it with a final file name for submitting to your instructor, saving it to a location designated by your instructor. The following steps save a file with a different file name.

1 With your USB flash drive connected to one of the computer's USB ports, click File on the Ribbon to open the Backstage view.

2 Click Save As in the Backstage view to display the Save As dialog box.

3 Type **Brain Busters Rental Summary** in the File name text box (Save As dialog box) to change the file name. Do not press the ENTER key after typing the file name because you do not want to close the dialog box at this time.

4 Navigate to the desired save location (the Excel folder in the CIS 101 folder [or your class folder] on the USB flash drive, in this case). For specific instructions, perform the tasks in steps 4a through 4g.

4a If a navigation pane is not displayed in the Save As dialog box, click the Browse Folders button to expand the dialog box.

4b If Computer is not displayed in the navigation pane, drag the navigation pane scroll bar (Save As dialog box) until Computer appears.

4c If Computer is not expanded in the navigation pane, double-click Computer to display a list of available storage devices in the navigation pane.

4d If necessary, scroll through the Save As dialog box until your USB flash drive appears in the list of available storage devices in the navigation pane.

4e If your USB flash drive is not expanded, double-click the USB flash drive in the list of available storage devices in the navigation pane to select that drive as the new save location and display its contents in the right pane.

4f If your class folder (CIS 101, in this case) is not expanded, double-click the CIS 101 folder to select the folder and display its contents.

4g Double-click the Excel folder to select it and display its contents in the right pane.

5 Click the Save button (Save As dialog box) to save the file in the selected folder on the selected drive with the new file name.

To Quit an Office Program

You are finished using Excel. The following steps quit Excel.

1 If you have one Office document open, click the Close button on the right side of the title bar to close the document and quit the Office program; or if you have multiple Office documents open, click File on the Ribbon to open the Backstage view and then click Exit in the Backstage view to close all open documents and quit the Office program.

2 If a dialog box appears, click the Save button to save any changes made to the file since the last save.

Access

The term **database** describes a collection of data organized in a manner that allows access, retrieval, and use of that data. **Microsoft Access 2010**, usually referred to as simply **Access,** is a database management system. A **database management system** is software that allows you to use a computer to create a database; add, change, and delete data in the database; create queries that allow you to ask questions concerning the data in the database; and create forms and reports using the data in the database.

To Start a Program

The following steps, which assume Windows 7 is running, start the Access program based on a typical installation. You may need to ask your instructor how to start programs for your computer.

1 Click the Start button on the Windows 7 taskbar to display the Start menu.

2 Type the name of the program, `Microsoft Access` in this case, as the search text in the 'Search programs and files' text box and watch the search results appear on the Start menu.

3 Click the name of the program, Microsoft Access 2010 in this case, in the search results on the Start menu to start Access.

4 If the program window is not maximized, click the Maximize button on its title bar to maximize the window (Figure 74).

Q&A Do I have to start Access using these steps?

No. You can use any previously discussed method of starting an Office program to start Access.

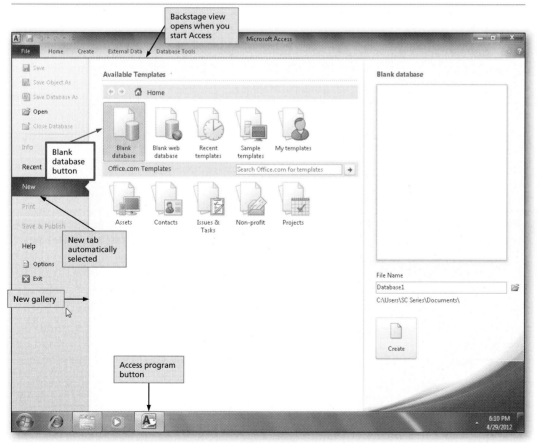

Figure 74

Unique Elements in Access

You work on objects such as tables, forms, and reports in the **Access work area**. In Figure 74, the Access window contains no open objects. Figure 75 shows a work area with multiple objects open. **Object tabs** for the open objects appear at the top of the work area. You select an open object by clicking its tab. In the figure, the Suppliers Split Form is the selected object. To the left of the work area is the Navigation Pane, which contains a list of all the objects in the database. You use this pane to open an object. You also can customize the way objects are displayed in the Navigation Pane.

Because the Navigation Pane can take up space in the window, you may not have as much open space for working as you would with Word or Excel. You can use the Shutter Bar Open/Close button to minimize the Navigation Pane when you are not using it, which allows more space to work with tables, forms, reports, and other database elements.

Figure 75

Ribbon When you start Access, the Ribbon displays five main tabs: File, Home, Create, External Data, and Database Tools. Access has unique groupings such as Sort & Filter and Records that are designed specifically for working with databases. Many of the formatting options are reserved for the tool tabs that appear when you are working with forms and reports.

To Create an Access Database

Unlike the other Office programs, Access saves a database when you first create it. When working in Access, you will add data to an Access database. As you add data to a database, Access automatically saves your changes rather than waiting until you manually save the database or quit Access. Recall that in Word and Excel, you entered the data first and then saved it.

Because Access automatically saves the database as you add and change data, you do not have to always click the Save button. In fact, the Save button in Access is used for saving the objects (including tables, queries, forms, reports, and other database objects) a database contains. You can use either the Blank Database option or a template to create a new database. If you already know the organization of your database, you would use the Blank Database option. If not, you can use a template. Templates can guide you by suggesting some commonly used database organizations.

The following steps use the Blank Database option to create a database named Charmed Excursions in the Access folder in the class folder (CIS 101, in this case) on a USB flash drive.

1

- If necessary, click the Blank database button in the New gallery (shown in Figure 74 on page OFF 53) in the Backstage view to select the template type.

- Click the File Name text box to select the default database name.

- Type **Charmed Excursions** in the File Name text box to enter the new file name. Do not press the ENTER key after typing the file name because you do not want to create the database at this time (Figure 76).

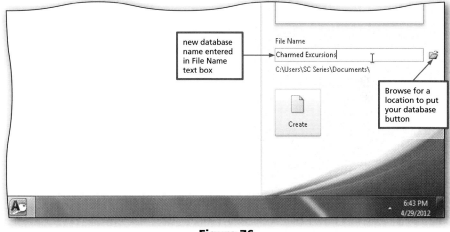

Figure 76

Q&A | Why is the Backstage view automatically open when you start Access?

Unlike other Office programs, you first must save a database before adding any data. For this reason, the Backstage view opens automatically when you start Access.

2

- Click the 'Browse for a location to put your database' button to display the File New Database dialog box.

- Navigate to the location for the database, that is, the USB flash drive, then to the folder identifying your class (CIS 101, in this case), and then to the Access folder (Figure 77). For detailed steps about navigating, see Steps 3a – 3c on pages OFF 28 and OFF 29.

Q&A | Why does the 'Save as type' box say Microsoft Access 2007 Databases?

Microsoft Access database formats change with some new versions of Microsoft Access. The most recent format is the Microsoft Access 2007 Databases format, which was released with Access 2007.

Figure 77

3

- Click the OK button (File New Database dialog box) to select the Access folder as the location for the database and close the dialog box (Figure 78).

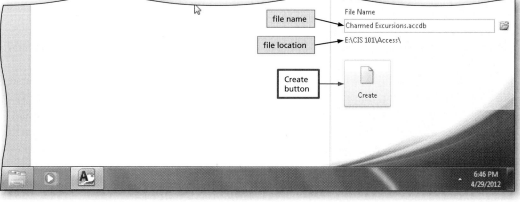

Figure 78

4

- Click the Create button in the Backstage view to create the database on the selected drive in the selected folder with the file name, Charmed Excursions. If necessary, click the Enable Content button (Figure 79).

Q&A

How do I know that the Charmed Excursions database is created?

The name of the database appears on the title bar.

Figure 79

To Close an Office File

Assume you need to close the Access database and return to it later. The following step closes an Office file.

1 Click File on the Ribbon to open the Backstage view and then click Close Database in the Backstage view to close the open file (Charmed Excursions, in this case) without quitting the active program.

Q&A

Why is Access still on the screen?

When you close a database, the program remains open.

To Open an Existing Office File

Assume you wish to continue working on an existing file, that is, a file you previously saved. Earlier in this chapter, you learned how to open a recently used file through the Backstage view. The following steps open a database, specifically the Charmed Excursions database, from the USB flash drive.

1

- With your USB flash drive connected to one of the computer's USB ports, if necessary, click File on the Ribbon to open the Backstage view.

- Click Open in the Backstage view to display the Open dialog box (Figure 80).

2

- Navigate to the location of the file to be opened (in this case, the USB flash drive, then to the CIS 101 folder [or your class folder], and then to the Access folder). For detailed steps about navigating, see Steps 3a – 3c on pages OFF 28 and OFF 29.

Q&A

What if I did not save my file in a folder?

If you did not save your file in a folder, the file you wish to open should be displayed in the Open dialog box before navigating to any folders.

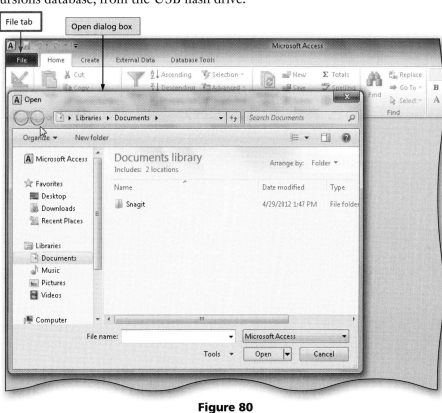

Figure 80

3

- Click the file to be opened, Charmed Excursions in this case, to select the file (Figure 81).

4

- Click the Open button (Open dialog box) to open the selected file and display the opened file in the current program window (shown in Figure 79).

Other Ways

1. Click File on the Ribbon, click Recent in Backstage view, double-click file

2. Press CTRL+O

3. Navigate to file in Windows Explorer, double-click file

Figure 81

To Quit an Office Program

You are finished using Access. The following step quits Access.

1 Click the Close button on the right side of the title bar to close the file and quit the Office program.

Other Office Programs

In addition to the Office programs discussed thus far, three other programs are useful when collaborating and communicating with others: Outlook, Publisher, and OneNote.

Outlook

Outlook is a powerful communications and scheduling program that helps you communicate with others, keep track of contacts, and organize your calendar. Personal information manager (PIM) programs such as Outlook provide a way for individuals and workgroups to organize, find, view, and share information easily. Outlook allows you to send and receive electronic mail (e-mail) and permits you to engage in real-time messaging with family, friends, or coworkers using instant messaging. Outlook also provides a means to organize contacts. Users can track e-mail messages, meetings, and notes related to a particular contact. Outlook's Calendar, Contacts, Tasks, and Notes components aid in this organization. Contact information readily is available from the Outlook Calendar, Mail, Contacts, and Task components by accessing the Find a Contact feature.

Electronic mail (e-mail) is the transmission of messages and files over a computer network. E-mail has become an important means of exchanging information and files between business associates, classmates and instructors, friends, and family. Businesses find that using e-mail to send documents electronically saves both time and money. Parents with students away at college or relatives who live across the country find that communicating by e-mail is an inexpensive and easy way to stay in touch with their family members. Exchanging e-mail messages is one of the more widely used features of the Internet.

The Outlook Window   Figure 82 shows an Outlook window, which is divided into six panes: the Favorites folder pane, Mail folder pane, and Navigation Pane on the left side of the window, the Inbox message pane to the left of center, the Reading Pane to the right of center, and the People Pane just below the Reading Pane.

When an e-mail message is open in Outlook, it is displayed in a Message window (Figure 83). When you open a message, the Message window Ribbon displays the Message tab, which contains the more frequently used commands.

Figure 82

Figure 83

Publisher

Publisher is a powerful desktop publishing (DTP) program that assists you in designing and producing professional-quality documents that combine text, graphics, illustrations, and photos. DTP software provides additional tools beyond those typically found in word processing programs, including design templates, graphic manipulation tools, color schemes or libraries, advanced layout and printing tools, and Web components. For large jobs, businesses use DTP software to design publications that are camera ready, which means the files are suitable for outside commercial printing. In addition, DTP software can be used to create Web pages and interactive Web forms.

Publisher is used by people who regularly produce high-quality color publications, such as newsletters, brochures, flyers, logos, signs, catalogs, cards, and business forms. Saving publications as Web pages or complete Web sites is a powerful component of Publisher. All publications can be saved in a format that easily is viewed and manipulated using a browser.

Publisher has many features designed to simplify production and make publications visually appealing. Using Publisher, you easily can change the shape, size, and color of text and graphics. You can include many kinds of graphical objects, including mastheads, borders, tables, images, pictures, charts, and Web objects in publications, as well as integrate spreadsheets and databases.

BTW

Starting Publisher
When you first start Publisher, the New templates gallery usually is displayed in the Backstage view. If it is not displayed, click File on the Ribbon, click Options in the Backstage view, click General (Options dialog box), and then click Show the New template gallery when starting Publisher to select the check box in the General panel.

The Publisher Window On the right side of the Backstage view, Publisher displays the New template gallery, which includes a list of publication types. **Publication types** are typical publications used by desktop publishers. The more popular types are displayed in the center of the window. Each publication type is a link to display various templates and blank publications from which you may choose.

Once you select a publication type, the window changes to allow you to select a specific template (Figure 84). Some templates are installed with Publisher, and others are available online. Clicking a publication type causes template previews to be displayed in the center of the window. The templates are organized by purpose (for example, Sales) and then alphabetically by design type. On the right, Publisher will display a larger preview of the selected template, along with some customization options if the template is installed or a download option if the template is online. In Figure 84, the installed Arrows template is selected so that the customize options appear.

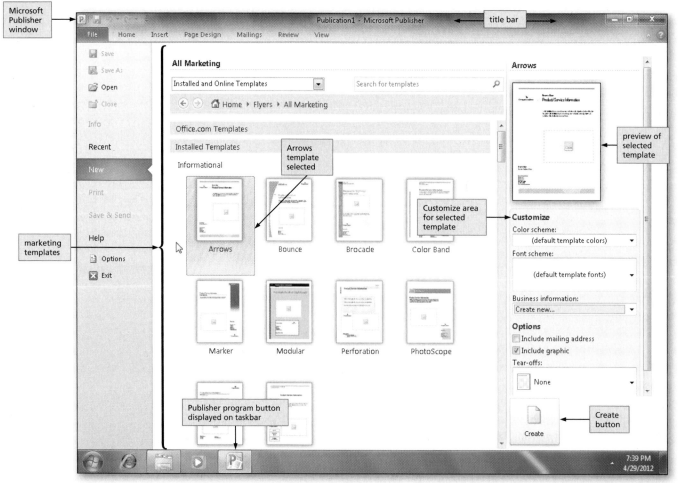

Figure 84

When you click the Create button, Publisher creates the document and sets it up for you to edit. Figure 85 shows the Arrows document that Publisher creates when default options are selected.

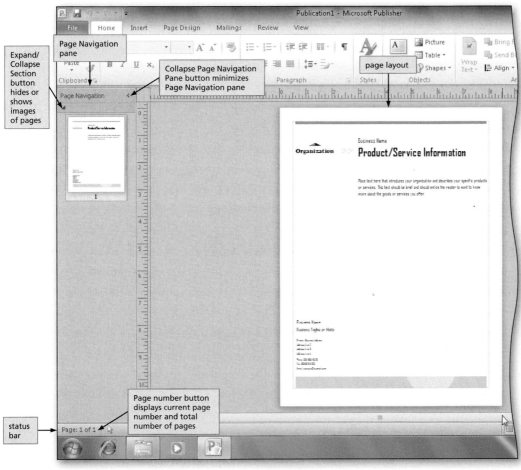

Figure 85

OneNote

OneNote is a note taking program that assists you in entering, saving, organizing, searching, and using notes. It enables you to create pages, which are organized in sections, just as in a physical notebook. In OneNote, you can type notes anywhere on a page and then easily move the notes around on the page. You can create lists and outlines, use handwriting to enter notes, and create drawings. If you use a Tablet PC to add handwritten notes to a document, OneNote can convert the handwriting to text. It also can perform searches on the handwritten entries. Pictures and data from other programs easily are incorporated in your notes.

In addition to typing and handwriting, you can take audio notes. For example, you could record conversations during a meeting or lecture. As you record, you can take additional notes. When you play back the audio notes, you can synchronize the additional notes you took; that is, OneNote will show you during playback the exact points at which you added the notes. A variety of note flags, which are symbols that call your attention to notes on a page, enable you to flag notes as being important. You then can use the Note Flags summary to view the flagged notes, which can be sorted in a variety of ways.

OneNote includes tools to assist you with organizing a notebook and navigating its contents. It also includes a search facility, making it easy to find the specific notes in which you are interested. For short notes that you always want to have available readily, you can use Side Notes, which are used much like the sticky notes that you might use in a physical notebook.

OneNote Window All activity in OneNote takes place in the **notebook** (Figure 86). Like a physical notebook, the OneNote notebook consists of notes that are placed on **pages**. The pages are grouped into **sections**, which can be further grouped into **folders**. (No folders are shown in the notebook in the figure.) You can use the Search All Notebooks box to search for specific text in your notes.

You can add pages to the notebook using the New Page button in the Page Tabs pane. If Page Tabs are displayed, then you can switch to a page by clicking its tab. Figure 86 shows the Top Uses page being displayed for the General notebook.

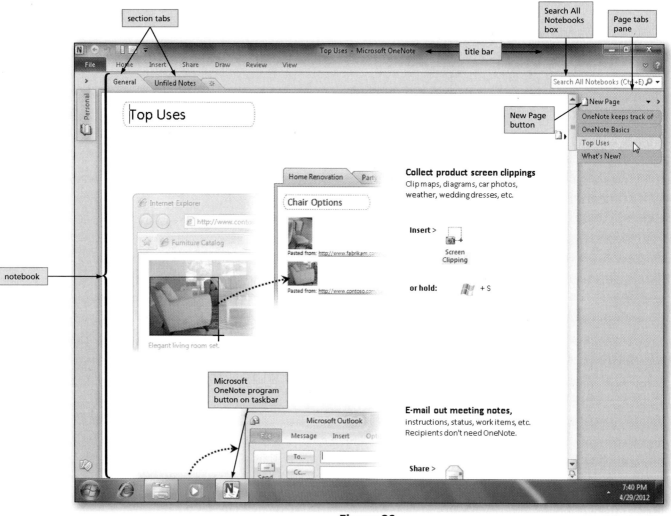

Figure 86

Break Point: If you wish to take a break, this is a good place to do so. To resume at a later time, continue to follow the steps from this location forward.

Moving, Renaming, and Deleting Files

Earlier in this chapter, you learned how to organize files in folders, which is part of a process known as **file management**. The following sections cover additional file management topics including renaming, moving, and deleting files.

To Rename a File

In some circumstances, you may want to change the name of, or rename, a file or a folder. For example, you may want to distinguish a file in one folder or drive from a copy of a similar file, or you may decide to rename a file to better identify its contents. The Word folder shown in Figure 87 contains the Word document, Koala Exhibit. The following steps change the name of the Koala Exhibit file in the Word folder to Koala Exhibit Flyer.

1

• If necessary, click the Windows Explorer program button on the taskbar to display the folder window in Windows Explorer.

• Navigate to the location of the file to be renamed (in this case, the Word folder in the CIS 101 [or your class folder] folder on the USB flash drive) to display the file(s) it contains in the right pane.

• Right-click the Koala Exhibit icon or file name in the right pane to select the Koala Exhibit file and display a shortcut menu that presents a list of commands related to files (Figure 87).

Figure 87

2

• Click Rename on the shortcut menu to place the current file name in a text box.

• Type **Koala Exhibit Flyer** in the text box and then press the ENTER key (Figure 88).

Q&A Are any risks involved in renaming files that are located on a hard disk?

If you inadvertently rename a file that is associated with certain programs, the programs may not be able to find the file and, therefore, may not execute properly. Always use caution when renaming files.

Q&A Can I rename a file when it is open?

No, a file must be closed to change the file name.

Figure 88

Other Ways
1. Select file, press F2, type new file name, press ENTER

To Move a File

At some time, you may want to move a file from one folder, called the source folder, to another, called the destination. When you move a file, it no longer appears in the original folder. If the destination and the source folders are on the same disk drive, you can move a file by dragging it. If the folders are on different disk drives, then you will need to right-drag the file. The following step moves the Brain Busters Rental Summary file from the Excel folder to the OneNote folder.

1

- In Windows Explorer, navigate to the location of the file to be moved (in this case, the Excel folder in the CIS 101 folder [or your class folder] on the USB flash drive).

- Click the Excel folder in the navigation pane to display the files it contains in the right pane (Figure 89).

- Drag the Brain Busters Rental Summary file in the right pane to the OneNote folder in the navigation pane.

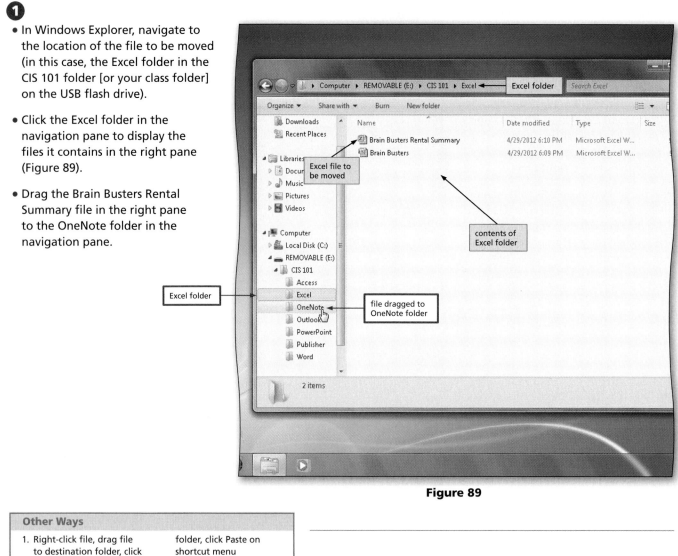

Figure 89

Other Ways

1. Right-click file, drag file to destination folder, click Move here
2. Right-click file to copy, click Cut on shortcut menu, right-click destination folder, click Paste on shortcut menu
3. Select file to copy, press CTRL+X, select destination folder, press CTRL+V

To Delete a File

A final task you may want to perform is to delete a file. Exercise extreme caution when deleting a file or files. When you delete a file from a hard disk, the deleted file is stored in the Recycle Bin where you can recover it until you empty the Recycle Bin. If you delete a file from removable media, such as a USB flash drive, the file is deleted permanently. The next steps delete the Koala Exhibit Gala file from the PowerPoint folder.

1

- In Windows Explorer, navigate to the location of the file to be deleted (in this case, the PowerPoint folder in the CIS 101 folder [or your class folder] on the USB flash drive).

- Click the PowerPoint folder in the navigation pane to display the files it contains in the right pane.

- Right-click the Koala Exhibit Gala icon or file name in the right pane to select the file and display a shortcut menu (Figure 90).

Figure 90

2

- Click Delete on the shortcut menu to display the Delete File dialog box (Figure 91).

- Click the Yes button (Delete File dialog box) to delete the selected file.

Q&A

Can I use this same technique to delete a folder?

Yes. Right-click the folder and then click Delete on the shortcut menu. When you delete a folder, all of the files and folders contained in the folder you are deleting, together with any files and folders on lower hierarchical levels, are deleted as well.

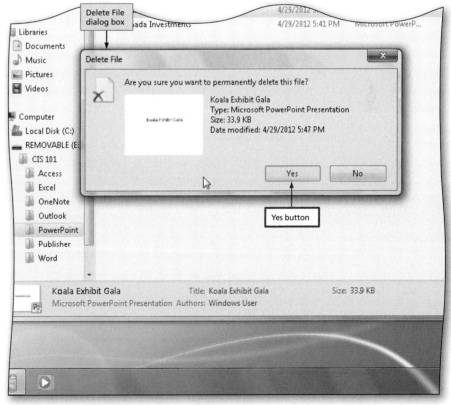

Figure 91

Other Ways

1. Select icon, press DELETE

Microsoft Office and Windows Help

At any time while you are using one of the Microsoft Office 2010 programs, you can use Office Help to display information about all topics associated with the program. To illustrate the use of Office Help, this section uses Word. Help in other Office 2010 programs operates in a similar fashion.

In Office 2010, Help is presented in a window that has Web-browser-style navigation buttons. Each Office 2010 program has its own Help home page, which is the starting Help page that is displayed in the Help window. If your computer is connected to the Internet, the contents of the Help page reflect both the local help files installed on the computer and material from Microsoft's Web site.

To Open the Help Window in an Office Program

The following step opens the Word Help window.

1

- Start an Office program, in this case Word.

- Click the Office program's Help button near the upper-right corner of the program window (the Microsoft Word Help button, in this case) to open the program's Help window (Figure 92).

Figure 92

Other Ways
1. Press F1

Moving and Resizing Windows

Up to this point, this chapter has used minimized and maximized windows. At times, however, it is useful, or even necessary, to have more than one window open and visible on the screen at the same time. You can resize and move these open windows so that you can view different areas of and elements in the window. In the case of the Help window, for example, it could be covering document text in the Word window that you need to see.

To Move a Window by Dragging

You can move any open window that is not maximized to another location on the desktop by dragging the title bar of the window. The following step drags the Word Help window to the top left of the desktop.

1

- Drag the window title bar (the Word Help window title bar, in this case) so that the window moves to the top left of the desktop, as shown in Figure 93.

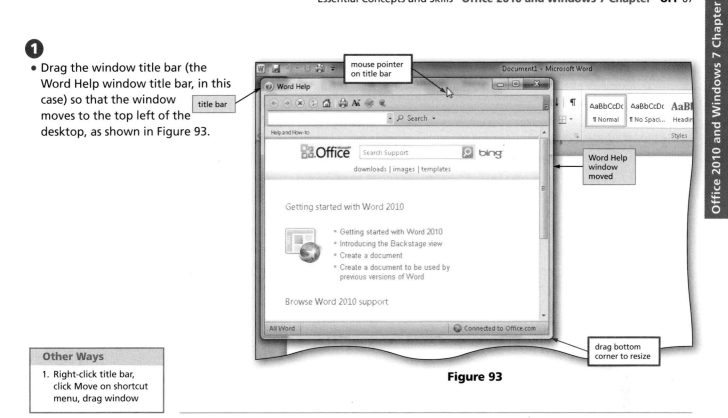

Figure 93

Other Ways

1. Right-click title bar, click Move on shortcut menu, drag window

To Resize a Window by Dragging

Sometimes, information is not visible completely in a window. A method used to change the size of the window is to drag the window borders. The following step changes the size of the Word Help window by dragging its borders.

1

- Point to the lower-right corner of the window (the Word Help window, in this case) until the mouse pointer changes to a two-headed arrow.

- Drag the bottom border downward to display more of the active window (Figure 94).

Q&A Can I drag other borders on the window to enlarge or shrink the window?

Yes, you can drag the left, right, and top borders and any window corner to resize a window.

Q&A Will Windows 7 remember the new size of the window after I close it?

Yes. When you reopen the window, Windows 7 will display it at the same size it was when you closed it.

Figure 94

Using Office Help

Once an Office program's Help window is open, several methods exist for navigating Help. You can search for help by using any of the three following methods from the Help window:

1. Enter search text in the 'Type words to search for' text box
2. Click the links in the Help window
3. Use the Table of Contents

To Obtain Help Using the 'Type words to search for' Text Box

Assume for the following example that you want to know more about the Backstage view. The following steps use the 'Type words to search for' text box to obtain useful information about the Backstage view by entering the word, Backstage, as search text.

1

- Type **Backstage** in the 'Type words to search for' text box at the top of the Word Help window to enter the search text.

- Click the Search button arrow to display the Search menu (Figure 95).

- If it is not selected already, click All Word on the Search menu, so that Help performs the most complete search of the current program (Word, in this case). If All Word already is selected, click the Search button arrow again to close the Search menu.

Figure 95

Q&A

Why select All Word on the Search menu?

Selecting All Word on the Search menu ensures that Word Help will search all possible sources for information about your search term. It will produce the most complete search results.

2

- Click the Search button to display the search results (Figure 96).

Q&A Why do my search results differ?

If you do not have an Internet connection, your results will reflect only the content of the Help files on your computer. When searching for help online, results also can change as material is added, deleted, and updated on the online Help Web pages maintained by Microsoft.

Q&A Why were my search results not very helpful?

When initiating a search, be sure to check the spelling of the search text; also, keep your search specific, with fewer than seven words, to return the most accurate results.

Figure 96

3

- Click the Introducing Backstage link to open the Help document associated with the selected topic (Figure 97).

Figure 97

4

- Click the Home button on the toolbar to clear the search results and redisplay the Help home page (Figure 98).

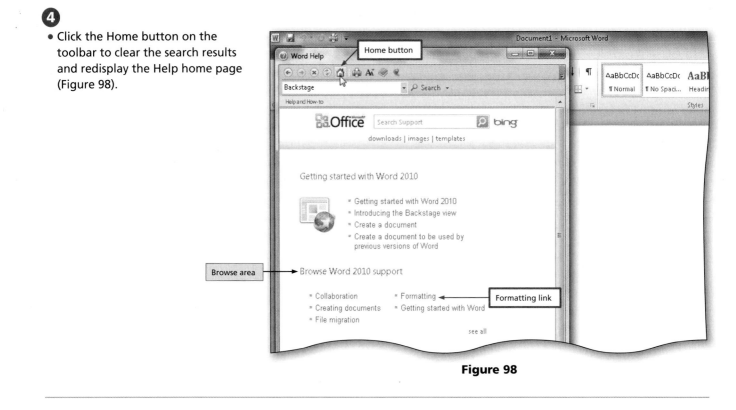

Figure 98

To Obtain Help Using the Help Links

If your topic of interest is listed in the Browse area of the Help window, you can click the link to begin browsing the Help categories instead of entering search text. You browse Help just as you would browse a Web site. If you know which category contains your Help information, you may wish to use these links. The following step finds the Formatting Help information using the category links from the Word Help home page.

1

- Click the Formatting link on the Help home page (shown in Figure 98) to display the Formatting page (Figure 99).

Figure 99

To Obtain Help Using the Help Table of Contents

A third way to find Help in Office programs is through the Help Table of Contents. You can browse through the Table of Contents to display information about a particular topic or to familiarize yourself with an Office program. The following steps access the Help information about themes by browsing through the Table of Contents.

1

- Click the Home button on the toolbar to display the Help home page.

- Click the Show Table of Contents button on the toolbar to display the Table of Contents pane on the left side of the Help window. If necessary, click the Maximize button on the Help title bar to maximize the window (Figure 100).

Q&A
Why does the appearance of the Show Table of Contents button change?

When the Table of Contents is displayed in the Help window, the Hide Table of Contents button replaces the Show Table of Contents button.

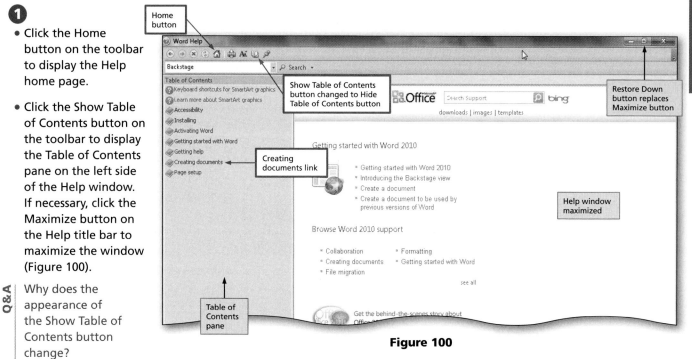

Figure 100

2

- Click the Creating documents link in the Table of Contents pane to view a list of Help subtopics.

- Click the Apply themes to Word documents link in the Table of Contents pane to view the selected Help document in the right pane (Figure 101).

- After reviewing the page, click the Close button to quit Help.

- Click the Office program's Close button (Word, in this case) to quit the Office program.

Figure 101

Q&A
How do I remove the Table of Contents pane when I am finished with it?

The Show Table of Contents button acts as a toggle. When the Table of Contents pane is visible, the button changes to Hide Table of Contents. Clicking it hides the Table of Contents pane and changes the button to Show Table of Contents.

Obtaining Help while Working in an Office Program

Help in the Office programs provides you with the ability to obtain help directly, without the need to open the Help window and initiate a search. For example, you may be unsure about how a particular command works, or you may be presented with a dialog box that you are not sure how to use.

Figure 102 shows one option for obtaining help while working in Word. If you want to learn more about a command, point to the command button and wait for the Enhanced ScreenTip to appear. If the Help icon appears in the Enhanced ScreenTip, press the F1 key while pointing to the command to open the Help window associated with that command.

Figure 102

Figure 103 shows a dialog box that contains a Help button. Pressing the F1 key while the dialog box is displayed opens a Help window. The Help window contains help about that dialog box, if available. If no help file is available for that particular dialog box, then the main Help window opens.

Figure 103

Using Windows Help and Support

One of the more powerful Windows 7 features is Windows Help and Support. **Windows Help and Support** is available when using Windows 7 or when using any Microsoft program running under Windows 7. This feature is designed to assist you in using Windows 7 or the various programs. Table 4 describes the content found in the Help and Support Center. The same methods used for searching Microsoft Office Help can be used in Windows Help and Support. The difference is that Windows Help and Support displays help for Windows 7, instead of for Microsoft Office.

Table 4 Windows Help and Support Center Content Areas

Area	Function
Find an answer quickly	This area contains instructions about how to do a quick search using the search box.
Not sure where to start?	This area displays three topics to help guide a user: How to get started with your computer, Learn about Windows Basics, and Browse Help topics. Clicking one of the options navigates to corresponding Help and Support pages.
More on the Windows Website	This area contains links to online content from the Windows Web site. Clicking the links navigates to the corresponding Web pages on the Web site.

To Start Windows Help and Support

The following steps start Windows Help and Support and display the Windows Help and Support window, containing links to more information about Windows 7.

1

• Click the Start button on the taskbar to display the Start menu (Figure 104).

Q&A

Why are the programs that are displayed on the Start menu different?

Windows adds the programs you have used recently to the left pane on the Start menu. You have started several programs while performing the steps in this chapter, so those programs now are displayed on the Start menu.

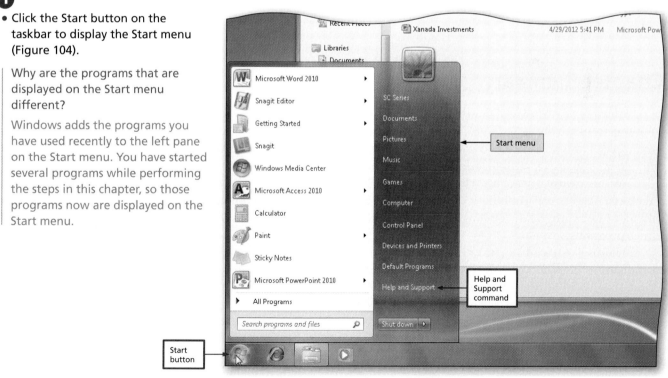

Figure 104

2

- Click Help and Support on the Start menu to open the Windows Help and Support window (Figure 105).

- After reviewing the Windows Help and Support window, click the Close button to quit Windows Help and Support.

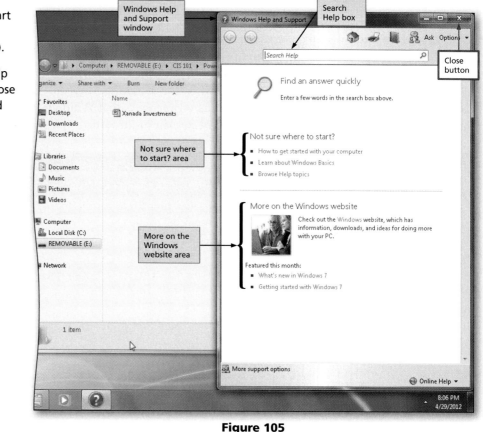

Figure 105

Other Ways

1. Press CTRL+ESC, press RIGHT ARROW, press UP ARROW, press ENTER
2. Press WINDOWS+F1

Chapter Summary

In this chapter, you learned about the Windows 7 interface. You started Windows 7, were introduced to the components of the desktop, and learned several mouse operations. You opened, closed, moved, resized, minimized, maximized, and scrolled a window. You used folder windows to expand and collapse drives and folders, display drive and folder contents, create folders, and rename and then delete a file.

You also learned some basic features of some Microsoft Office 2010 programs, including Word, PowerPoint, Excel, and Access. As part of this learning process, you discovered the common elements that exist among these different Office programs. You now can save basic document, presentation, spreadsheet, and database files. Additional Office programs, including Outlook, Publisher, and OneNote also were discussed.

Microsoft Office Help was demonstrated, and you learned how to use the Office Help window. You were introduced to the Windows 7 Help and Support Center and learned how to use it to obtain more information about Windows 7.

The items listed below include all of the new Windows 7 and Office 2010 skills you have learned in this chapter.

1. Log On to the Computer (OFF 6)
2. Start a Program Using the Start Menu (OFF 10)
3. Maximize a Window (OFF 12)
4. Display a Different Tab on the Ribbon (OFF 16)
5. Minimize, Display, and Restore the Ribbon (OFF 17)
6. Display and Use a Shortcut Menu (OFF 18)
7. Customize the Quick Access Toolbar (OFF 19)
8. Enter Text in a Document (OFF 20)
9. Create a Folder (OFF 22)
10. Create a Folder within a Folder (OFF 24)
11. Expand a Folder, Scroll through Folder Contents, and Collapse a Folder (OFF 26)
12. Switch from One Program to Another (OFF 27)
13. Save a File in a Folder (OFF 27)
14. Minimize and Restore a Window (OFF 30)
15. Change the Screen Resolution (OFF 33)

16. Quit an Office Program with One Document Open (OFF 35)
17. Start a Program Using the Search Box (OFF 37)
18. Enter Content in a Title Slide (OFF 40)
19. Create a New Office Document from the Backstage View (OFF 41)
20. Close an Office File Using the Backstage View (OFF 44)
21. Open a Recent Office File Using the Backstage View (OFF 45)
22. Create a New Blank Office Document from Windows Explorer (OFF 47)
23. Start a Program from Windows Explorer and Open a File (OFF 48)
24. Enter a Worksheet Title (OFF 50)
25. Save an Existing Document with the Same File Name (OFF 51)

26. Create an Access Database (OFF 55)
27. Open an Existing Office File (OFF 57)
28. Rename a File (OFF 63)
29. Move a File (OFF 64)
30. Delete a File (OFF 64)
31. Open the Help Window in an Office Program (OFF 66)
32. Move a Window by Dragging (OFF 66)
33. Resize a Window by Dragging (OFF 67)
34. Obtain Help Using the 'Type words to search for' Text Box (OFF 68)
35. Obtain Help Using the Help Links (OFF 70)
36. Obtain Help Using the Help Table of Contents (OFF 71)
37. Start Windows Help and Support (OFF 73)

If you have a SAM 2010 user profile, your instructor may have assigned an autogradable version of this assignment. If so, log into the SAM 2010 Web site at www.cengage.com/sam2010 to download the instruction and start files.

Learn It Online

Test your knowledge of chapter content and key terms.

Instructions: To complete the Learn It Online exercises, start your browser, click the Address bar, and then enter the Web address `scsite.com/office2010/learn`. When the Office 2010 Learn It Online page is displayed, click the link for the exercise you want to complete and then read the instructions.

Chapter Reinforcement TF, MC, and SA
A series of true/false, multiple choice, and short answer questions that test your knowledge of the chapter content.

Flash Cards
An interactive learning environment where you identify chapter key terms associated with displayed definitions.

Practice Test
A series of multiple choice questions that test your knowledge of chapter content and key terms.

Who Wants To Be a Computer Genius?
An interactive game that challenges your knowledge of chapter content in the style of a television quiz show.

Wheel of Terms
An interactive game that challenges your knowledge of chapter key terms in the style of the television show *Wheel of Fortune*.

Crossword Puzzle Challenge
A crossword puzzle that challenges your knowledge of key terms presented in the chapter.

STUDENT ASSIGNMENTS

Apply Your Knowledge

Reinforce the skills and apply the concepts you learned in this chapter.

Creating a Folder and a Document

Instructions: You will create a Word folder and then create a Word document and save it in the folder.

Perform the following tasks:

1. Connect a USB flash drive to an available USB port and then open the USB flash drive window.
2. Click the New folder button on the toolbar to display a new folder icon and text box for the folder name.
3. Type **Word** in the text box to name the folder. Press the ENTER key to create the folder on the USB flash drive.
4. Start Word.
5. Enter the text shown in Figure 106.
6. Click the Save button on the Quick Access Toolbar. Navigate to the Word folder on the USB flash drive and then save the document using the file name, Apply 1 Class List.
7. If your Quick Access Toolbar does not show the Quick Print button, add the Quick Print button to the Quick Access Toolbar. Print the document using the Quick Print button on the Quick Access Toolbar. When you are finished printing, remove the Quick Print button from the Quick Access Toolbar.
8. Submit the printout to your instructor.
9. Quit Word.

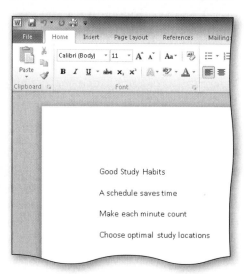

Figure 106

Extend Your Knowledge

Extend the skills you learned in this chapter and experiment with new skills. You will use Help to complete the assignment.

Using Help

Instructions: Use Office Help to perform the following tasks.

Perform the following tasks:

1. Start Word.
2. Click the Microsoft Word Help button to open the Word Help window (Figure 107).
3. Search Word Help to answer the following questions.
   a. What are the steps to add a new group to the Ribbon?
   b. What are Quick Parts?
4. With the Word program still running, start PowerPoint.

Figure 107

5. Click the Microsoft PowerPoint Help button on the title bar to open the PowerPoint Help window.

6. Search PowerPoint Help to answer the following questions.

   a. What is a slide master?

   b. How do you copy slides from another presentation into the existing presentation?

7. Quit PowerPoint.

8. Start Excel.

9. Click the Microsoft Excel Help button to open the Excel Help window.

10. Search Excel Help to answer the following questions.

    a. What are three different functions available in Excel?

    b. What are sparklines?

11. Quit Excel.

12. Start Access.

13. Click the Microsoft Access Help button to open the Access Help window.

14. Search Access Help to answer the following questions.

    a. What is SQL?

    b. What is a data macro?

15. Quit Access.

16. Type the answers from your searches in the Word document. Save the document with a new file name and then submit it in the format specified by your instructor.

17. Quit Word.

Make It Right

Analyze a file structure and correct all errors and/or improve the design.

Organizing Vacation Photos

Instructions: See the inside back cover of this book for instructions on downloading the Data Files for Students, or contact your instructor for information on accessing the required files.

Traditionally, you have stored photos from past vacations together in one folder. The photos are becoming difficult to manage, and you now want to store them in appropriate folders. You will create the folder structure shown in Figure 108. You then will move the photos to the folders so that they will be organized properly.

1. Connect a USB flash drive to an available USB port to open the USB flash drive window.

2. Using the techniques presented in the chapter, create the hierarchical folder structure shown in Figure 108.

3. Using the techniques presented in the chapter, move the vacation photos to their appropriate folders.

4. Submit your work in the format specified by your instructor.

Figure 108

In the Lab

Use the guidelines, concepts, and skills presented in this chapter to increase your knowledge of Windows 7 and Office 2010. Labs are listed in order of increasing difficulty.

Lab 1: Using Windows Help and Support

Problem: You have a few questions about using Windows 7 and would like to answer these questions using Windows Help and Support.

Instructions: Use Windows Help and Support to perform the following tasks:

1. Display the Start menu and then click Help and Support to start Windows Help and Support.

2. Use the Help and Support Content page to answer the following questions.

   a. How do you reduce computer screen flicker?

   b. Which dialog box do you use to change the appearance of the mouse pointer?

   c. How do you minimize all windows?

   d. What is a VPN?

3. Use the Search Help text box in Windows Help and Support to answer the following questions.

   a. How can you minimize all open windows on the desktop?

   b. How do you start a program using the Run command?

   c. What are the steps to add a toolbar to the taskbar?

   d. What wizard do you use to remove unwanted desktop icons?

4. The tools to solve a problem while using Windows 7 are called **troubleshooters**. Use Windows Help and Support to find the list of troubleshooters (Figure 109), and answer the following questions.

   a. What problems does the HomeGroup troubleshooter allow you to resolve?

   b. List five Windows 7 troubleshooters that are not listed in Figure 109.

5. Use Windows Help and Support to obtain information about software licensing and product activation, and answer the following questions.

   a. What is genuine Windows?

   b. What is activation?

   c. What steps are required to activate Windows?

   d. What steps are required to read the Microsoft Software License Terms?

   e. Can you legally make a second copy of Windows 7 for use at home, work, or on a mobile computer or device?

   f. What is registration?

6. Close the Windows Help and Support window.

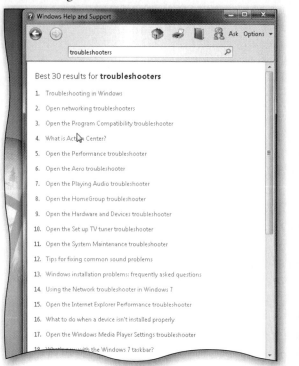

Figure 109

In the Lab

Lab 2: Creating Folders for a Pet Supply Store

Problem: Your friend works for Pete's Pet Supplies. He would like to organize his files in relation to the types of pets available in the store. He has five main categories: dogs, cats, fish, birds, and exotic. You are to create a folder structure similar to Figure 110.

Instructions: Perform the following tasks:

1. Connect a USB flash drive to an available USB port and then open the USB flash drive window.

2. Create the main folder for Pete's Pet Supplies.

3. Navigate to the Pete's Pet Supplies folder.

4. Within the Pete's Pet Supplies folder, create a folder for each of the following: Dogs, Cats, Fish, Birds, and Exotic.

5. Within the Exotic folder, create two additional folders, one for Primates and the second for Reptiles.

6. Submit the assignment in the format specified by your instructor.

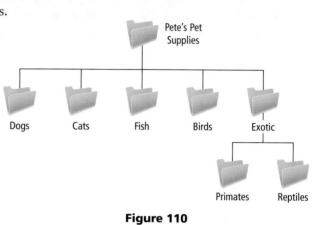

Figure 110

In the Lab

Lab 3: Creating Office Documents

Problem: You are taking a class that requires you to create a Word, PowerPoint, Excel, and Access file. You will save these files to folders named for four different Office programs (Figure 111).

Instructions: Create the folders shown in Figure 111. Then, using the respective Office program, create a small file to save in each folder (i.e., create a Word document to save in the Word folder, a PowerPoint presentation to save in the PowerPoint folder, and so on).

1. Connect a USB flash drive to an available USB port and then open the USB flash drive window.

2. Create the folder structure shown in Figure 111.

3. Navigate to the Word folder.

4. Create a Word document containing the text, My First Word Document, and then save it in the Word folder.

5. Navigate to the PowerPoint folder.

6. Create a PowerPoint presentation containing the title text, My First PowerPoint Presentation, and then save it in the PowerPoint folder.

7. Navigate to the Excel folder.

Figure 111

Continued >

In the Lab *continued*

8. Create an Excel spreadsheet containing the text, My First Excel Spreadsheet, in cell A1 and then save it in the Excel folder.

9. Navigate to the Access folder.

10. Save an Access database named, My First Database, in the Access folder.

11. Close all open Office programs.

12. Submit the assignment in the format specified by your instructor.

Cases and Places

Apply your creative thinking and problem solving skills to design and implement a solution.

Note: To complete these assignments, you may be required to use the Data Files for Students. See the inside back cover of this book for instructions on downloading the Data Files for Students, or contact your instructor for information about accessing the required files.

1: Creating Beginning Files for Classes

Academic

You are taking the following classes: Introduction to Engineering, Beginning Psychology, Introduction to Biology, and Accounting. Create folders for each of the classes. Use the following folder names: Engineering, Psychology, Biology, and Accounting, when creating the folder structure. In the Engineering folder, use Word to create a Word document with the name of the class and the class meeting location and time (MW 10:30 – 11:45, Room 317). In the Psychology folder, use PowerPoint to create your first lab presentation. It should begin with a title slide containing the text, Behavioral Observations. In the Biology folder, save a database named Research in the Biology folder. In the Accounting folder, create an Excel spreadsheet with the text, Tax Information, in cell A1. Use the concepts and techniques presented in this chapter to create the folders and files.

2: Using Help

Personal

Your parents enjoy working and playing games on their home computers. Your mother uses a notebook computer downstairs, and your father uses a desktop computer upstairs. They expressed interest in sharing files between their computers and sharing a single printer, so you offered to research various home networking options. Start Windows Help and Support, and search Help using the keywords, home networking. Use the link for installing a printer on a home network. Start Word and then type the main steps for installing a printer. Use the link for setting up a HomeGroup and then type the main steps for creating a HomeGroup in the Word document. Use the concepts and techniques presented in this chapter to use Help and create the Word document.

3: Creating Folders

Professional

Your boss at the bookstore where you work part-time has asked for help with organizing her files. After looking through the files, you decided upon a file structure for her to use, including the following folders: books, magazines, tapes, DVDs, and general merchandise. Within the books folder, create folders for hardback and paperback books. Within magazines, create folders for special issues and periodicals. In the tapes folder, create folders for celebrity and major release. In the DVDs folder, create a folder for book to DVD. In the general merchandise folder, create folders for novelties, posters, and games. Use the concepts and techniques presented in this chapter to create the folders.

1 Databases and Database Objects: An Introduction

Objectives

You will have mastered the material in this chapter when you can:

- Design a database to satisfy a collection of requirements
- Describe the features of the Access window
- Create a database
- Create tables in Datasheet and Design views
- Add records to a table

- Close a database
- Open a database
- Print the contents of a table
- Create and use a query
- Create and use a form
- Create and print custom reports
- Modify a report in Layout view

1 | Databases and Database Objects: An Introduction

Introduction

The term **database** describes a collection of data organized in a manner that allows access, retrieval, and use of that data. Microsoft Access 2010, usually referred to as simply Access, is a database management system. A **database management system**, such as Access, is software that allows you to use a computer to create a database; add, change, and delete data in the database; ask and answer questions concerning the data in the database; and create forms and reports using the data in the database.

Project Planning Guidelines

> The process of developing a database that communicates specific information requires careful analysis and planning. As a starting point, establish why the database is needed. Once the purpose is determined, analyze the intended users of the database and their unique needs. Then, gather information about the topic and decide what to include in the database. Finally, determine the database design and style that will be most successful at delivering the message. Details of these guidelines are provided in Appendix A. In addition, each project in this book provides practical applications of these planning considerations.

Project — Database Creation

Camashaly Design Group is a small company that provides custom marketing solutions for the service, nonprofit, and retail sectors. Alyssa Morgan, Camden Scott, and Ashton James started the business after they graduated from a local university. The three owners, all computer graphics design majors and business minors, worked on a service learning project during college that produced a Web site for a nonprofit organization. Alyssa, Camden, and Ashton worked well together. Upon researching the local area for competing businesses, they decided to form their own company. The company specializes in designing and maintaining Web sites and using social networking Web sites for online marketing. They also conduct market research and develop printed media. Camashaly already has received one award for its design work. Camashaly is also recognized for its efforts in providing work opportunities to individuals who want flexible schedules and to student interns.

Camashaly uses business analysts to work collaboratively with clients. Business analysts are employees who translate business requirements into marketing specifications and serve as the interface between clients and Camashaly. Business analysts are paid a base salary and can earn incentive pay for maintaining and expanding client relationships.

Camashaly charges a one-time fee for Web site development. Clients can pay for Web site maintenance by contracting for a specified number of hours or can pay for maintenance on an hour-by-hour basis. Other fees vary depending on the specific scope of work.

To ensure that operations run smoothly, Camashaly organizes data on its clients and business analysts in a database managed by Access. In this way, Camashaly keeps its data current and accurate while the owners can analyze the data for trends and produce a variety of useful reports. In this chapter, you will create the Camashaly database.

BTW

BTWs
For a complete list of the BTWs found in the margins of this book, visit the Access 2010 BTW Web page (scsite.com/ac2010/btw).

In a **relational database** such as those maintained by Access, a database consists of a collection of tables, each of which contains information on a specific subject. Figure 1–1 shows the database for Camashaly Design. It consists of two tables: the Client table (Figure 1–1a) contains information about the clients to whom Camashaly provides services, and the Business Analyst table (Figure 1–1b) contains information about the business analysts to whom these clients are assigned.

Client table

CL #	Client Name	Street	City	State	Postal Code	Amount Paid	Current Due	Hrs YTD	BA #
BA53	Bavant Animal Hospital	134 Main	Burles	NC	28817	$0.00	$7,500.00	0.00	11
BB32	Babbage CPA Firm	464 Linnell	Austin	SC	28796	$1,500.00	$500.00	5.00	14
BC76	Buda Community Clinic	867 Ridge	Buda	NC	27032	$2,500.00	$750.00	2.50	11
CJ29	Catering by Jenna	123 Second	Granger	NC	27036	$3,000.00	$1,000.00	15.80	27
GA74	Grant Antiques	78 Catawba	Georgetown	NC	28794	$5,500.00	$3,200.00	34.50	14
GF56	Granger Foundation	65 Simpson	Granger	NC	27036	$0.00	$6,500.00	0.00	11
HC10	Hendley County Hospital	216 Rivard	Austin	SC	28796	$3,100.00	$1,200.00	12.00	27
KD21	KAL Design Studio	116 Pine	Georgetown	NC	28794	$6,000.00	$3,200.00	30.50	14
KG04	Kyle Grocery Cooperative	421 First	Kyle	SC	28798	$3,200.00	$0.00	5.00	11
ME14	Mike's Electronic Stop	234 Gilham	Georgetown	NC	28794	$2,500.00	$1,500.00	8.50	27
PJ34	Patricia Jean Florist	345 Magee	Kyle	SC	28798	$0.00	$5,200.00	0.00	27
SL77	Smarter Law Associates	764 Main	Burles	NC	28817	$3,800.00	$0.00	10.50	11
TB17	The Bikeshop	346 Austin	Buda	NC	27032	$2,750.00	$1,200.00	14.00	27
WE05	Walburg Energy Alternatives	12 Polk	Walburg	NC	28819	$4,500.00	$1,450.00	19.50	14
WS01	Woody Sporting Goods	578 Central	Walburg	NC	28819	$2,250.00	$1,600.00	18.50	14

(a) Client table

caption for Client Number field

fields

records

BA # (Business Analyst Number) is 11

caption for Business Analyst Number field

Business Analyst Table

BA #	Last Name	First Name	Street	City	State	Postal Code	Salary YTD	Incentive YTD
11	Kerry	Cordelia	251 Painter	Georgetown	NC	28794	$3,200.00	$3,450.00
14	Martinez	Manuel	3125 Steel	Kyle	SC	28797	$3,100.00	$2,430.00
27	Liu	Jan	265 Marble	Byron	SC	28795	$3,400.00	$2,280.00
35	Scott	Jeff	1925 Pine	Georgetown	NC	28794	$500.00	$0.00

(b) Business Analyst table

BA # (Business Analyst Number) for Cordelia Kerry is 11

Figure 1–1

The rows in the tables are called **records**. A record contains information about a given person, product, or event. A row in the Client table, for example, contains information about a specific client, such as the client's name, address information, and other data.

The columns in the tables are called fields. A **field** contains a specific piece of information within a record. In the Client table, for example, the fourth field, City, contains the name of the city where the client is located.

The first field in the Client table is CL #, which is an abbreviation for Client Number. Camashaly Design assigns each client a client number. As is common to the way in which many organizations format client numbers, Camashaly Design calls it a number, although it actually contains letters. The Camashaly client numbers consist of two uppercase letters followed by a two-digit number.

The client numbers are unique; that is, no two clients are assigned the same number. Such a field can be used as a **unique identifier**. A unique identifier, as its name suggests, is a way of uniquely identifying each record in the database. A given client number will appear only in a single record in the table. Only one record exists, for example, in which the client number is BB32. A unique identifier also is called a **primary key**. Thus, the Client Number field is the primary key for the Client table.

The next eight fields in the Client table are Client Name, Street, City, State, Postal Code, Amount Paid, Current Due, and Hrs YTD, which is an abbreviation for Contract Hours YTD. YTD is an abbreviation for year to date. The Amount Paid column contains the amount that the client has paid Camashaly Design YTD prior to the current period. The Current Due column contains the amount due to Camashaly for the current period. The Hrs YTD column contains the number of hours the client has contracted for Web site maintenance so far this year. For example, client BB32 is Babbage CPA Firm. The address is 464 Linnell in Austin, South Carolina. The postal code is 28796. The client has paid $1,500.00 for services so far this year. The amount due for the current period is $500.00. The client has contracted for 5.00 hours of Web site maintenance.

Camashaly assigns a single business analyst to work with each client. The last column in the Client table, BA #, which is an abbreviation for Business Analyst Number, gives the number of the client's business analyst.

The first field in the Business Analyst table is also BA #, an abbreviation for Business Analyst Number. The business analyst numbers are unique, so the Business Analyst Number field is the primary key of the Business Analyst table.

The other fields in the Business Analyst table are Last Name, First Name, Street, City, State, Postal Code, Salary YTD, and Incentive YTD. The Salary YTD field gives the salary paid to the analyst thus far this year. The Incentive YTD gives the incentive for which the analyst qualified thus far this year. For example, business analyst 14 is Manuel Martinez. His address is 3125 Steel in Kyle, South Carolina. The Postal Code is 28797. So far this year, he has been paid $3,100.00 in salary. He has earned $2,430.00 in incentive pay.

The business analyst number appears in both the Client table and the Business Analyst table, and relates clients and business analysts. For example, in the Client table, you see that the business analyst number for client Babbage CPA Firm is 14. To find the name of this business analyst, look for the row in the Business Analyst table that contains 14 in the BA # column. After you have found it, you know the client is assigned to Manuel Martinez. To find all the clients assigned to Cordelia Kerry, you would first look in the Business Analyst table to find that her number is 11. You would then look through the Client table for all the clients that contain 11 in the BA # column. Her clients are BA53 (Bavant Animal Hospital), BC76 (Buda Community Clinic), GF56 (Granger Foundation), KG04 (Kyle Grocery Cooperative), and SL77 (Smarter Law Associates).

The last business analyst in the Business Analyst table, Jeff Scott, has not been assigned any clients yet; therefore, his business analyst number, 35, does not appear on any row in the Client table.

Overview

As you read this chapter, you will learn how to create the database shown in Figure 1–1 by performing these general tasks:

- Design the database.
- Create a new blank database.
- Create a table and add the records.
- Preview and print the contents of a table.
- Create a second table and import the records.
- Create a simple query.
- Create a simple form.
- Create and modify a report.

Database Design Guidelines

Database design refers to the arrangement of data into tables and fields. In the example in this chapter, the design is specified, but in many cases, you will have to determine the design based on what you want the system to accomplish.

Plan
Ahead

When designing a database to satisfy a given set of requirements, the actions you take and the decisions you make will determine the tables and fields that will be included in the database. As you create a database, such as the one shown in Figure 1–1 on page AC 3, you should follow these general guidelines:

1. **Identify the tables.** Examine the requirements for the database to identify the main objects that are involved. There will be a table for each object you identify.

   In one database, for example, the main objects might be departments and employees. Thus, there would be two tables: one for departments and the other for employees. In another database, the main objects might be clients and business analysts. In this case, there also would be two tables: one for clients and the other for business analysts. In still another database, the main objects might be books, publishers, and authors. This database would require three tables: one for books, a second for publishers, and a third for authors.

2. **Determine the primary keys.** Recall that the primary key is the unique identifier for records in the table. For each table, determine the unique identifier. In a Department table, for example, the unique identifier might be the Department Code. For a Book table, the unique identifier might be the ISBN.

3. **Determine the additional fields.** The primary key will be a field or combination of fields in a table. A table typically will contain many additional fields, each of which contains a type of data. Examine the project requirements to determine these additional fields. For example, in an Employee table, the additional fields might include such fields as Employee Name, Street Address, City, State, Postal Code, Date Hired, Salary, and so on.

4. **Determine relationships between the tables.** Examine the list of tables you have created to see which tables are related. When you determine that two tables are related, include matching fields in the two tables. For example, in a database containing employees and departments, there is a relationship between the two tables because one department can have many employees assigned to it. Department Code could be the matching field in the two tables.

5. **Determine data types for the fields.** For each field, determine the type of data the field can contain. One field, for example, might contain only numbers. Another field might contain currency amounts, while a third field might contain only dates. Some fields contain text data, meaning any combination of letters, numbers, and special characters (!, ;, ‘, &, and so on). For example, in an Employee table, the Date Hired field would contain dates, the Salary field would contain currency amounts, and the Hours Worked field would contain numbers. The other fields in the Employee table would contain text data, such as Employee Name and Department Code.

6. **Identify and remove any unwanted redundancy.** Redundancy is the storing of a piece of data in more than one place. Redundancy usually, but not always, causes problems, such as wasted space, difficulties with update, and possible data inconsistency. Examine each table you have created to see if it contains redundancy and, if so, determine whether the redundancy causes the problems described. If it does, remove the redundancy by splitting the table into two tables. For example, you might have a single table of employees. In addition to typical employee data (name, address, earnings, and so on), the table might contain Department Number and Department Name. If so, the Department Name could repeat multiple times. Every employee whose department number is 12, for example, would have the same department name. It would be better to split the table into two tables: one for Employees and one for Department. In the Department table, the Department Name is stored only once.

7. **Determine a storage location for the database.** The database you have designed will be stored in a single file. You need to determine a location in which to store the file.

8. **Determine additional properties for fields.** Before creating the database, determine any other properties you should specify for the fields. These could include a field size, which is

(continued)

Plan
Ahead

(continued)

the maximum number of characters that can be stored in the field. If you want something other than the field name to appear at the top of a column (such as an abbreviation), you can change the caption to the desired heading. You also can add a description, which is a message that appears on the screen concerning a field whenever the field is selected.

9. **Determine the best method for distributing the database objects.** The traditional method of distributing database objects uses a printer to produce a hard copy of a table or report on paper. You also can distribute the table as an electronic image that mirrors the original table's appearance.

When necessary, more specific details concerning the above guidelines are presented at appropriate points in the chapter. The chapter also will identify the actions performed and decisions made regarding these guidelines during the creation of the database shown in Figure 1–1 on page AC 3.

Designing a Database

This section illustrates the database design process by showing how you would design the database for Camashaly Design from a set of requirements. In this section, you will use commonly accepted shorthand to represent the tables and fields that make up the database as well as the primary keys for the tables. For each table, you give the name of the table followed by a set of parentheses. Within the parentheses is a list of the fields in the table separated by columns. You underline the primary key. For example,

Product (<u>Product Code</u>, Description, On Hand, Price)

represents a table called Product. The Product table contains four fields: Product Code, Description, On Hand, and Price. The Product Code field is the primary key.

Database Requirements

The Camashaly Design database must maintain information on both clients and business analysts. The business currently keeps this data in two Word tables and two Excel workbooks, as shown in Figure 1–2. They use Word tables for address information and Excel workbooks for financial information.

Client Number	Client Name	Street	City	State	Postal Code
BA53	Bavant Animal Hospital	134 Main	Burles	NC	28817
BB32	Babbage CPA Firm	464 Linnell	Austin	SC	28796
BC76	Buda Community Clinic	867 Ridge	Buda	NC	27032
CJ29	Catering by Jenna	123 Second	Granger	NC	27036
GA74	Grant Antiques	78 Catawba	Georgetown	NC	28794
GF56	Granger Foundation	65 Simpson	Granger	NC	27036
HC10	Hendley County Hospital	216 Rivard	Austin	SC	28796
KD21	KAL Design Studio	116 Pine	Georgetown	NC	28794
KG04	Kyle Grocery Cooperative	421 First	Kyle	SC	28798
ME14	Mike's Electronic Stop	234 Gilham	Georgetown	NC	28794
PJ34	Patricia Jean Florist	345 Magee	Kyle	SC	28798
SL77	Smarter Law Associates	764 Main	Burles	NC	28817
TB17	The Bikeshop	346 Austin	Buda	NC	27032
WE05	Walburg Energy Alternatives	12 Polk	Walburg	NC	28819
WS01	Woody Sporting Goods	578 Central	Walburg	NC	28819

Figure 1–2   (a) Client Address Information (Word Table)

▲	A	B	C	D	E	F	G	H
1	Client Number	Client Name	Amount Paid	Current Due	Contract Hours YTD			
2	BA53	Bavant Animal Hospital	0.00	7,500.00	0			
3	BB32	Babbage CPA Firm	1,500.00	500.00	5			
4	BC76	Buda Community Clinic	2,500.00	750.00	2.5			
5	CJ29	Catering by Jenna	3,000.00	1,000.00	15.5			
6	GA74	Grant Antiques	5,500.00	3,200.00	34.5			
7	GF56	Granger Foundation	0.00	6,500.00	0			
8	HC10	Hendley County Hospital	3,100.00	1,200.00	12			
9	KD21	KAL Design Studio	6,000.00	3,200.00	30.5			
10	KG04	Kyle Grocery Cooperative	3,200.00	0.00	5			
11	ME14	Mike's Electronic Stop	2,500.00	1,500.00	8.5			
12	PJ34	Patricia Jean Florist	0.00	5,200.00	0			
13	SL77	Smarter Law Associates	3,800.00	0.00	10.5			
14	TB17	The Bikeshop	2,750.00	1,200.00	14			
15	WE05	Walburg Energy Alternatives	4,500.00	1,450.00	19.5			
16	WS01	Woody Sporting Goods	2,250.00	1,600.00	18.5			

Figure 1–2   (b) Client Financial Information (Excel Worksheet)

Business Analyst Number	Last Name	First Name	Street	City	State	Postal Code
11	Kerry	Cordelia	251 Painter	Georgetown	NC	28794
14	Martinez	Manuel	3125 Steel	Kyle	SC	28797
27	Liu	Jan	265 Marble	Byron	SC	28795
35	Scott	Jeff	1925 Pine	Georgetown	NC	28794

Figure 1–2   (c) Business Analyst Address Information (Word Table)

▲	A	B	C	D	E	F	G	H	I
1	Business Analyst Number	Last Name	First Name	Salary YTD	Incentive YTD				
2	11	Kerry	Cordelia	3,200.00	3,450.00				
3	14	Martinez	Manuel	3,100.00	2,430.00				
4	27	Liu	Jan	3,400.00	2,280.00				
5	35	Scott	Jeff	500.00	0.00				

Figure 1–2   (d) Business Analyst Financial Information (Excel Worksheet)

For clients, Camashaly needs to maintain address data. It currently keeps this address data in a Word table (Figure 1–2a). It also maintains financial data for each client. This includes the amount paid, current amount due, and contract hours YTD for the client. It keeps these amounts, along with the client name and number, in the Excel workbook shown in Figure 1–2b.

Camashaly keeps business analyst address data in a Word table, as shown in Figure 1–2c. Just as with clients, it keeps financial data for business analysts, including their salary YTD and incentive YTD, in a separate Excel workbook, as shown in Figure 1–2d.

Finally, it keeps track of which clients are assigned to which business analysts. Each client is assigned to a single business analyst, but each business analyst might be assigned many clients. Currently, for example, clients BA53 (Bavant Animal Hospital), BC76 (Buda Community Clinic), GF56 (Granger Foundation), KG04 (Kyle Grocery Cooperative), and SL77 (Smarter Law Associates) are assigned to business analyst 11 (Cordelia Kerry). Clients BB32 (Babbage CPA Firm), GA74 (Grant Antiques), KD21 (KAL Design Studio), WE05 (Walburg Energy Alternatives), and WS01 (Woody Sporting Goods) are assigned to business analyst 14 (Manuel Martinez). Clients CJ29 (Catering by Jenna), HC10 (Hendley County Hospital), ME14 (Mike's Electronic Stop), PJ34 (Patricia Jean Florist), and TB17 (The Bikeshop) are assigned to business analyst 27 (Jan Liu). Camashaly has an additional business analyst, Jeff Scott, whose number has been assigned as 35, but who has not yet been assigned any clients.

BTW

Additional Data for Camashaly
There are many other types of data that Camashaly could include in a database. For example, they might keep all employee information in a database as well as information on client contracts and an inventory of hardware and software.

BTW

Naming Files
The following characters cannot be used in a file name: question mark (?), quotation mark ("), slash (/), backslash (\ ), colon (:), asterisk (*), vertical bar (|), greater than symbol (>), and less than symbol (<).

Naming Tables and Fields

In designing your database, you must name the tables and fields. Thus, before beginning the design process, you must understand the rules Access applies to table and field names. These rules are:

1. Names can be up to 64 characters in length.
2. Names can contain letters, digits, and spaces, as well as most of the punctuation symbols.
3. Names cannot contain periods (.), exclamation points (!), accent graves (`), or square brackets ([ ]).
4. The same name cannot be used for two different fields in the same table.

The approach to naming tables and fields used in this text is to begin the names with an uppercase letter and to use lowercase for the other letters. In multiple-word names, each word begins with an uppercase letter, and there is a space between words (for example, Client Number). You should know that other approaches exist, all of which are acceptable in Access. Some people omit the space (ClientNumber). Still others use an underscore in place of the space (Client_Number). Finally, some use an underscore in place of a space, but use the same case for all letters (CLIENT_NUMBER or client_number).

Identifying the Tables

BTW

Naming Fields
Access 2010 has a number of reserved words, words that have a special meaning to Access. You cannot use these reserved words as field names. For example, Name is a reserved word and could not be used in the Client table to describe a client's name. For a complete list of reserved words in Access 2010, consult Access Help.

Now that you know the rules for naming tables and fields, you are ready to begin the design process. The first step is to identify the main objects involved in the requirements. For the Camashaly Design database, the main objects are clients and business analysts. This leads to two tables, which you must name. Reasonable names for these two tables are:

Client
Business Analyst

Determining the Primary Keys

The next step is to identify the fields that will be the unique identifiers, or primary keys. Client numbers uniquely identify clients, and business analyst numbers uniquely identify business analysts. Thus, the primary key for the Client table is the client number, and the primary key for the Business Analyst table is the business analyst number. Reasonable names for these fields would be Client Number and Business Analyst Number, respectively. Adding these primary keys to the tables gives:

Client (<u>Client Number</u>)
Business Analyst (<u>Business Analyst Number</u>)

Determining Additional Fields

After identifying the primary keys, you need to determine and name the additional fields. In addition to the client number, the Client Address Information shown in Figure 1–2a on page AC 6 contains the client name, street, city, state, and postal code. These would be fields in the Client table. The Client Financial Information shown in Figure 1–2b also contains the client number and client name, which are already included in the Client table. The financial information also contains the amount paid, current due, and contract hours YTD. Adding the amount paid, current due, and contract hours YTD fields to those already identified in the Client table and assigning reasonable names gives:

Client (<u>Client Number</u>, Client Name, Street, City, State, Postal Code, Amount Paid, Current Due, Contract Hours YTD)

Similarly, examining the Business Analyst Address Information in Figure 1–2c adds the last name, first name, street, city, state, and postal code fields to the Business Analyst table. In addition to the business analyst number, last name, and first name, the Business Analyst Financial Information in Figure 1–2d would add the salary YTD and Incentive YTD. Adding these fields to the Business Analyst table and assigning reasonable names gives:

Business Analyst (<u>Business Analyst Number</u>, Last Name, First Name, Street, City, State, Postal Code, Salary YTD, Incentive YTD)

Determining and Implementing Relationships Between the Tables

Plan
Ahead

> **Determine relationships between the tables.**
> The most common type of relationship you will encounter between tables is the **one-to-many relationship**. This means that each row in the first table may be associated with many rows in the second table, but each row in the second table is associated with only one row in the first. The first table is called the "one" table and the second is called the "many" table. For example, there may be a relationship between departments and employees, in which each department can have many employees, but each employee is assigned to only one department. In this relationship, there would be two tables, Department and Employee. The Department table would be the "one" table in the relationship. The Employee table would be the "many" table.
>   To determine relationships between tables, you can follow these general guidelines:
>
> * Identify the "one" table.
> * Identify the "many" table.
> * Include the primary key from the "one" table as a field in the "many" table.

According to the requirements, each client has one business analyst, but each business analyst can have many clients. Thus, the Business Analyst table is the "one" table, and the Client table is the "many" table. To implement this one-to-many relationship between business analysts and clients, add the Business Analyst Number field (the primary key of the Business Analyst table) to the Client table. This produces:

Client (<u>Client Number</u>, Client Name, Street, City, State, Postal Code, Amount Paid, Current Due, Contract Hours YTD, Business Analyst Number)

Business Analyst (<u>Business Analyst Number</u>, Last Name, First Name, Street, City, State, Postal Code, Salary YTD, Incentive YTD)

BTW

Database Design Language (DBDL)
DBDL is a commonly accepted shorthand representation for showing the structure of a relational database. You write the name of the table and then within parentheses you list all the columns in the table. If the columns continue beyond one line, indent the subsequent lines.

Determining Data Types for the Fields

Each field has a **data type**. This indicates the type of data that can be stored in the field. Three of the most commonly used data types are:

1. **Text** — The field can contain any characters. A maximum number of 255 characters is allowed in a field whose data type is Text.

2. **Number** — The field can contain only numbers. The numbers either can be positive or negative. Fields are assigned this type so they can be used in arithmetic operations. Fields that contain numbers but will not be used for arithmetic operations (such as postal codes) usually are assigned a data type of Text.

3. **Currency** — The field can contain only monetary data. The values will appear with currency symbols, such as dollar signs, commas, and decimal points, and with two digits following the decimal point. Like numeric fields, you can use currency fields in arithmetic operations. Access assigns a size to currency fields automatically.

Table 1–1 shows the other data types that are available in Access.

BTW

Data Types
Different database
management systems have
different available data
types. Even data types that
are essentially the same
can have different names.
The Currency data type
in Access, for example, is
referred to as Money in
SQL Server.

Table 1–1 Additional Data Types

Data Type	Description
Memo	Field can store a variable amount of text or combinations of text and numbers where the total number of characters may exceed 255.
Date/Time	Field can store dates and times.
AutoNumber	Field can store a unique sequential number that Access assigns to a record. Access will increment the number by 1 as each new record is added.
Yes/No	Field can store only one of two values. The choices are Yes/No, True/False, or On/Off.
OLE Object	Field can store an OLE object, which is an object linked to or embedded in the table.
Hyperlink	Field can store text that can be used as a hyperlink address.
Attachment	Field can contain an attached file. Images, spreadsheets, documents, charts, and so on can be attached to this field in a record in the database. You can view and edit the attached file.
Calculated	Field specified as a calculation based on other fields. The value is not actually stored.

In the Client table, because the Client Number, Client Name, Street, City, and State can all contain letters, their data types should be Text. The data type for Postal Code is Text instead of Number because postal codes are not used in arithmetic operations; you do not add postal codes or find an average postal code, for example. The Amount Paid and Current Due fields both contain monetary data, so their data types should be Currency. The Contract Hours YTD field contains a number that is not a currency amount, so its data type should be Number.

Similarly, in the Business Analyst table, the data type for the Business Analyst Number, Last Name, First Name, Street, City, State, and Postal Code fields all should be Text. The Salary YTD and Incentive YTD fields both contain monetary amounts, so their data types should be Currency.

Fields whose data type is Number often require you to change the field size, which is the storage space assigned to the field by Access. Table 1–2 shows the possible field sizes for Number fields. If the size were Byte, Integer, or Long Integer, for example, only integers could be stored. If you try to store a value that has decimal places, such as 2.50, the portion to the right of the decimal point would be removed, giving a result of 2. To address this problem, you would change to a size such as Single.

Table 1–2 Field Sizes for Number Fields

Field Size	Description
Byte	Integer value in the range of 0 to 255
Integer	Integer value in the range of –32,768 to 32,767
Long Integer	Integer value in the range of –2,147,483,648 to 2,147,483,647
Single	Numeric values with decimal places to seven significant digits — requires 4 bytes of storage
Double	Numeric values with decimal places to more accuracy than Single — requires 8 bytes of storage
Replication ID	Special identifier required for replication
Decimal	Numeric values with decimal places to more accuracy than Single or Double — requires 12 bytes of storage.

Identifying and Removing Redundancy

Redundancy means storing the same fact in more than one place. It usually results from placing too many fields in a table — fields that really belong in separate tables — and often causes serious problems. If you had not realized there were two objects, clients and business analysts, for example, you might have placed all the data in a single Client table. Figure 1–3 shows an example of a table that includes both client and business analyst information. Notice that the data for a given business analyst (number, name, address, and so on) occurs on more than one record. The data for analyst 11, Cordelia Kerry, is repeated in the figure.

Client Table

Client Number	Client Name	Street	...	Business Analyst Number	Last Name	First Name	...
BA53	Bavant Animal Hospital	134 Main	...	11	Kerry	Cordelia	...
BB32	Babbage CPA Firm	464 Linnell	..	14	Martinez	Manuel	...
BC76	Buda Community Clinic	867 Ridge	...	11	Kerry	Cordelia	...
...	...	...	...	...	...	..	...

business analyst numbers are 11

name of business analyst 11 appears more than once

Figure 1–3

Storing this data on multiple records is an example of redundancy, which causes several problems, including:

1. Wasted storage space. The name of business analyst 11, Cordelia Kerry, for example, should be stored only once. Storing this fact several times is wasteful.

2. More difficult database updates. If, for example, Cordelia Kerry's name is spelled wrong and needs to be changed in the database, her name would need to be changed in several different places.

3. A possibility of inconsistent data. Nothing prohibits the business analyst's last name from being Kerry on client BA53's record and Bronson on client BC76's record. The data would be inconsistent. In both cases, the business analyst number is 11, but the last names are different.

The solution to the problem is to place the redundant data in a separate table, one in which the data no longer will be redundant. If, for example, you place the data for business analysts in a separate table (Figure 1–4), the data for each business analyst will appear only once.

Client Table

Client Number	Client Name	Street	...	Business Analyst Number
BA53	Bavant Animal Hospital	134 Main	...	11
BB32	Babbage CPA Firm	464 Linnell	...	14
BC76	Buda Community Clinic	867 Ridge	...	11
..	...		...	

business analyst numbers are 11

Business Analyst Table

Business Analyst Number	Last Name	First Name	...
11	Kerry	Cordelia	...
14	Martinez	Manuel	...
...	...		...

name of business analyst 11 appears only once

Figure 1–4

BTW

Postal Codes
Some organizations with customers throughout the country have a separate table of postal codes, cities, and states. When placing an order, you typically are asked for your postal code (or ZIP code), rather than city, state, and postal code. You then are asked to confirm that the city and state correspond to that postal code.

Notice that you need to have the business analyst number in both tables. Without it, there would be no way to tell which business analyst is associated with which client. The remaining business analyst data, however, was removed from the Client table and placed in the Business Analyst table. This new arrangement corrects the problems of redundancy in the following ways:

1. Because the data for each business analyst is stored only once, space is not wasted.
2. Changing the name of a business analyst is easy. You have only to change one row in the Business Analyst table.
3. Because the data for a business analyst is stored only once, inconsistent data cannot occur. Designing to omit redundancy will help you to produce good and valid database designs.

You should always examine your design to see if it contains redundancy. If it does, you should decide whether you need to remove the redundancy by creating a separate table.

If you examine your design, you'll see that there is one area of redundancy (see the data in Figure 1–1 on page AC 3). Cities and states are both repeated. Every client whose postal code is 28794, for example, has Georgetown as the city and NC as the state. To remove this redundancy, you would create a table whose primary key is Postal Code and that contains City and State as additional fields. City and State would be removed from the Client table. Having City, State, and Postal Code in a table is very common, however, and usually you would not take such action. No other redundancy exists in your tables.

To Start Access

For an introduction to Windows 7 and instruction about how to perform basic Windows 7 tasks, read the Office 2010 and Windows 7 chapter at the beginning of this book, where you can learn how to resize windows, change screen resolution, create folders, move and rename files, use Windows Help, and much more.

If you are using a computer to step through the project in this chapter and you want your screens to match the figures in this book, you should change your screen's resolution to 1024 × 768. For information about how to change a computer's resolution, refer to the Office 2010 and Windows 7 chapter at the beginning of this book.

The following steps, which assume Windows 7 is running, start Access based on a typical installation. You may need to ask your instructor how to start Access for your computer. For a detailed example of the procedure summarized below, refer to the Office 2010 and Windows 7 chapter.

1 Click the Start button on the Windows 7 taskbar to display the Start menu.

2 Type `Microsoft Access` as the search text in the 'Search programs and files' text box and watch the search results appear on the Start menu.

3 Click Microsoft Access 2010 in the search results on the Start menu to start Access and display the Backstage view for Access.

4 If the Access window is not maximized, click the Maximize button next to the Close button on its title bar to maximize the window.

Creating a Database

In Access, all the tables, reports, forms, and queries that you create are stored in a single file called a database. Thus, you first must create the database to hold the tables, reports, forms, and queries. You can use either the Blank database option or a template to create a new database. If you already know the tables and fields you want in your database, you would use the Blank database option. If not, you can use a template. Templates can guide you by suggesting some commonly used databases.

Determine a storage location for the database.
When creating a database, you must decide which storage medium to use.

If you always work on the same computer and have no need to transport your database to a different location, then your computer's hard drive will suffice as a storage location. It is a good idea, however, to save a backup copy of your database on a separate medium in case the file becomes corrupted or the computer's hard drive fails.

If you plan to work on your database in various locations or on multiple computers, then you can consider saving your projects on a portable medium, such as a USB flash drive or CD. The projects in this book are stored on a USB flash drive, which saves files quickly and reliably and can be reused. CDs are easily portable and serve as good backups for the final versions of projects because they generally can save files only one time.

Plan Ahead

For an introduction to Office 2010 and instruction about how to perform basic tasks in Office 2010 programs, read the Office 2010 and Windows 7 chapter at the beginning of this book, where you can learn how to start a program, use the Ribbon, save a file, open a file, quit a program, use Help, and much more.

To Create a Database

Because you already know the tables and fields you want in the Camashaly Design database, you would use the Blank database option rather than using a template. The following steps assume you already have created folders for storing your files, for example, a CIS 101 folder (for your class) that contains an Access folder (for your assignments). Thus, these steps save the document in the Access folder in the CIS 101 folder on a USB flash drive using the file name, Camashaly Design. For a detailed example of the procedure summarized below, refer to the Office 2010 and Windows 7 chapter at the beginning of this book.

1 With a USB flash drive connected to one of the computer's USB ports, ensure the New tab is selected in the Backstage view and that Blank database is selected in the New gallery.

2 Click the Browse button in the right pane of the New gallery to display the File New Database dialog box.

3 Type `Camashaly Design` in the File New Database dialog box to change the file name. Do not press the ENTER key after typing the file name.

4 Navigate to the desired save location (in this case, the Access folder in the CIS 101 folder [or your class folder] on the USB flash drive).

5 Click the OK button, which returns you to the New gallery. (Your screen may show Camashaly Design.accdb.)

6 Click the Create button in the right pane of the New gallery to create the database on the selected drive with the entered file name (Figure 1–5).

BTW

Q&As
For a complete list of the Q&As found in many of the step-by-step sequences in this book, visit the Access 2010 Q&A Web page (scsite.com/ac2010/qa).

Q&A

The title bar for my Navigation Pane contains All Tables rather than All Access Objects, as in the figure. Is that a problem?

It is not a problem. The title bar indicates how the Navigation Pane is organized. You can carry out the steps in the text with either organization. To make your screens match the ones in the text, click the Navigation Pane arrow and then click Object Type.

Q&A

I do not have the Search bar that appears on the figure. Is that a problem?

It is not a problem. If your Navigation Pane does not display a Search bar and you want your screens to match the ones in the text, right-click the Navigation Pane title bar arrow to display a shortcut menu, and then click Search Bar.

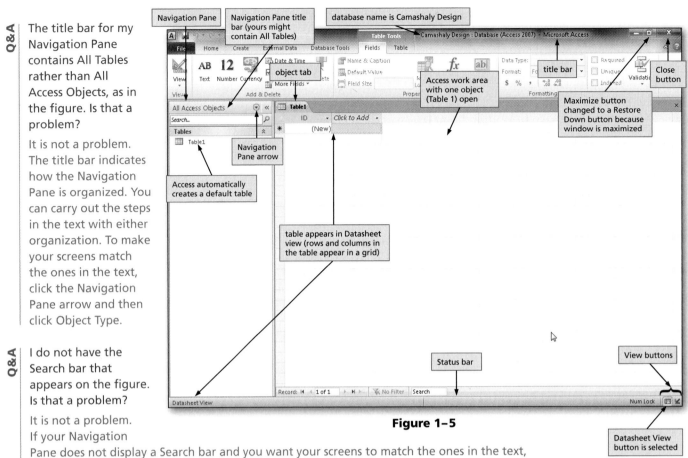

Figure 1–5

BTW

Available Templates
The Blank web database button on the New tab in the Backstage view allows you to create a database that you can publish to a SharePoint server running Access Services. Access 2010 also includes five Web-based templates. To display previously used templates, click the My templates button.

TO CREATE A DATABASE USING A TEMPLATE

Ideally, you will design your own database, create a blank database, and then create the tables you have determined that your database should contain. If you are not sure what database design you will need, you could use a template. Templates can guide you by suggesting some commonly used databases. To create a database using a template, you would use the following steps.

1. After starting Access, be sure the Backstage view is open. If it is not, click File on the Ribbon to open it.
2. Click the New tab if it is not already selected.
3. Click Sample templates to display a list of templates stored locally or search Microsoft Office online for additional templates.
4. Click the template you want to use.
5. Enter a file name (or accept the suggested file name) and select a location for the database.
6. Click the Create button to create the database or the Download button to download the database and create the database, if necessary.

The Access Window

The Access window consists of a variety of components to make your work more efficient and documents more professional. These include the Navigation Pane, Access work area, Ribbon, shortcut menus, and Quick Access Toolbar. Some of these components are common to other Microsoft Office 2010 programs; others are unique to Access.

Navigation Pane and Access Work Area

You work on objects such as tables, forms, and reports in the **Access work area**. In the work area in Figure 1–5, a single table, Table1, is open in the work area. **Object tabs** for the open objects appear at the top of the work area. If you have multiple objects open at the same time, you can select one of the open objects by clicking its tab. To the left of the work area is the Navigation Pane. The **Navigation Pane** contains a list of all the objects in the database. You use this pane to open an object. You also can customize the way objects are displayed in the Navigation Pane.

The **Status bar**, located at the bottom of the Access window, presents information about the database object, the progress of current tasks, and the status of certain commands and keys; it also provides controls for viewing the object. As you type text or perform certain commands, various indicators may appear on the Status bar. The left edge of the Status bar in Figure 1–5 shows that the table object is open in Datasheet view. Toward the right edge are View buttons, which you can use to change the view that currently is displayed.

Creating a Table

To create a table, you must describe the structure of the table to Access. That is, you must describe all the fields that make up the table and their characteristics. You must also indicate the primary key.

In Access, you can use two different views to create a table: Datasheet view and Design view. In **Datasheet view**, the data in the table is presented in rows and columns, similar to a spreadsheet. Although the main reason to use Datasheet view is to add or update records in a table, you can also use it to create a table or to later modify its structure. The other view, **Design view**, is only used to create a table or to modify the structure of the table.

As you might expect, Design view has more functionality for creating a table than Datasheet view. That is, there are certain actions that can only be performed in Design view. If creating your table requires such actions, you must use Design view. If not, you can choose either view. In this chapter, you will create the first table, the Business Analyst table, in Datasheet view. You will create the second table, the Client table, in Design view.

Whichever view you choose to use, before creating the table, you need to determine the names and data types of the fields that will make up the table. You already have determined the types for the Camashaly fields. You also need to determine additional properties for the fields.

BTW

The Ribbon and Screen Resolution
Access may change how the groups and buttons within the groups appear on the Ribbon, depending on the computer's screen resolution. Thus, your Ribbon may look different from the ones in this book if you are using a screen resolution other than 1024 × 768.

Plan
Ahead

Determine additional properties for fields.

- **Determine if a special caption is warranted.** Normally, the field name will appear as the label for a field on a form or report and as the column name in Datasheet view. If you would rather have a different name appear, you can change the field's caption to the desired name. One common use of captions is to shorten the column heading. If the data in a column is considerably shorter than the column heading, you could change the caption to a shorter heading. This would enable you to reduce the width of the column and yet still be able to see the entire column heading.

- **Determine if a special description is warranted.** Determine whether to include a description that would appear in the Status bar whenever the field is selected.

- **Determine field sizes.** For Text fields, determine the field size; that is, the maximum number of characters that can be entered in the field. Users will be prohibited from entering a value that has more characters than the field size.

- **Determine formats.** Determine whether the data in the field should be formatted in any particular way. You could, for example, specify that a number field is to be formatted with precisely two decimal places.

BTW

Naming Tables
Database users typically have their own guidelines for naming tables. Some use the singular version of the object being described while others use the prefix tbl with a table name. This book uses the singular version of the object (Client, Business Analyst) but adds the word Table to the name for the Business Analyst table to illustrate another possible approach. Including the word Table can assist visually impaired users when viewing the Navigation Pane.

The results of these decisions for the fields in the Business Analyst table are shown in Table 1–3. The table also shows the data types and field sizes of the fields as well as any special properties that need to be changed. The Business Analyst Number field has a caption of BA #, enabling the width of the Business Analyst Number column to be reduced in the datasheet.

Table 1–3 Structure of Business Analyst Table

Field Name	Data Type	Field Size	Description
Business Analyst Number	Text	2	**Primary Key** **Description:** Business Analyst Number **Caption:** BA #
Last Name	Text	15	
First Name	Text	15	
Street	Text	15	
City	Text	15	
State	Text	2	
Postal Code	Text	5	
Salary YTD	Currency		
Incentive YTD	Currency		

To Modify the Primary Key

When you first create your database, Access automatically creates a table for you. You can immediately begin defining the fields. If, for any reason, you do not have this table or inadvertently delete it, you can create the table by clicking Create on the Ribbon and then clicking the Table button (Create tab | Tables group). In either case, you are ready to define the fields.

The following steps define the first field, the Business Analyst Number field, which is the primary key. Access has already created a primary key field, which it has named ID. Thus, the steps will change the name, data type, and other properties of this field to match the Business Analyst field in Table 1–3.

1

- Right-click the column heading for the ID field to display a shortcut menu (Figure 1–6).

Q&A

Why does my shortcut menu look different?

You right-clicked within the column instead of right-clicking the column heading.

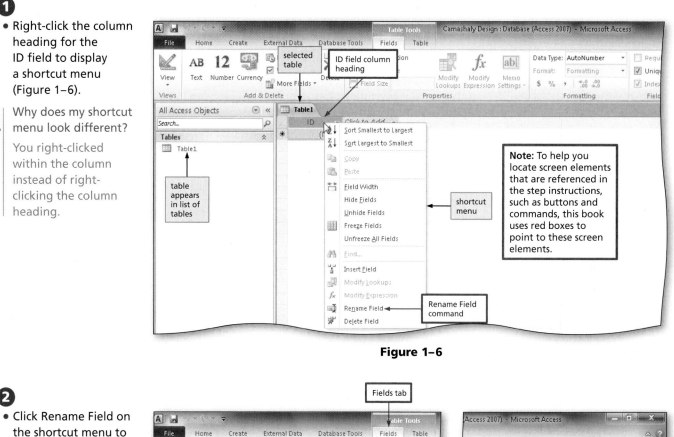

Note: To help you locate screen elements that are referenced in the step instructions, such as buttons and commands, this book uses red boxes to point to these screen elements.

Figure 1–6

2

- Click Rename Field on the shortcut menu to highlight the current name.

- Type **Business Analyst Number** to assign a name to the new field.

- Click the white space immediately below the field name to complete the addition of the field (Figure 1–7).

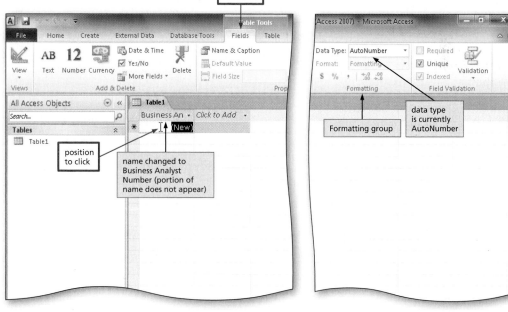

Figure 1–7

Q&A

Why doesn't the whole name appear?

The default column size is not large enough for Business Analyst Number to appear in its entirety. You will address this issue in later steps.

3

- Because the data type needs to be changed from AutoNumber to Text, click the Data Type box arrow (Table Tools Fields tab | Formatting group) to display a menu of available data types (Figure 1–8).

Figure 1–8

4

- Click Text to select the data type for the field (Figure 1–9).

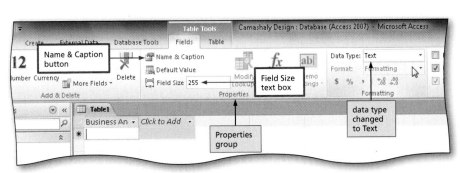

Figure 1–9

5

- Click the Field Size text box (Table Tools Fields tab | Properties group) to select the current field size, use either the DELETE or BACKSPACE keys to erase the current field size, and then type   2   as the new field size.

- Click the Name & Caption button (Table Tools Fields tab | Properties group) to display the Enter Field Properties dialog box.

- Click the Caption text box (Enter Field Properties dialog box), and then type   **BA #**   as the caption.

Figure 1–10

- Click the Description text box, and then type   **Unique identifier of business analyst**   as the description (Figure 1–10).

6

- Click the OK button (Enter Field Properties dialog box) to change the caption and description (Figure 1–11).

Figure 1–11

To Define the Remaining Fields in a Table

To define an additional field, you click the Click to Add column heading, select the data type, and then type the field name. This is different from the process you used to modify the ID field, which was an existing field. The following steps define the remaining fields shown in Table 1–3 on page AC 16.

1

• Click the Click to Add column heading to display a menu of available data types (Figure 1–12).

Q&A Why don't I rename the field like I renamed the ID field?

The ID field was an existing field, created automatically by Access. For a new field, you need to click the Click to Add heading.

Figure 1–12

2

• Click Text in the menu of available data types to select the Text data type.

• Type Last Name to enter a field name.

• Click the white space below the field name to complete the change of the name. Click the white space a second time to select the field (Figure 1–13).

Q&A I realized after I entered the field name that I selected the wrong data type. How can I correct it?

Click the Data Type box arrow and then select the correct type.

Q&A I inadvertently clicked the white space before entering the field name. How can I correct the name?

Right-click the field name, click Rename Field on the shortcut menu, and then type the new name.

Figure 1–13

3

• Change the field size to 15 just as you changed the field size of the Business Analyst Number field.

• Using the same technique, add the remaining fields in the Business Analyst table. For the First Name, Street, City, State, and Postal Code fields, the Text data type is correct, but you will need to change the field size to match Table 1–3. For the Salary YTD and Incentive YTD fields, you need to change the data type to Currency. Before defining the Incentive YTD field, you may need to click the right scroll arrow to bring the column for the field to the screen (Figure 1–14).

Figure 1–14

Q&A Why does Currency appear twice?

The second Currency is the format, which indicates how the data will be displayed. For the Currency data type, Access automatically sets the format to Currency, which is usually what you would want. You could change it to something else, if desired, by clicking the arrow and selecting the desired format.

Q&A I have an extra row between the row containing the field names and the row that begins with the asterisk. What happened? Is this a problem? If so, how do I fix it?

You inadvertently added a record to the table by pressing some key. Even pressing the SPACEBAR would add a record. You now have a record you do not want. To fix it, you need to delete the record, which you will do in Step 4.

4

- If you have an additional record between the field names and the asterisk, click the record selector (the box at the beginning of the record), press the DELETE key, and then click the Yes button when Access asks you if you want to delete the record.

BTW

Currency Symbols
To show the symbol for the Euro (€) instead of the dollar sign, change the Format property for the field whose data type is currency. To change the default symbols for currency, change the settings in the operating system using the control panel.

Making Changes to the Structure

When creating a table, check the entries carefully to ensure they are correct. If you discover a mistake while still typing the entry, you can correct the error by repeatedly pressing the BACKSPACE key until the incorrect characters are removed. Then, type the correct characters. If you do not discover a mistake until later, you can use the following techniques to make the necessary changes to the structure:

- To undo your most recent change, click the Undo button on the Quick Access Toolbar. If there is nothing that Access can undo, this button will be dim, and clicking it will have no effect.
- To delete a field, right-click the column heading for the field (the position containing the field name), and then click Delete Field on the shortcut menu.
- To change the name of a field, right-click the column heading for the field, click Rename Field on the shortcut menu, and then type the desired field name.
- To insert a field as the last field, click the Click to Add column heading, click the appropriate data type on the menu of available data types, type the desired field name, and, if necessary, change the field size.
- To insert a field between existing fields, right-click the column heading for the field that will follow the new field, and then click Insert Field on the shortcut menu. Right-click the column heading for the field, click Rename Field on the shortcut menu, and then type the desired field name.
- To move a field, click the column heading for the field to be moved to select the field, and then drag the field to the desired position.

As an alternative to these steps, you may want to start over. To do so, click the Close button for the table, and then click the No button in the Microsoft Access dialog box. Click Create on the Ribbon and then click the Table button to create a table. You then can repeat the process you used earlier to define the fields in the table.

To Save a Table

The Business Analyst table structure now is complete. The final step is to save the table within the database. As part of the process, you will give the table a name. The following steps save the table, giving it the name, Business Analyst Table.

1
- Click the Save button on the Quick Access Toolbar to display the Save As dialog box (Figure 1–15).

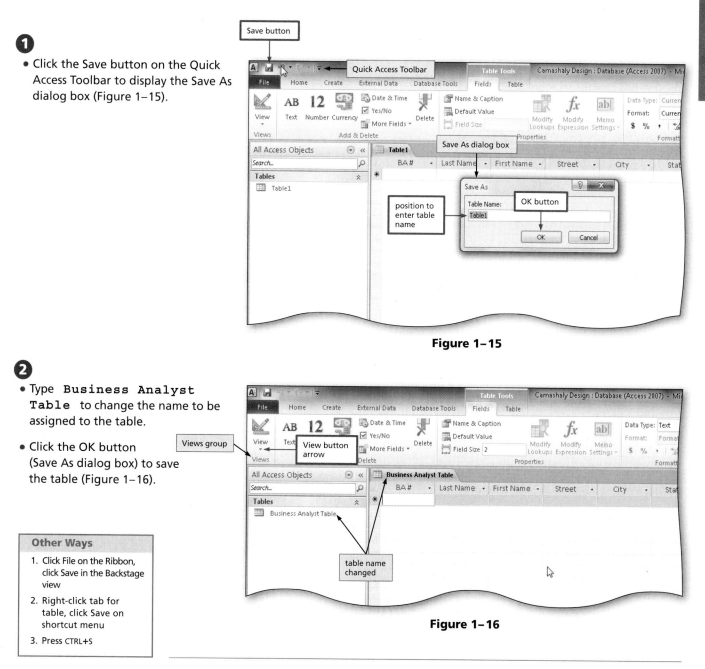

Figure 1–15

2
- Type **Business Analyst Table** to change the name to be assigned to the table.

- Click the OK button (Save As dialog box) to save the table (Figure 1–16).

Other Ways

1. Click File on the Ribbon, click Save in the Backstage view
2. Right-click tab for table, click Save on shortcut menu
3. Press CTRL+S

Figure 1–16

To View the Table in Design View

Even when creating a table in Datasheet view, Design view can be helpful. You should view the fields, data types, and properties to ensure you have entered them correctly. This viewing is easier to do in Design view. It is also easier to determine the primary key in Design view. The following steps view the structure of the Business Analyst Table in Design view so that you can verify the design is correct.

1

• Click the View button arrow (Table Tools Fields tab | Views group) to display the View button menu (Figure 1–17).

Q&A

Could I just click the View button rather than the arrow?

Yes. Clicking the button is equivalent to clicking the command represented by the icon currently appearing on the button. Because the icon on the button in Figure 1–17 is the icon for Design view, clicking the button would display the table in Design view. If you are uncertain, you can always click the arrow and select from the menu.

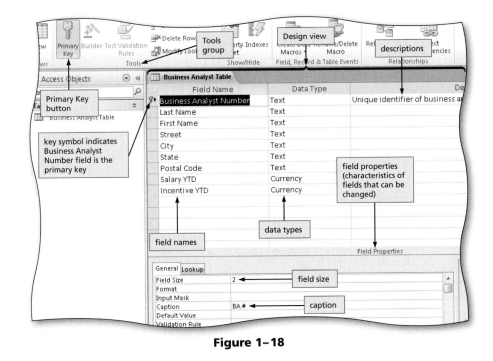

Figure 1–17

2

• Click Design View on the View button menu to view the table in Design view (Figure 1–18).

Figure 1–18

Other Ways

1. Click Design View button on Status bar

Checking the Structure in Design View

You should use Design view to carefully check the entries you have made. In Figure 1–18, for example, you can see that the Business Analyst Number field is the primary key of the Business Analyst Table by the key symbol in front of the field name. If your table does not have a key symbol, you can click the Primary Key button (Table Tools Design tab | Tools group) to designate the field as the primary key. You also can check that the data type, the description, the field size, and the caption are all correct.

For the other fields, you can see the field name, data type, and description without taking any special action. To see the field size and/or caption for a field, click the field's **row selector**, the small box that precedes the field. Clicking the row selector for the Last Name field, for example, displays the field properties for the field (Figure 1–19). You then can check to see that the field size is correct. In addition, if the field has a caption, you can check to see if that is correct as well. If you find any mistakes, you can make the necessary corrections on this screen. When you have finished, you would click the Save button to save your changes.

To Close the Table

Once you are sure that your entries are correct and you have saved your changes, you can close the table.

1

• Click the Close button for the Business Analyst Table to close the table (Figure 1–19).

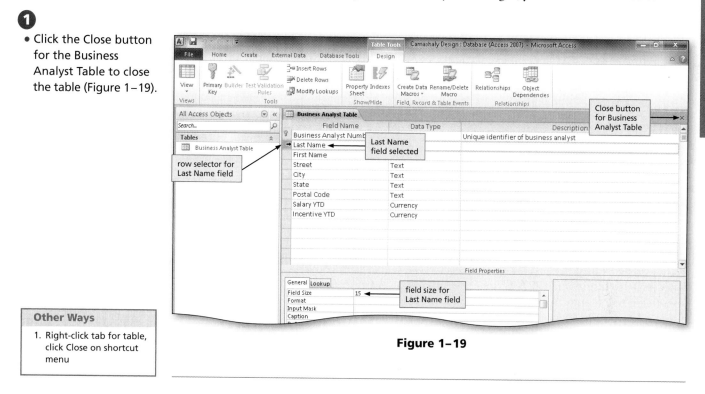

Figure 1–19

Other Ways

1. Right-click tab for table, click Close on shortcut menu

To Add Records to a Table

Creating a table by building the structure and saving the table is the first step in a two-step process. The second step is to add records to the table. To add records to a table, the table must be open. When making changes to tables, you work in Datasheet view. In Datasheet view, the table is represented as a collection of rows and columns called a **datasheet**.

You often add records in phases. For example, you might not have enough time to add all the records in one session. The following steps open the Business Analyst Table in Datasheet view and then add the first two records in the Business Analyst Table (Figure 1–20).

BA #	Last Name	First Name	Street	City	State	Postal Code	Salary YTD	Incentive YTD
11	Kerry	Cordelia	251 Painter	Georgetown	NC	28794	$3,200.00	$3,450.00
14	Martinez	Manuel	3125 Steel	Kyle	SC	28797	$3,100.00	$2,430.00

Figure 1–20

1

• Right-click the Business Analyst Table in the Navigation Pane to display the shortcut menu (Figure 1–21).

Figure 1–21

2

- Click Open on the shortcut menu to open the table in Datasheet view.

Q&A

What if I want to return to Design view?

You can open Design view by clicking Design View on the shortcut menu.

- Click the Shutter Bar Open/Close Button to close the Navigation Pane (Figure 1–22).

Shutter Bar Open/Close Button opens Navigation Pane if it is currently closed

record selector (box that, when clicked, selects the entire record) currently positioned on first record

Datasheet view

position to enter business analyst number on first record

positioned on record 1 out of 1

Record: 1 of 1 | No Filter | Search

Unique identifier of business analyst

Num Lock

Figure 1–22

3

- Click the BA # field if necessary to display an insertion point, and type 11 to enter the first business analyst number (Figure 1–23).

pencil icon in the record selector column indicates that the record is being edited but changes to the record are not saved yet

business analyst number on first record

Access creates row for a new record

Figure 1–23

4

- Press the TAB key to move to the next field.

- Enter the last name, first name, street, city, state, and postal code by typing the following entries, pressing the TAB key after each one: **Kerry** as the last name, **Cordelia** as the first name, **251 Painter** as the street, **Georgetown** as the city, **NC** as the state, and **28794** as the postal code.

- Type **3200** in the Salary YTD field (Figure 1–24).

Salary YTD field still selected

last name entered

first name entered

street entered

city entered

state entered

postal code entered

salary YTD in process of being entered

Figure 1–24

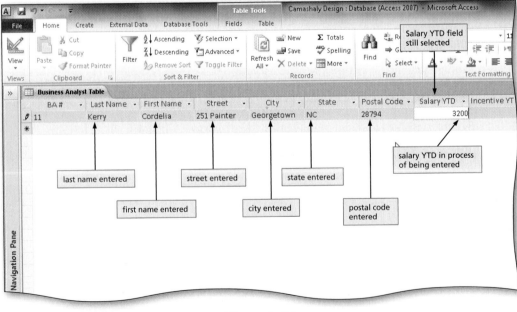

Q&A

Do I need to type a dollar sign?

You do not need to type dollar signs or commas. In addition, because the digits to the right of the decimal point are both zeros, you do not need to type either the decimal point or the zeros.

5

- Press the TAB key to complete the entry for the field.

- Type 3450 in the Incentive YTD field, and then press the TAB key to complete the entry of the first record (Figure 1–25).

Q&A

How and when do I save the record?

As soon as you have entered or modified a record and moved to another record, the original record is saved. This is different from other applications. The rows entered in an Excel worksheet, for example, are not saved until the entire worksheet is saved.

Business Analyst Number field selected

position to enter business analyst number on second record

first record entered and saved

currently positioned on record 2 out of 2

Figure 1–25

6

- Use the techniques shown in Steps 3 through 5 to enter the data for the second record (Figure 1–26).

Experiment

- Click the Salary YTD field on either of the records. Be sure the Table Tools Fields tab is selected. Click the Format box arrow and then click each of the formats in the Format box menu to see the effect on the values in the Salary YTD field. When finished, click Currency in the Format box menu.

Close button for Business Analyst Table

record selector

second record entered and saved

Figure 1–26

Making Changes to the Data

As you enter data, check your entries carefully to ensure they are correct. If you make a mistake and discover it before you press the TAB key, correct it by pressing the BACKSPACE key until the incorrect characters are removed, and then type the correct characters. If you do not discover a mistake until later, you can use the following techniques to make the necessary corrections to the data:

- To undo your most recent change, click the Undo button on the Quick Access Toolbar. If there is nothing that Access can undo, this button will be dimmed, and clicking it will have no effect.

- To add a record, click the New (blank) record button, click the position for the Business Analyst Number field on the first open record, and then add the record. Do not worry about it being in the correct position in the table. Access will reposition the record based on the primary key, in this case, the Business Analyst Number.

BTW

Adding Records
You can add records in any order. When you close a table and re-open it, the records will be in order by primary key.

- To delete a record, click the record selector, shown in Figure 1–26, for the record to be deleted. Then press the DELETE key to delete the record, and click the Yes button when Access asks you to verify that you do indeed want to delete the record.

- To change the contents of one or more fields in a record, the record must be on the screen. If it is not, use any appropriate technique, such as the UP ARROW and DOWN ARROW keys or the vertical scroll bar, to move to it. If the field you want to correct is not visible on the screen, use the horizontal scroll bar along the bottom of the screen to shift all the fields until the one you want appears. If the value in the field is currently highlighted, you can simply type the new value. If you would rather edit the existing value, you must have an insertion point in the field. You can place the insertion point by clicking in the field or by pressing F2. You then can use the arrow keys, the DELETE key, and the BACKSPACE key for making the correction. You also can use the INSERT key to switch between Insert and Overtype mode. When you have made the change, press the TAB key to move to the next field.

If you cannot determine how to correct the data, you may find that you are "stuck" on the record, in which case Access neither allows you to move to another record nor allows you to close the table until you have made the correction. If you encounter this situation, simply press the ESC key. Pressing the ESC key will remove from the screen the record you are trying to add. You then can move to any other record, close the table, or take any other action you desire.

To Close a Table

Now that you have created and saved the Business Analyst Table, you can close it. The following step closes the table.

1 Click the Close button for the Business Analyst Table, shown in Figure 1–26, to close the table (Figure 1–27).

Figure 1–27

To Quit Access

The following steps quit Access. For a detailed example of the procedure summarized below, refer to the Office 2010 and Windows 7 chapter at the beginning of this book.

1 Click the Close button on the right side of the title bar to quit Access.

2 If a Microsoft Access dialog box appears, click the Save button to save any changes made to the object since the last save.

Break Point: If you wish to take a break, this is a good place to do so. To resume at a later time, continue following the steps from this location forward.

Starting Access and Opening a Database

Once you have created and later closed a database, you will need to open it in the future in order to use it. Opening a database requires that Access is running on your computer.

To Start Access

1 Click the Start button on the Windows 7 taskbar to display the Start menu.

2 Type `Microsoft Access` as the search text in the 'Search programs and files' text box and watch the search results appear on the Start menu.

3 Click Microsoft Access 2010 in the search results on the Start menu to start Access.

To Open a Database from Access

Earlier in this chapter, you saved your database on a USB flash drive using the file name, Camashaly Design. The following steps open the Camashaly Design database from the Access folder in the CIS 101 folder on the USB flash drive. For a detailed example of the procedure summarized below, refer to the Office 2010 and Windows 7 chapter at the beginning of this book.

1 With your USB flash drive connected to one of the computer's USB ports, click File on the Ribbon to open the Backstage view, if necessary.

2 Click Open in the Backstage view to display the Open dialog box.

3 Navigate to the location of the file to be opened (in this case, the USB flash drive, then to the CIS 101 folder [or your class folder], and then to the Access folder).

4 Click Camashaly Design to select the file to be opened.

5 Click the Open button (Open dialog box) to open the selected file and display the opened database in the Access window.

6 If a Security Warning appears, click the Enable Content button (Figure 1–28).

BTW

Organizing Files and Folders
You should organize and store files in folders so that you easily can find the files later. For a discussion of folders and detailed examples of creating folders, refer to the Office 2010 and Windows 7 chapter at the beginning of this book.

Q&A

When would I not want to enable the content?

You would want to disable the content if you suspected that your database might contain harmful content or damaging macros. Because you are the one who created the database and no one else has used it, you should have no such suspicions.

Figure 1–28

Other Ways

1. Click File on the Ribbon, click Recent in the Backstage view, click file name

To Add Additional Records to a Table

You can add records to a table that already contains data using a process almost identical to that used to add records to an empty table. The only difference is that you place the insertion point after the last record before you enter the additional data. To do so, use the **Navigation buttons**, which are buttons used to move within a table, found near the lower-left corner of the screen when a table is open. The purpose of each of the Navigation buttons is described in Table 1–4.

Table 1–4 Navigation Buttons in Datasheet View	
Button	**Purpose**
First record	Moves to the first record in the table
Previous record	Moves to the previous record
Next record	Moves to the next record
Last record	Moves to the last record in the table
New (blank) record	Moves to the end of the table to a position for entering a new record

The following steps add the remaining records (Figure 1–29) to the Business Analyst table.

BA # ▾	Last Name ▾	First Name ▾	Street ▾	City ▾	State ▾	Postal Code ▾	Salary YTD ▾	Incentive YTD ▾
27	Liu	Jan	265 Marble	Byron	SC	28795	$3,400.00	$2,280.00
35	Scott	Jeff	1925 Pine	Georgetown	NC	28794	$500.00	$0.00

Business Analyst Table

Figure 1–29

1
- If the Navigation Pane is closed, click the Shutter Bar Open/ Close Button, shown in Figure 1–27, to open the Navigation Pane (Figure 1–30).

Figure 1–30

2
- Right-click the Business Analyst table in the Navigation Pane to display a shortcut menu.

- Click Open on the short-cut menu to open the table in Datasheet view.

- Close the Navigation Pane by clicking the Shutter Bar Open/Close Button (Figure 1–31).

Figure 1–31

3

- Click the New (blank) record button to move to a position to enter a new record (Figure 1–32).

Q&A

Could you just click the Business Analyst Number (BA #) on the first open record and then add the record?

Yes, but it's a good habit to use the New (blank) Record button. Once a table contains more records than will fit on the screen, it is easier to click the New (blank) record button.

Figure 1–32

4

- Add the records shown in Figure 1–29, using the same techniques you used to add the first two records (Figure 1–33).

Figure 1–33

Other Ways

1. Click New button (Home tab | Records group)
2. Press CTRL+PLUS SIGN (+)

To Resize Columns in a Datasheet

Access assigns default column sizes, which do not always allow all the data in the field to appear. In some cases, the data might appear but not the entire field name. You can correct this problem by **resizing** the column (changing its size) in the datasheet. In some instances, you may want to reduce the size of a column. The State field, for example, is short enough that it does not require all the space on the screen that is allotted to it. Changing a column width changes the **layout**, or design, of a table.

The following steps resize the columns in the Business Analyst table and save the changes to the layout.

1

- Point to the right boundary of the field selector for the Business Analyst (BA #) field (Figure 1–34) so that the mouse pointer becomes a two-headed arrow.

Figure 1–34

2

- Double-click the right boundary of the field selector to resize the field so that it best fits the data.

- Use the same technique to resize all the other fields to best fit the data (Figure 1–35).

3

- Save the changes to the layout by clicking the Save button on the Quick Access Toolbar (Figure 1–35).

- Click the table's Close button (shown in Figure 1–33) to the table.

Figure 1–35

Q&A What if I closed the table without saving the layout changes?
You would be asked if you want to save the changes.

Other Ways
1. Right-click field name, click Field Width

Plan Ahead

Determine the best method for distributing the database objects.
The traditional method of distributing database objects uses a printer to produce a hard copy of a table. A **hard copy** or **printout** is information that exists on a physical medium such as paper. For users who can receive fax documents, you can elect to print a hard copy on a remote fax machine. Hard copies can be useful for the following reasons:

- Many people prefer proofreading a hard copy of a document rather than viewing it on the screen to check for errors and readability.

- Hard copies can serve as reference material if your storage medium is lost or becomes corrupted and you need to re-create the document.

Instead of distributing a hard copy, users can choose to distribute the document as an electronic image that mirrors the original document's appearance. The electronic image of the document can be e-mailed, posted on a Web site, or copied to a portable medium such as a USB flash drive. Two popular electronic image formats, sometimes called fixed formats, are PDF by Adobe Systems and XPS by Microsoft. In Access, you can create PDF and XPS files through the External Data tab on the Ribbon. Electronic images of documents, such as PDF and XPS, can be useful for the following reasons:

- Users can view electronic images of documents without the software that created the original document (i.e., Access). Specifically, to view a PDF file, you use a program called Acrobat Reader, which can be downloaded free from Adobe's Web site. Similarly, to view an XPS file, you use a program called an XPS Viewer, which is included in the latest versions of Windows and Internet Explorer.

- Sending electronic documents saves paper and printer supplies. Society encourages users to contribute to **green computing**, which involves reducing the environmental waste generated when using a computer.

BTW

Changing Printers
To change the default printer that appears in the Print dialog box, click File on the Ribbon, click the Print tab in the Backstage view, click Print in the Print gallery, then click the Name box arrow and select the desired printer.

Previewing and Printing the Contents of a Table

When working with a database, you often will need to print a copy of the table contents. Figure 1–36 shows a printed copy of the contents of the Business Analyst table. (Yours may look slightly different, depending on your printer.) Because the Business Analyst table is substantially wider than the screen, it also will be wider than the normal printed page in portrait orientation. **Portrait orientation** means the printout is across the width of the page. **Landscape orientation** means the printout is across the height of the page. Thus, to print the wide database table, you might prefer to use landscape orientation. A convenient way to change to landscape orientation is to preview what the printed copy will look like by using Print Preview. This allows you to determine whether landscape orientation is necessary and, if it is, to change the orientation easily to landscape. In addition, you also can use Print Preview to determine whether any adjustments are necessary to the page margins.

Business Analyst Table   4/12/2012

BA #	Last Name	First Name	Street	City	State	Postal Code	Salary YTD	Incentive YTD
11	Kerry	Cordelia	251 Painter	Georgetown	NC	28794	$3,200.00	$3,450.00
14	Martinez	Manuel	3125 Steel	Kyle	SC	28797	$3,100.00	$2,430.00
27	Liu	Jan	265 Marble	Byron	SC	28795	$3,400.00	$2,280.00
35	Scott	Jeff	1925 Pine	Georgetown	NC	28794	$500.00	$0.00

Figure 1–36

To Preview and Print the Contents of a Table

The following steps use Print Preview to preview and then print the contents of the Business Analyst table.

1

- If the Navigation Pane is closed, open the Navigation Pane by clicking the Shutter Bar Open/Close Button.

- Be sure the Business Analyst table is selected.

Q&A

Why do I have to be sure the Business Analyst table is selected? It is the only object in the database.

When the database contains only one object, you don't have to worry about selecting the object. Ensuring that the correct object is selected is a good habit to form, however, to make sure that the object you print is the one you want.

Figure 1–37

- Click File on the Ribbon to open the Backstage view.

- Click the Print tab in the Backstage view to display the Print gallery (Figure 1–37).

2

- Click the Print Preview button in the Print gallery to display a preview of what the table will look like when printed.

- Close the Navigation Pane to free up more of the screen for the preview (Figure 1–38).

Q&A

I can't read the table. Can I magnify a portion of the table?

Yes. Point the mouse pointer, whose shape will change to a magnifying glass, at the portion of the table that you want to magnify, and then click.

You can return the view of the table to the one shown in the figure by clicking a second time.

Figure 1–38

3

- Click the mouse pointer in the position shown in Figure 1–38 to magnify the upper-right section of the table (Figure 1–39).

Q&A

My table was already magnified in a different area. How can I see the area shown in the figure?

One way is to use the scroll bars to move to the desired portion of the table. You also can click the mouse pointer anywhere in the table to produce a screen like the one in Figure 1–38, and then click in the location shown in the figure.

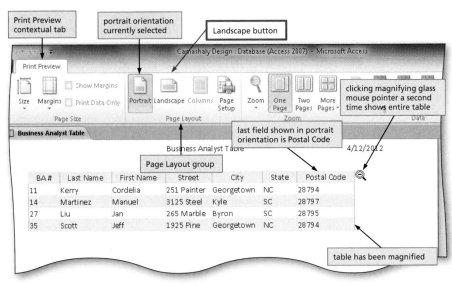

Figure 1–39

4

- Click the Landscape button to change to landscape orientation (Figure 1–40).

- Click the Print button (Print Preview tab | Print group) to display the Print dialog box.

- Click the OK button (Print dialog box) to print the table.

- When the printer stops, retrieve the hard copy of the Business Analyst Table.

- Click the Close Print Preview button (Print Preview tab | Close Preview group) to close the Print Preview window.

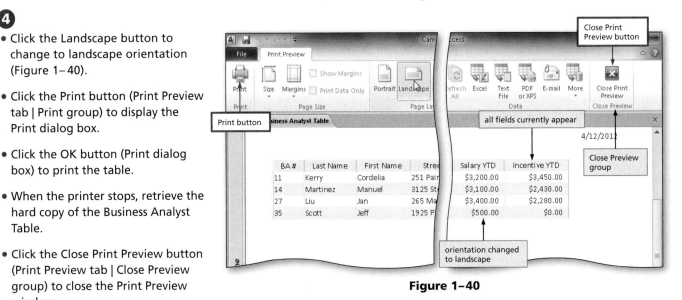

Figure 1–40

Other Ways

1. Press CTRL+P, click OK button (Print dialog box)

Creating Additional Tables

The Camashaly Design database contains two tables, the Business Analyst table and the Client table. You still need to create the Client table and add records to it. You created the Business Analyst table in Datasheet view. You will create the Client table in Design view.

Recall that the fields for the Client table are Client Number, Client Name, Street, City, State, Postal Code, Amount Paid, Current Due, Contract Hours YTD, and Business Analyst Number. The details that must be entered for these fields are shown in Table 1–5. The Client Number is the primary key. The Client Number field and the Business Analyst Number fields have both descriptions and captions. The Contract Hours YTD has a caption.

Because the values in the Contract Hours YTD field have decimal places, only Single, Double, or Decimal would be possible field size choices. (See Table 1–2 on Page AC 10 for a description of the possible field sizes for Number fields.) The difference between these choices concerns the amount of accuracy. Double is more accurate than Single, for example,

Field Size box
▼ the Field
arrow.

Field Size box
display the
box menu
–48).

uld happen if
field size set
r?

d size is
o decimal
n be stored.
lue of 2.50
stored as 2.

ter your hours and none of the values have decimal places, probably you did not
he field size.

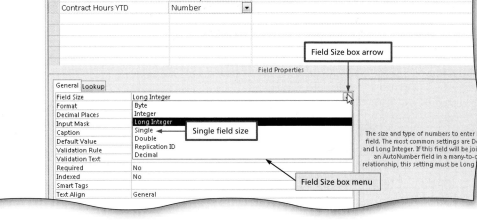

Figure 1–48

le to select
ecision as the

Format box
y the Format
w.

Format box
display the
ox menu
–49).

Figure 1–49

ed to select
the format.

Decimal
ox to display
mal Places box

Decimal
ox arrow to
e number of
places.

o select 2
umber of
places.

Caption text
roduce an insertion point, and then type `Hrs YTD` to enter a caption
–50).

Figure 1–50

but requires more storage space. Because the rates are only two decimal places, Single is a
perfectly acceptable choice.

In addition to changing the field size for the Contract Hours YTD, you will also change
the format to Fixed (a fixed number of decimal places) and the number of decimal places to 2.

Table 1– 5 Structure of Client Table			
Field Name	**Data Type**	**Field Size**	**Notes**
Client Number	Text	4	**Primary Key** **Description:** Client Number (two uppercase letters followed by 2-digit number) **Caption:** CL #
Client Name	Text	30	
Street	Text	15	
City	Text	15	
State	Text	2	
Postal Code	Text	5	
Amount Paid	Currency		
Current Due	Currency		
Contract Hours YTD	Number	Single	**Caption:** Hrs YTD **Format:** Fixed **Decimal Places:** 2
Business Analyst Number	Text	2	**Caption:** BA # **Description:** Business Analyst Number (number of business analyst for client)

To Create a Table in Design View

The next step in creating the table is to define the fields by specifying the required details in Design view. You
will make entries in the Field Name, Data Type, and Description columns and enter additional information in the Field
Properties box in the lower portion of the Table window. As you define the fields, the row selector (Figure 1–19 on page
AC 23) indicates the field you currently are describing. Clicking the row selector selects the entire row. It is positioned
on the first field, indicating Access is ready for you to enter the name of the first field in the Field Name column.

The following steps use Design view to define the fields in the table.

1
• Open the Navigation Pane.

• Click Create on the Ribbon to display
the Create tab (Figure 1–41).

Figure 1–41

2
- Click the Table Design button (Create tab | Tables group) to create a new table in Design view (Figure 1–42).

Q&A

Could I save the table now so I can assign it the name I want, rather than Table1?

You certainly could. Be aware, however, that you will still need to save it again once you have added all your fields.

Figure 1–42

3
- Type **Client Number** (the name of the first field) in the Field Name column and then press the TAB key to accept the field name and move to the Data Type column (Figure 1–43).

Figure 1–43

4
- Click the Primary Key button (Table Tools Design tab | Tools group) to designate the Client Number field as the primary key (Figure 1–44).

Figure 1–44

5
- Press the TAB key to move to the Description column, and then type **Client Number (two uppercase letters followed by a two-digit number)** as the description.

- Click the Field Size text box in the Field Properties pane to produce an insertion point, use either the BACKSPACE or DELETE key as necessary to erase the current entry (255), and then type **4** to change the field size.

- Click the Caption text box to produce an insertion point, and then type **CL #** to enter a caption (Figure 1–45).

Figure 1–45

6
- Click the Field Name column on the second row to produce an insertion point and then make the entries for the Client Name field.

- Use the techniques illustrated in Steps 1 through 5 to make the entries for the remaining fields in the Client table structure, shown in Table 1–5 on page AC 33, up through and including the name of the Amount Paid field.

- Click the Data Type box arrow to display a menu of available data types (Figure 1–46).

Figure 1–46

7
- Click Currency to select the data type.

- Enter the Current Due field and select the Currency data type.

- Enter the Contract Hours YTD field and select the Number data type (Figure 1–47).

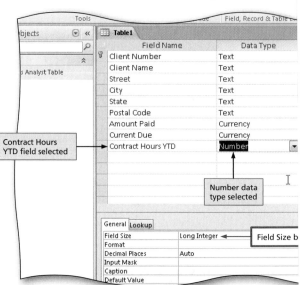

Figure 1–47

8
- Click t___ to disp___ Size b___

- Click t___ arrow ___ Field S___ (Figure ___

Q&A

What ___ I left t___ to Inte___

If the ___ Intege___ places ___ Thus a___ would ___ If you ___ change___

9
- Click S___ single ___ field s___

- Click t___ to disp___ box ar___

- Click t___ arrow ___ Forma___ (Figure ___

10
- Click F___ fixed a___

- Click t___ Places ___ the De___ arrow ___

- Click t___ Places ___ enter ___ decim___

- Click 2___ as the ___ decim___

- Click t___ box to ___ (Figure ___

⑪

- Enter the Business Analyst Number field from Table 1–5. Be sure to change the description, field size, and caption to the ones shown in the table.

- Click the Save button on the Quick Access Toolbar to display the Save As dialog box, type Client as the name of the table, and then click the OK button (Save As dialog box) to save the table (Figure 1–51).

Figure 1–51

Correcting Errors in the Structure

When creating a table, check the entries carefully to ensure they are correct. If you make a mistake and discover it before you press the TAB key, you can correct the error by repeatedly pressing the BACKSPACE key until the incorrect characters are removed. Then, type the correct characters. If you do not discover a mistake until later, you can click the entry, type the correct value, and then press the ENTER key. You can use the following techniques to make changes to the structure:

- If you accidentally add an extra field to the structure, select the field by clicking the row selector (the leftmost column on the row that contains the field to be deleted). Once you have selected the field, press the DELETE key. This will remove the field from the structure.

- If you forget to include a field, select the field that will follow the field you want to add by clicking the row selector, and then press the INSERT key. The remaining fields move down one row, making room for the missing field. Make the entries for the new field in the usual manner.

- If you made the wrong field a primary key field, click the correct primary key entry for the field and then click the Primary Key button (Table Tools Design tab | Tools group).

- To move a field, click the row selector for the field to be moved to select the field, and then drag the field to the desired position.

As an alternative to these steps, you may want to start over. To do so, click the Close button for the window containing the table, and then click the No button in the Microsoft Access dialog box. Click Create on the Ribbon and then click the Table Design button to create a table. You then can repeat the process you used earlier to define the fields in the table.

Other Ways

1. Press F6 to move between the upper pane and the lower pane in the Table Design window

AutoCorrect Feature
The AutoCorrect feature of Access corrects common mistakes when entering text in a cell. AutoCorrect corrects two capital letters by changing the second letter to lowercase and capitalizes the first letter in the names of days. It also corrects more than 400 commonly misspelled words.

Other AutoCorrect Options
Using the Office AutoCorrect feature, you can create entries that will replace abbreviations with spelled-out names and phrases automatically. To specify AutoCorrect rules, click File to open the Backstage view, click Options, and then click Proofing in the Access Options dialog box.

To Close the Table

Now that you have completed and saved the Client table, you can close it. The following step closes the table.

1 Click the Close button for the Client table (see Figure 1–51) to close the table.

Importing Data from Other Applications to Access

Now that you have created the Client table, you could add the records to it just as you did with the Business Analyst table. Access provides an alternative, however, that is available because Camashaly Design has already stored the necessary data in an Excel workbook (Figure 1–52). The data is stored in the form of an Excel **list**; that is, the first row contains column headings describing the data in each of the columns, and the remaining rows contain the data. Camashaly can **import** the data, which means to make a copy of the data in a table in the Access database.

When importing data, you have two choices. You can create a new table, in which case the column headings in the worksheet become the field names in the table. Access will attempt to assign appropriate data types. You would need to review the data types, adjust field sizes, captions, descriptions, and formats after the data was imported. The other option is to add the records to an existing table. This method is appropriate if you have already created the table, provided the column headings in the worksheet match the field names in the table, as they do in the case of the Client table.

	A	B	C	D	E	F	G	H	I	J	K
1	Client Number	Client Name	Street	City	State	Postal Code	Amount Paid	Current Due	Contract Hours YTD	Business Analyst Number	
2	BA53	Bavant Animal Hospital	134 Main	Burles	NC	28817	$0.00	$7,500.00	0.00	11	
3	BB32	Babbage CPA Firm	464 Linnell	Austin	SC	28796	$1,500.00	$500.00	5.00	14	
4	BC76	Buda Community Clinic	867 Ridge	Buda	NC	27032	$2,500.00	$750.00	2.50	11	
5	CJ29	Catering by Jenna	123 Second	Granger	NC	27036	$3,000.00	$1,000.00	15.50	27	
6	GA74	Grant Antiques	78 Catawba	Georgetown	NC	28794	$5,500.00	$3,200.00	34.50	14	
7	GF56	Granger Foundation	65 Simpson	Granger	NC	27036	$0.00	$6,500.00	0.00	11	
8	HC10	Hendley County Hospital	216 Rivard	Austin	SC	28796	$3,100.00	$1,200.00	12.00	27	
9	KD21	KAL Design Studio	116 Pine	Georgetown	NC	28794	$6,000.00	$3,200.00	30.50	14	
10	KG04	Kyle Grocery Cooperative	421 First	Kyle	SC	28798	$3,200.00	$0.00	5.00	11	
11	ME14	Mike's Electronic Stop	234 Gilham	Georgetown	NC	28794	$2,500.00	$1,500.00	8.50	27	
12	PJ34	Patricia Jean Florist	345 Magee	Kyle	SC	28798	$0.00	$5,200.00	0.00	27	
13	SL77	Smarter Law Associates	764 Main	Burles	NC	28817	$3,800.00	$0.00	10.50	11	
14	TB17	The Bikeshop	346 Austin	Buda	NC	27032	$2,750.00	$1,200.00	14.00	27	
15	WE05	Walburg Energy Alternatives	12 Polk	Walburg	NC	28819	$4,500.00	$1,450.00	19.50	14	
16	WS01	Woody Sporting Goods	578 Central	Walburg	NC	28819	$2,250.00	$1,600.00	18.50	14	
17											

Figure 1–52

The process of importing into an Access database uses a wizard. Specifically, if the data is imported from an Excel worksheet, the process will use the Import Spreadsheet Wizard. The wizard takes you through some basic steps, asking a few simple questions. After you have answered the questions, the wizard will import or link the data.

To Import an Excel Worksheet

To import the data in the Camashaly Client Data workbook, you use the Import Spreadsheet Wizard to place the rows from an Excel worksheet into an existing table. The following steps import the Camashaly Client Data Excel workbook, which is provided as a data file. See the inside back cover of this book for instructions on downloading the Data Files for Students, or contact your instructor for more information about accessing the required files.

1

• Click External Data on the Ribbon to display the External Data tab (Figure 1–53).

Figure 1–53

2

• Click the Excel button (External Data tab | Import & Link group) to display the Get External Data – Excel Spreadsheet dialog box.

• Click the Browse button (Get External Data – Excel Spreadsheet dialog box) to display the File Open dialog box.

• Navigate to the USB flash drive (or the location of your data files).

• Double-click your USB flash drive, and then click Camashaly Client Data to select the file to be opened.

• Click the Open button (File Open dialog box), which will return you to the Get External Data dialog box with the Camashaly Client Data workbook selected.

3

• Click the option button to append a copy of records to a table (Figure 1–54).

Q&A

What happens if I select the option button to import records into a new table?

Instead of the records being added to an existing table, they will be placed in a new table. Access will assign all the data types. You would then need to ensure they are correct. You also would need to change any field sizes, descriptions, captions, formats, or number of decimal places to the ones you want.

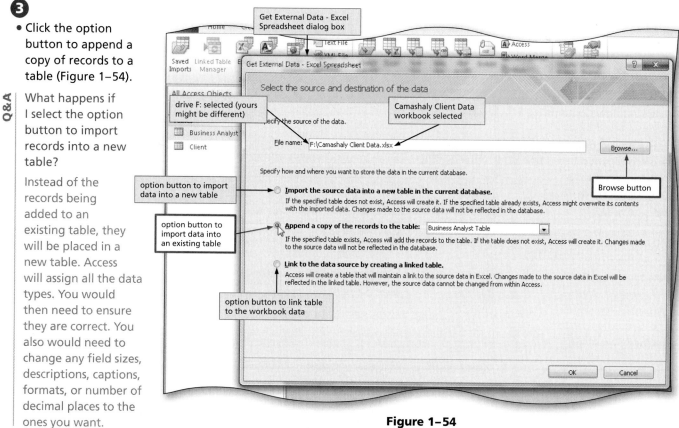

Figure 1–54

4

- Click the arrow to produce a menu of available tables.

- Click the Client table to select the table to which a copy of the records will be appended (Figure 1–55).

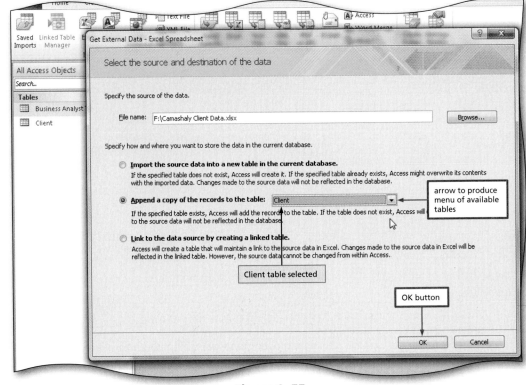

Figure 1–55

5

- Click the OK button to move to the next Import Spreadsheet Wizard screen (Figure 1–56).

Q&A

The First Row Contains Column Headings check box is checked, but it is dimmed. What if I want to remove the check mark?

When you are appending records to an existing table, the first row must contain column headings. If instead you were creating a new table, the first row might not contain column headings. In that case, you would have control over this check box.

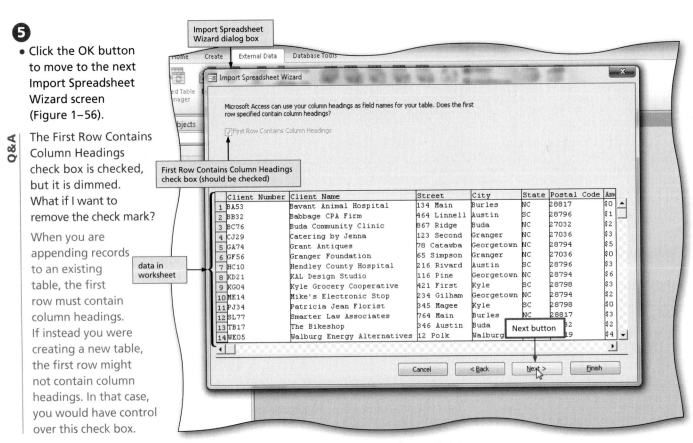

Figure 1–56

6

- Click the Next button to move to the next Import Spreadsheet Wizard screen (Figure 1–57).

Q&A What happens if I later realize I have selected the wrong table?

If you have not yet clicked the Finish button, you can click the Back button to return to the screen where you selected the table, and then select the correct table.

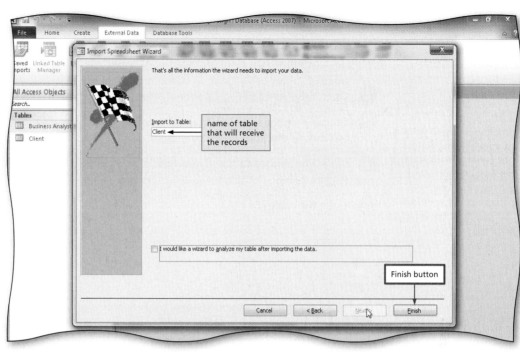

Figure 1–57

7

- Because the table name is correct, click the Finish button to import the data (Figure 1–58).

Q&A I got an error message that stated that a particular field did not exist in the Client table. What did I do wrong? How do I fix it?

When you created the table, you did not name that particular field correctly. Open the table in Design view and change the field name to the correct name. Check other field names as well. When you are done, save and close the table. Then, repeat the import process.

Figure 1–58

8

- Because you will not save the import steps, click the Close button.

Q&A When would I save the import steps?

If you think you might need to repeat these steps in the future, you can save time by saving the steps.

Other Ways

1. Right-click table in Navigation Pane, click Import on shortcut menu.

To Resize Columns in a Datasheet

You can resize the columns in the datasheet for the Client table just as you resized the columns in the datasheet for the Business Analyst table. The following steps resize the columns in the Client table to best fit the data.

BTW

Resizing Columns
To resize all columns in a datasheet to best fit simultaneously, select the column heading for the first column, hold down the SHIFT key and select the last column in the datasheet. Then, double-click the right boundary of any field selector.

1 Open the Client table in Datasheet view and then close the Navigation Pane.

2 Double-click the right boundary of the field selectors of each of the fields to resize the columns so that they best fit the data.

3 Save the changes to the layout by clicking the Save button on the Quick Access Toolbar (Figure 1–59).

4 Close the table.

Figure 1–59

Break Point: If you wish to take a break, this is a good place to do so. You can quit Access now. To resume at a later time, start Access, open the database called Camashaly Design, and continue following the steps from this location forward.

Additional Database Objects

A computerized database such as Access contains many types of objects. Tables are the objects you use to store and manipulate data. Access supports other important types of objects as well; each of these objects has a specific purpose that assists in maximizing the benefits of a database. Through queries (questions), Access makes it possible to ask complex questions concerning the data in the database and then receive instant answers. Access also allows the user to produce attractive and useful forms for viewing and updating data. Additionally, Access includes report creation tools that make it easy to produce sophisticated reports for presenting data.

To Use the Simple Query Wizard to Create a Query

Queries are simply questions, the answers to which are in the database. Access contains a powerful query feature that helps you find the answers to a wide variety of questions. Once you have examined the question you want to ask to determine the fields involved in the question, you can begin creating the query. If there are no restrictions involved in the query, nor any special order or calculations, you can use the Simple Query Wizard.

The following steps use the Simple Query Wizard to create a query that Camashaly Design might use to obtain financial information on its clients. The query displays the number, name, amount paid, current due, contract hours YTD, and business analyst number of all clients.

1

- If the Navigation Pane is closed, click the Shutter Bar Open/Close Button to open the Navigation Pane.

- Be sure the Client table is selected.

- Click Create on the Ribbon to display the Create tab.

- Click the Query Wizard button (Create tab | Queries group) to display the New Query dialog box (Figure 1–60).

Figure 1–60

2

- Be sure Simple Query Wizard is selected, and then click the OK button (New Query dialog box) to display the Simple Query Wizard dialog box (Figure 1–61).

Q&A What would happen if the Business Analyst Table were selected instead of the Client table?

The list of available fields would contain fields from the Business Analyst Table rather than the Client table.

Q&A If the list contained Business Analyst Table fields, how could I make it contain Client table fields?

Click the arrow in the Tables/Queries box and then click the Client table in the list that appears.

Figure 1–61

3

- With the Client Number field selected, click the Add Field button to add the field to the query.

- With the Client Name field selected, click the Add Field button a second time to add the field.

- Click the Amount Paid field, and then click the Add Field button to add the field.

- In a similar fashion, add the Current Due, Contract Hours YTD, and Business Analyst Number fields (Figure 1–62).

Figure 1–62

4

- Click the Next button to move to the next screen.

- Ensure that the Detail (shows every field of every record) option button is selected (Figure 1–63).

Q&A What is the difference between Detail and Summary?

Detail shows all the records and fields. Summary only shows computations (for example, the total amount paid).

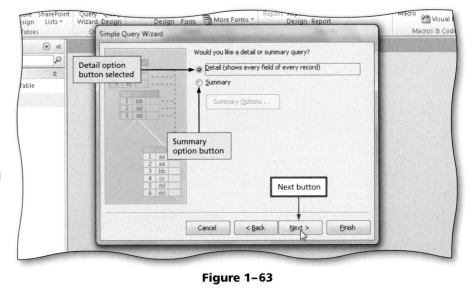

Figure 1–63

5

- Click the Next button to move to the next screen.

- Ensure the title of the query is Client Query (Figure 1–64).

Figure 1–64

6

- Click the Finish button to create the query (Figure 1–65).

- Click the Close button for the Client Query to remove the query results from the screen.

Q&A

If I want to use this query in the future, do I need to save the query?

Normally you would. The one exception is a query created by the wizard. The wizard automatically saves the query it creates.

Figure 1–65

Using Queries

After you have created and saved a query, Access stores it as a database object and makes it available for use in a variety of ways:

- To view the results of the query, open it by right-clicking the query in the Navigation Pane and clicking Open on the shortcut menu.

- To print the results with the query open, click File on the Ribbon, click the Print tab, and then click either Print or Quick Print.

- If you want to change the design of the query, right-click the query in the Navigation Pane and then click Design View on the shortcut menu to open the query in Design view.

- To print the query without first opening it, be sure the query is selected in the Navigation Pane and click File on the Ribbon, click the Print tab, and then click either Print or Quick Print.

You can switch between views of a query using the View button (Home tab | Views group). Clicking the arrow in the bottom of the button produces the View button menu. You then click the desired view in the menu. The two query views you will use in this chapter are Datasheet view (see the results) and Design view (change the design). You also can click the top part of the View button, in which case, you will switch to the view identified by the icon on the button. In the figure, the button contains the icon for Design view, so clicking the button would change to Design view. For the most part, the icon on the button represents the view you want, so you can usually simply click the button.

To Use a Criterion in a Query

After you have determined the fields to be included in a query, you will determine whether there are any restrictions on the records that are to be included. For example, you might only want to include those clients whose business analyst number is 14. In such a case, you need to enter the 14 as a **criterion**, which is a condition that the records to be included must satisfy. To do so, you will open the query in Design view, enter the criterion below the appropriate field, and then view the results of the query. The following steps enter a criterion to include only the clients of business analyst 14 and then view the query results.

- Right-click the Client Query in the Navigation Pane to produce a shortcut menu (Figure 1–66).

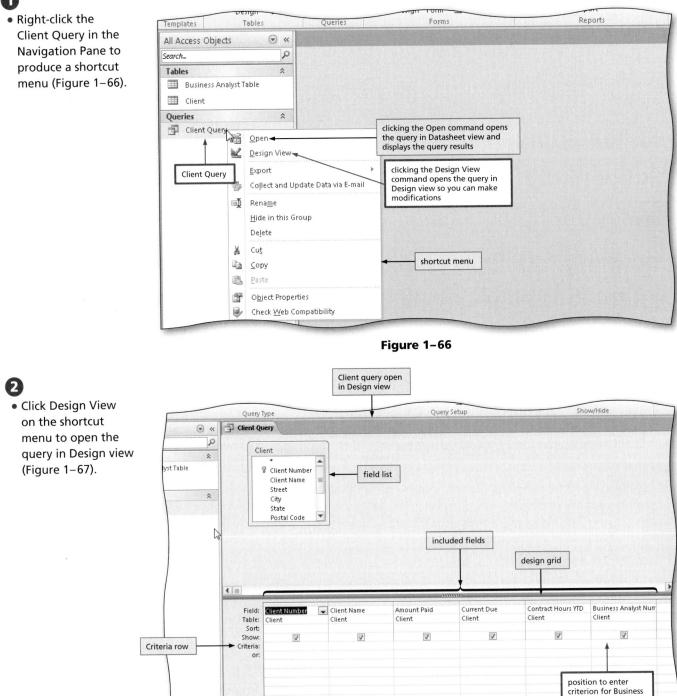

Figure 1–66

- Click Design View on the shortcut menu to open the query in Design view (Figure 1–67).

Figure 1–67

3

- Click the Criteria row in the Business Analyst Number column of the grid, and then type **14** as the criterion (Figure 1–68).

Q&A

The Business Analyst Number field is a text field. Do I need to enclose the value for a text field in quotation marks?

You could, but it is not necessary, because Access inserts the quotation marks for you automatically.

Figure 1–68

4

- Click the View button to display the query results in Datasheet view (Figure 1–69).

Q&A

Could I click the View button arrow and then click Datasheet view?

Yes, if the icon representing the view you want appears on the View button; however, it is easier just to click the button.

Figure 1–69

5

- Click the Close button for the Client Query to close the query.

- When asked if you want to save your changes, click the No button.

Q&A

If I saved the query, what would happen the next time I ran the query?

You would see only clients of business analyst 14.

Q&A

Could I save the query with another name?

Yes. To save the query with another name, click File on the Ribbon, click Save Object As, enter a new file name in the Save As dialog box and click OK (Save As dialog box).

Other Ways

1. Click Run button (Query Tools Design tab | Results group)
2. Click Datasheet View button on Status bar

To Print the Results of a Query

The following steps print the results of a saved query.

1 With the Client Query selected in the Navigation Pane, click File on the Ribbon to open the Backstage view.

2 Click the Print tab in the Backstage view to display the Print gallery.

3 Click the Quick Print button to print the query.

Creating and Using Forms

In Datasheet view, you can view many records at once. If there are many fields, however, only some of the fields in each record might be visible at a time. In **Form view**, where data is displayed in a form on the screen, you usually can see all the fields, but only for one record.

To Create a Form

Like a paper form, a **form** in a database is a formatted document with fields that contain data. Forms allow you to view and maintain data. Forms also can be used to print data, but reports are more commonly used for that purpose. The simplest type of form in Access is one that includes all the fields in a table stacked one above the other. The following steps create a form, use the form to view records, and then save the form.

1

- Select the Client table in the Navigation Pane.

- If necessary, click Create on the Ribbon to display the Create tab (Figure 1–70).

Figure 1–70

2

- Click the Form button (Create tab | Forms group) to create a simple form (Figure 1–71).

Q&A

A Field list appeared on my screen. What should I do?

Click the Add Existing Fields button (Form Layout Tools Design tab | Tools group) to remove the Field list from the screen.

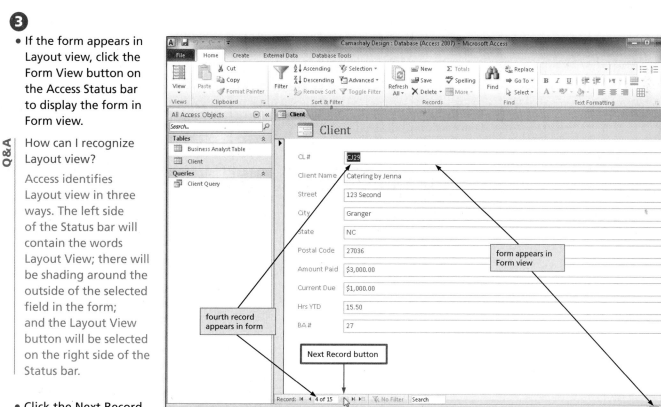

Figure 1–71

3

- If the form appears in Layout view, click the Form View button on the Access Status bar to display the form in Form view.

Q&A

How can I recognize Layout view?

Access identifies Layout view in three ways. The left side of the Status bar will contain the words Layout View; there will be shading around the outside of the selected field in the form; and the Layout View button will be selected on the right side of the Status bar.

- Click the Next Record button three times to move to record 4 (Figure 1–72).

Figure 1–72

4

- Click the Save button on the Quick Access Toolbar to display the Save As dialog box (Figure 1–73).

Figure 1–73

Q&A

Did I have to click the Next Record button before saving?

No. The only reason you were asked to click the button was so that you could experience navigation within the form.

5

- Type **Client Form** as the form name, and then click the OK button to save the form.

- Click the Close button for the form to close the form.

Other Ways

1. Click View button (Form Layout Tools Design tab | Views group)

Using a Form

After you have saved a form, you can use it at anytime by right-clicking the form in the Navigation Pane and then clicking Open in the shortcut menu. In addition to viewing data in the form, you can also use it to enter or update data, a process that is very similar to updating data using a datasheet. If you plan to use the form to enter or revise data, you must ensure you are viewing the form in Form view.

Break Point: If you wish to take a break, this is a good place to do so. You can quit Access now. To resume at a later time, start Access, open the database called Camashaly Design, and continue following the steps from this location forward.

Creating and Printing Reports

Camashaly Design wants to create the Client Financial Report shown in Figure 1–74. Just as you can create a form containing all fields by clicking a single button, you can click a button to create a report containing all the fields. Doing so will not match the report shown in Figure 1–74, however, which does not contain all the fields. Some of the column headings are different. In addition, some of the headings in the report in Figure 1–74 are split over multiple lines, whereas the ones in the report created by clicking the button will not be split. Fortunately, you can later modify the report design to make it precisely match the figure. To do so, you use Layout view for the report.

| | Client Financial Report | | | | | Thursday, April 12, 2012 |
| | | | | | | 5:17:00 PM |

Client Number	Client Name	Amount Paid	Current Due	Hrs YTD	Business Analyst Number
BA53	Bavant Animal Hospital	$0.00	$7,500.00	0.00	11
BB32	Babbage CPA Firm	$1,500.00	$500.00	5.00	14
BC76	Buda Community Clinic	$2,500.00	$750.00	2.50	11
CJ29	Catering by Jenna	$3,000.00	$1,000.00	15.50	27
GA74	Grant Antiques	$5,500.00	$3,200.00	34.50	14
GF56	Granger Foundation	$0.00	$6,500.00	0.00	11
HC10	Hendley County Hospital	$3,100.00	$1,200.00	12.00	27
KD21	KAL Design Studio	$6,000.00	$3,200.00	30.50	14
KG04	Kyle Grocery Cooperative	$3,200.00	$0.00	5.00	11
ME14	Mike's Electronic Stop	$2,500.00	$1,500.00	8.50	27
PJ34	Patricia Jean Florist	$0.00	$5,200.00	0.00	27
SL77	Smarter Law Associates	$3,800.00	$0.00	10.50	11
TB17	The Bikeshop	$2,750.00	$1,200.00	14.00	27
WE05	Walburg Energy Alternatives	$4,500.00	$1,450.00	19.50	14
WS01	Woody Sporting Goods	$2,250.00	$1,600.00	18.50	14
		$40,600.00	$34,800.00	176.00	

Figure 1–74

To Create a Report

You will first create a report containing all fields. The following steps create and save the initial report. They also modify the report title.

1

- Be sure the Client table is selected in the Navigation Pane.

- Click Create on the Ribbon to display the Create tab (Figure 1–75).

Q&A

Why do I need to select the Client table prior to clicking Create on the Ribbon?

You don't need to select it at that point. You do need to select it prior to clicking the Report button at the next step because Access will include all the fields in whichever table or query is currently selected.

Figure 1–75

2

- Click the Report button (Create tab | Reports group) to create the report (Figure 1–76).

Q&A

Why is the report title Client?

Access automatically assigns the name of the table or query as the title. It also automatically includes the date. You can change either of these later.

Figure 1–76

3

- Click the Save button on the Quick Access Toolbar to display the Save As dialog box and then type `Client Financial Report` as the name of the report (Figure 1–77).

Figure 1–77

4

- Click the OK button (Save As dialog box) to save the report (Figure 1–78).

Q&A

The name of the report changed. Why didn't the report title also change?

The report title just happens to begin with the same name as the report. If you change the name of the report, Access will not change the report title. You can change it at any time to any title you like.

Figure 1–78

5

- Close the report by clicking its Close button.

Using Layout View in a Report

When working with a report in Access, there are four different ways to view the report. They are Report view, Print Preview, Layout view, and Design view. Report view shows the report on the screen. Print Preview shows the report as it will appear when printed. Layout view is similar to Report view in that it shows the report on the screen, but it also allows you to make changes to the report. It is usually the easiest way to make such changes. Design view also allows you to make changes, but it does not show you the actual report. It is most useful when the changes you need to make are especially complex. In this chapter, you will use Layout view to modify the report.

To Modify Column Headings and Resize Columns

To make the report match the one in Figure 1–74, you need to change the title, remove some columns, modify the column headings, and also resize the columns. The following steps use Layout view to make the necessary modifications to the report.

1

- Right-click Client Financial Report in the Navigation Pane, and then click Layout View on the shortcut menu to open the report in Layout view.

- If a Field list appears, click the Add Existing Fields button (Report Layout Tools Design tab | Tools group) to remove the Field list from the screen.

- Close the Navigation Pane.

- Click the report title once to select it.

- Click the report title a second time to produce an insertion point (Figure 1–79).

Figure 1–79

Q&A

I clicked at a different position in the title and my insertion point is in the middle of Client. How do I produce an insertion point at the position shown in the figure?

You can use the RIGHT ARROW key to move the insertion point to the position in the figure or you can click the desired position.

2

- Press the SPACEBAR to insert a space and then type `Financial Report` to complete the title.

- Click the column heading for the Street field to select it.

- Hold the SHIFT key down and then click the column headings for the City field, the State field, and the Postal Code fields to select multiple column headings.

Q&A

What happens if I don't hold the SHIFT key down?

As soon as you click the column heading, it will be the only one that is selected. To select multiple objects, you need to hold the SHIFT key down for every object after the first one.

CL#	Client Name	Street	City	State	Postal Code	Amo
BA53	Bavant Animal Hospital	134 Main	Burles	NC	28817	
BB32	Babbage CPA Firm	464 Linnell	Austin	SC	28796	$
BC76	Buda Community Clinic	867 Ridge	Buda	NC	27032	$
CJ29	Catering by Jenna	123 Second	Granger	NC	27036	$
GA74	Grant Antiques	78 Catawba	Georgetown	NC	28794	$
GF56	Granger Foundation	65 Simpson	Granger	NC	27036	
HC10	Hendley County Hospital	216 Rivard	Austin	SC	28796	$
KD21	KAL Design Studio	116 Pine	Georgetown	NC	28794	$
KG04	Kyle Grocery Cooperative	421 First	Kyle	SC	28798	$
ME14	Mike's Electronic Stop	234 Gilham	Georgetown	NC	28794	$
PJ34	Patricia Jean Florist	345 Magee	Kyle	SC	28798	
SL77	Smarter Law Associates	764 Main	Burles	NC	28817	$
TB17	The Bikeshop	346 Austin	Buda	NC	27032	$
WE05	Walburg Energy Alternatives	12 Polk	Walburg	NC	28819	$
WS01	Woody Sporting Goods	578 Central	Walburg	NC	28819	$

Client Financial Report — Thursday, April 12, 2012 — 4:58:07 PM

Figure 1–80

I selected the wrong collection of objects. What should I do?

You can click somewhere else on the report so that the objects you want are not selected, and then begin the process again. Alternatively, you can repeatedly click the Undo button on the Quick Access Toolbar to undo your selections. Once you have done so, you can select the objects you want.

- Click Arrange on the Ribbon to display the Arrange tab (Figure 1–80).

3

- Click the Select Column button (Report Layout Tools Arrange tab | Rows & Columns group) to select the entire columns corresponding to the column headings you selected in the previous step.

- Press the DELETE key to delete the columns.

- Click the column heading for the Client Number field twice, once to select it and the second time to produce an insertion point (Figure 1–81).

I inadvertently selected the wrong field. What should I do?

Click somewhere outside the various fields to deselect the one you have selected. Then, click the Client Number field twice.

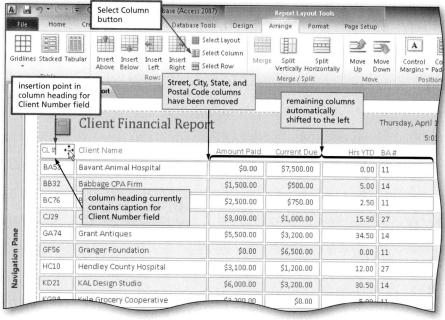

Figure 1–81

4

- Use the DELETE or BACKSPACE keys as necessary to erase the current entry and then type **Client Number** as the new entry.

- Click the heading for the Business Analyst Number field twice, erase the current entry, and then type **Business Analyst Number** as the new entry.

- Click the Client Number field heading to select it, point to the lower boundary of the heading for the Client Number field so that the mouse pointer changes to a two-headed arrow and then drag the lower boundary to the approximate position shown in Figure 1–82 to expand the column headings.

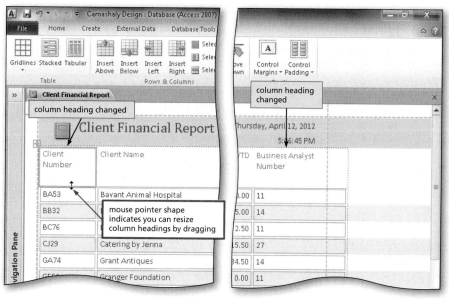

Figure 1–82

Do I have to be exact?

No. If you are in a slightly different position, your report would look a little different from the one in the figure, but the difference would not be significant.

5

- Point to the right boundary of the heading for the Client Number field so that the mouse pointer changes to a two-headed arrow and then drag the right boundary to the approximate position shown in Figure 1–83 to reduce the width of the column.

Q&A

Do I have to be exact?

No. Again, if you are in a slightly different position, the difference between your report and the one in the figure would not be significant.

Figure 1–83

6

- Using the same technique, resize the other columns to the sizes shown in Figure 1–84.

Figure 1–84

To Add Totals to a Report

The report in Figure 1–74 contains totals for the Amount Paid, Current Due, and Hrs YTD columns. You can use Layout view to add these totals. The following steps use Layout view to include totals for these three columns.

1

- Click the Amount Paid field heading (shown in Figure 1–84) to select the field.

Q&A Do I have to click the heading? Could I click the field on one of the records?

You do not have to click the heading. You also could click the Amount Paid field on any record.

- Click Design on the Ribbon to display the Design tab.

- Click the Totals button (Report Layout Tools Design tab | Grouping & Totals group) to display the list of available calculations (Figure 1–85).

Figure 1–85

2

- Click Sum to calculate the sum of the amount of paid values.

Q&A Is Sum the same as Total?

Yes.

- Using the same technique, add totals for the Current Due and Hrs YTD columns.

- Scroll down to the bottom of the report to verify that the totals are included. If necessary, expand the size of the total controls so they appear completely.

- Click the Page number to select it and then drag it to the approximate position shown in Figure 1–86.

Figure 1–86

Q&A Why did I need to move the page number?

The dotted line near the right-hand edge of the screen indicates the right-hand border of the available space on the printed page, based on whatever margins and orientation are currently selected. A portion of the page number extends beyond this border. By moving the page number, it no longer extends beyond the border.

3

- Click the Save button on the Quick Access Toolbar to save your changes to the report layout.

- Close the report.

To Print a Report

The following steps print the report.

1 With the Client Financial Report selected in the Navigation Pane, click File on the Ribbon to open the Backstage view.

2 Click the Print tab in the Backstage view to display the Print gallery.

3 Click the Quick Print button to print the report.

Q&A How can I print multiple copies of my report?

Click File on the Ribbon to open the Backstage view. Click the Print tab, click Print in the Print gallery to display the Print dialog box, increase the number in the Number of Copies box, and then click the OK button (Print dialog box).

Q&A How can I print a range of pages rather than printing the whole report?

Click File on the Ribbon to open the Backstage view. Click the Print tab, click Print in the Print gallery to display the Print dialog box, click the Pages option button in the Print Range area, enter the desired page range, and then click the OK button (Print dialog box).

BTW

Tabbed Documents Versus Overlapping Windows
By default, Access 2010 displays database objects in tabbed documents instead of overlapping windows. If your database is in overlapping windows mode, click File on the Ribbon, click Options in the Backstage view, click Current Database in the Access Options dialog box, and select the Display Document Tabs check box and the Tabbed Documents option button.

Database Properties

Access helps you organize and identify your databases by using **database properties**, which are the details about a file. Database properties, also known as **metadata**, can include such information as the file's author, title, or subject. **Keywords** are words or phrases that further describe the database. For example, a class name or database topic can describe the file's purpose or content.

Five different types of document properties exist, but the more common ones used in this book are standard and automatically updated properties. **Standard properties** are associated with all Microsoft Office documents and include author, title, and subject. **Automatically updated properties** include file system properties, such as the date you create or change a file, and statistics, such as the file size.

To Change Database Properties

The Database Properties dialog box contains areas where you can view and enter database properties. You can view and change information in this dialog box at anytime while you are working on your database. It is a good idea to add your name and class name as database properties. You also can add keywords that further describe your database. The following steps use the Properties dialog box to change database properties.

1

- Click File on the Ribbon to open the Backstage view.

- If necessary, click the Info tab in the Backstage view to display the Information gallery (Figure 1–87).

Q&A

How do I close the Backstage view?

Click File on the Ribbon or click the preview of the document in the Information gallery to return to the Access database window.

Figure 1–87

2

- Click the 'View and edit database properties' link in the right pane of the Info gallery to display the Camashaly Design.accdb Properties dialog box (Figure 1–88).

Q&A

Why are some of the database properties in my Properties dialog box already filled in?

The person who installed Microsoft Office 2010 on your computer or network may have set or customized the properties.

Figure 1–88

3

- If necessary, click the Summary tab.

- Click the Subject text box, if necessary delete any existing text, and then type **CIS 101, Section 20** as the Subject property.

- Click the Author text box and then type **Trevor Wilkins** as the Author property. If a name already is displayed in the Author text box, delete it before typing the new name.

- Click the Keywords text box, if necessary delete any existing text, and then type **online marketing, Web site design** as the Keywords property (Figure 1–89).

Q&A

What types of properties does Access collect automatically?

Access records such details as when the database was created, when it was last modified, total editing time, and the various objects contained in the database.

Figure 1–89

4

- Click the OK button to save your changes and remove the Camashaly Design.accdb Properties dialog box from the screen.

To Quit Access

The following steps quit Access.

1 Click the Close button on the right side of the title bar to quit Access.

2 If a Microsoft Access dialog box appears, click the Save button to save any changes made to the object since the last save.

Special Database Operations

The special operations involved in maintaining a database are backup, recovery, compacting a database, and repairing a database.

Backup and Recovery

It is possible to damage or destroy a database. Users can enter data that is incorrect; programs that are updating the database can end abnormally during an update; a hardware problem can occur; and so on. After any such event has occurred, the database may contain invalid data. It even might be totally destroyed.

Obviously, you cannot allow a situation in which data has been damaged or destroyed to go uncorrected. You must somehow return the database to a correct state. This process is called recovery; that is, you **recover** the database.

The simplest approach to recovery involves periodically making a copy of the database (called a **backup copy** or a **save copy**). This is referred to as **backing up** the database. If a problem occurs, you correct the problem by copying this backup copy over the actual database, often referred to as the **live database**.

To back up the database that is currently open, you use the Back Up Database command on the Save & Publish tab in the Backstage view. In the process, Access suggests a name that is a combination of the database name and the current date. For example, if you back up the Camashaly Design database on April 20, 2012, Access will suggest the name, Camashaly Design_2012-04-20. You can change this name if you desire, although it is a good idea to use this name. By doing so, it will be easy to distinguish between all the backup copies you have made to determine which is the most recent. In addition, if you discover that a critical problem occurred on April 18, 2012, you may want to go back to the most recent backup before April 18. If, for example, the database was not backed up on April 17 but was backed up on April 16, you would use Camashaly Design_2012-04-16.

To Back Up a Database

You would use the following steps to back up a database to a file on a hard disk or high-capacity removable disk.

1. Open the database to be backed up.
2. Click File on the Ribbon to open the Backstage view, and then click the Save & Publish tab.
3. With Save Database As selected in the File Types area, click Back Up Database in the Save Database As area, and then click the Save As button.
4. Selected the desired location in the Save As box. If you do not want the name Access has suggested, enter the desired name in the File name text box.
5. Click the Save button to back up the database.

Access creates a backup copy with the desired name in the desired location. Should you ever need to recover the database using this backup copy, you can simply copy it over the live version.

Compacting and Repairing a Database

As you add more data to a database, it naturally grows larger. When you delete an object (records, tables, forms, or queries), the space previously occupied by the object does not become available for additional objects. Instead, the additional objects are given new space; that is, space that was not already allocated. To remove this wasted space from the database, you must **compact** the database. The same option that compacts the database also repairs problems that might have occurred in the database.

To Compact and Repair a Database

You would use the following steps to compact and repair a database.

1. Open the database to be compacted.
2. Click File on the Ribbon to open the Backstage view, and then, if necessary, select the Info tab.
3. Click the Compact & Repair Database button in the Information gallery to compact and repair the database.

The database now is the compacted form of the original.

Additional Operations

Additional special operations include opening another database, closing a database without exiting Access, and saving a database with another name. They also include deleting a table (or other object) as well as renaming an object. Finally, you can change properties of a table or other object, such as the object's description.

When you open another database, Access will automatically close the database that previously was open. Before deleting or renaming an object, you should ensure that the object has no dependent objects; that is, other objects that depend on the object you want to delete.

TO OPEN ANOTHER DATABASE

To open another database, you would use the following steps.

1. Click File on the Ribbon to open the Backstage view.
2. Click Open.
3. Select the database to be opened.
4. Click the Open button.

TO CLOSE A DATABASE WITHOUT EXITING ACCESS

You would use the following steps to close a database without quitting Access.

1. Click File on the Ribbon to open the Backstage view.
2. Click Close Database.

TO SAVE A DATABASE WITH ANOTHER NAME

To save a database with another name, you would use the following steps.

1. Click File on the Ribbon to open the Backstage view, and then select the Save & Publish tab.
2. With Save Database As selected in the File Types area and Access Database selected in the Save Database As area, click the Save As button.
3. Enter a name and select a location for the new version.
4. Click the Save button.

TO DELETE A TABLE OR OTHER OBJECT IN THE DATABASE

You would use the following steps to delete a database object.

1. Right-click the object in the Navigation Pane.
2. Click Delete on the shortcut menu.
3. Click the Yes button in the Microsoft Access dialog box.

TO RENAME AN OBJECT IN THE DATABASE

You would use the following steps to rename a database object.

1. Right-click the object in the Navigation Pane.
2. Click Rename on the shortcut menu.
3. Type the new name and press the ENTER key.

Make It Right

Analyze a database and correct all errors and/or improve the design.

Correcting Errors in the Table Structure

Instructions: Start Access. Open the Beach Rentals database. See the inside back cover of this book for instructions for downloading the Data Files for Students, or see your instructor for information on accessing the files required in this book.

Beach Rentals is a database containing information on rental properties available at a beach resort. The Rentals table shown in Figure 1–92 contains a number of errors in the table structure. You are to correct these errors before any additional records can be added to the table. The Rental Code field is a Text field that contains a maximum of three characters. The field Address was omitted from the table. The Address field is a Text field with a maximum of 20 characters. It should appear after Rental Code. Only whole numbers should be allowed in the Bedrooms and Bathrooms fields. The column heading Weakly Rental is misspelled, and the field should contain monetary values. The Distance field represents the walking distance from the beach; the field should display two decimal places. The table name should be Rental Units, not Rentals.

Change the database properties, as specified by your instructor. Submit the revised database in the format specified by your instructor.

Rental Code	Bedrooms	Bathrooms	Distance	Weakly Rent	Click to Add
101	3	2	0	200	
*					

Figure 1–92

In the Lab

Design, create, modify, and/or use a database using the guidelines, concepts, and skills presented in this chapter. Labs are listed in order of increasing difficulty.

Lab 1: Creating Objects for the ECO Clothesline Database

Problem: ECO Clothesline is a local company that designs and manufactures eco-friendly casual wear, yoga clothing, and fitness apparel. All clothes are made from earth-friendly fabrics, such as bamboo, hemp, organic cotton, and natural silk. The company recently decided to store its customer and sales rep data in a database. Each customer is assigned to a single sales rep, but each sales rep may be assigned many customers. The database and the Customer table have been created, but there is no data in the Customer table. The Sales Rep table has not been created. The company plans to import the Customer data from an Excel workbook, shown in Figure 1–93a. The other Excel workbook (Figure 1–93b) contains information on the sales representatives that ECO employs. ECO would like to finish storing this data in a database and has asked for your help.

Instructions: Perform the following tasks: Start Access and open the ECO Clothesline database. See the inside back cover of this book for instructions for downloading the Data Files for Students, or see your instructor for information on accessing the files required in this book.

1. Import the Lab 1-1 Customer Data workbook into the Customer table.

2. Add the captions Cust # to the Customer Number field and SR # to the Sales Rep Number field in the Customer table and save the changes.

3. Open the Customer table in Datasheet view and resize the columns to best fit the data. Save the changes to the layout of the table.

4. Use Datasheet view to create a table in which to store the data related to sales reps. Use the name Sales Rep for the table. The fields and the data for the Sales Rep table are shown in Figure 1–93b.

Chapter Summary

In this chapter you have learned to design a database, create an Access database, create tables and add records to them, print the contents of tables, create queries, create forms, and create reports. You also have learned how to change database properties. The items listed below include all the new Access skills you have learned in this chapter.

1. Start Access (AC 12)
2. Create a Database (AC 13)
3. Create a Database Using a Template (AC 14)
4. Modify the Primary Key (AC 16)
5. Define the Remaining Fields in a Table (AC 19)
6. Save a Table (AC 21)
7. View the Table in Design View (AC 21)
8. Close the Table (AC 23)
9. Add Records to a Table (AC 23)
10. Quit Access (AC 26)
11. Open a Database from Access (AC 27)
12. Add Additional Records to a Table (AC 28)
13. Resize Columns in a Datasheet (AC 29)
14. Preview and Print the Contents of a Table (AC 31)
15. Create a Table in Design View (AC 33)
16. Import an Excel Worksheet (AC 38)
17. Use the Simple Query Wizard to Create a Query (AC 43)
18. Use a Criterion in a Query (AC 46)
19. Print the Results of a Query (AC 48)
20. Create a Form (AC 48)
21. Create a Report (AC 52)
22. Modify Column Headings and Resize Columns (AC 54)
23. Add Totals to a Report (AC 57)
24. Change Database Properties (AC 59)
25. Back Up a Database (AC 61)
26. Compact and Repair a Database (AC 61)
27. Open Another Database (AC 62)
28. Close a Database without Exiting Access (AC 62)
29. Save a Database with Another Name (AC 62)
30. Delete a Table or Other Object in the Database (AC 62)
31. Rename an Object in the Database (AC 62)

If you have a SAM 2010 user profile, your instructor may have assigned an autogradable version of this assignment. If so, log into the SAM 2010 Web site at www.cengage.com/sam2010 to download the instruction and start files.

Learn It Online

Test your knowledge of chapter content and key terms.

Instructions: To complete the Learn It Online exercises, start your browser, click the Address bar, and then enter the Web address **scsite.com/ac2010/learn**. When the Access 2010 Learn It Online page is displayed, click the link for the exercise you want to complete and then read the instructions.

Chapter Reinforcement TF, MC, and SA
A series of true/false, multiple choice, and short answer questions that test your knowledge of the chapter content.

Flash Cards
An interactive learning environment where you identify chapter key terms associated with displayed definitions.

Practice Test
A series of multiple choice questions that test your knowledge of chapter content and key terms.

Who Wants To Be a Computer Genius?
An interactive game that challenges your knowledge of chapter content in the style of a television quiz show.

Wheel of Terms
An interactive game that challenges your knowledge of chapter key terms in the style of the television show *Wheel of Fortune*.

Crossword Puzzle Challenge
A crossword puzzle that challenges your knowledge of key terms presented in the chapter.

Apply Your Knowledge

Reinforce the skills and apply the concepts you learned in this chapter.

Adding a Caption, Creating a Query, Creating a Form, and Creating a Report

Instructions: Start Access. Open the Babbage CPA Firm database. See the inside back cover of this book for instructions for downloading the Data Files for Students, or see your instructor for information on accessing the files required in this book.

The Babbage CPA Firm employs bookkeepers who maintain the books for those clients who need bookkeeping services. The Babbage CPA Firm has a database that keeps track of its bookkeepers and clients. Each client is assigned to a single bookkeeper, but each bookkeeper may be assigned many clients. The database has two tables. The Client table contains data on the clients who use the bookkeeping services of the Babbage CPA Firm. The Bookkeeper table contains data on the bookkeepers employed by Babbage CPA Firm.

Perform the following tasks:

1. Open the Bookkeeper table in Design view and add BKR # as the caption for Bookkeeper Number. Save the changes to the table.
2. Open the Bookkeeper table in Datasheet view and resize all columns to best fit the data. Save the changes to the layout of the table.
3. Use the Simple Query Wizard to create a query for the Client table that contains the Client Number, Client Name, Amount Paid, and Balance Due. Use the name, Client Query, for the query.
4. Create a simple form for the Bookkeeper table. Use the name, Bookkeeper, for the form.
5. Close the Bookkeeper form.
6. Create the report shown in Figure 1–90 for the Client table. The report includes totals for both the Amount Paid and Balance Due fields. Be sure the totals appear completely. You might need to expand the size of the controls. Move the page number so that it is within the margins.
7. Compact the database.
8. Back up the database.
9. Change the database properties, as specified by your instructor. Submit the revised database in the format specified by your instructor.

Client Financial Report — Thursday, April 12, 2012 — 8:38:16 PM

Client Number	Client Name	Amount Paid	Balance Due	Bookkeeper Number
A54	Afton Mills	$575.00	$315.00	22
A62	Atlas Suppliers	$250.00	$175.00	24
B26	Blake-Scripps	$875.00	$250.00	24
D76	Dege Grocery	$1,015.00	$325.00	22
G56	Grand Cleaners	$485.00	$165.00	24
H21	Hill Shoes	$0.00	$285.00	34
J77	Jones Plumbing	$685.00	$0.00	22
M26	Mohr Crafts	$125.00	$185.00	24
S56	SeeSaw Industries	$1,200.00	$645.00	22
T45	Tate Repair	$345.00	$200.00	34
W24	Woody Sporting Goods	$975.00	$0.00	34
C29	Catering by Jenna	$0.00	$250.00	34
		$6,530.00	$2,795.00	

Figure 1–90

Extend Your Knowledge

Extend the skills you learned in this chapter and experiment with new skills. You may need to use Help to complete the assignment.

Using a Database Template to Create a Students Database

Instructions: Access includes a number of templates that you can use to create a beginning database that can be modified to meet your specific needs. You will create a Students database using the Students template. The database includes sample tables, queries, forms, and reports. You will change the database and create the Student Birthdays Query, shown in Figure 1–91.

Figure 1–91

Perform the following tasks:

1. Start Access.
2. With a USB flash drive connected to one of the computer's USB ports, ensure the New tab is selected in the Backstage view and select Sample templates in the New gallery.
3. Select the Students template and create a new database on your USB drive with the file name, Students.
4. Close the Student List form and change the organization of the Navigation Pane to Tables and Related Views .
5. Delete the Student Details form.
6. Use the Query Wizard to create the query shown in Figure 1–91. Save the query as Student Birthdays Query.
7. Open the Student Phone List in Layout view and use the tools on the Format tab to make the Student Phone List title bold and change the font size to 24. Delete the control containing the time.
8. Save your changes to the report.
9. Compact the database.
10. Change the database properties, as specified by your instructor. Submit the revised database in the format specified by your instructor.

	A	B	C	D	E	F	G	H	I	J	K
1	Customer Number	Customer Name	Street	City	State	Postal Code	Balance	Amount Paid	Sales Rep Number		
2	AM23	Amy's Store	223 Johnson	Oxford	TN	37021	195.00	1,695.00	44		
3	BF34	Barbara's Fashions	1939 Jackson	Lowton	TN	37084	150.00	0.00	51		
4	BL15	Blondie's on Main	3294 Main	Oxford	TN	37021	555.00	1,350.00	49		
5	CM09	Casual by Marie	3140 Halsted	Ashton	VA	20123	295.00	1,080.00	51		
6	CY12	Curlin Yoga Studio	1632 Clark	Georgetown	NC	28794	145.00	710.00	49		
7	DG14	Della's Designs	312 Gilham	Granger	NC	27036	340.00	850.00	44		
8	EC07	Environmentally Casual	1805 Broadway	Pineville	VA	22503	0.00	1,700.00	44		
9	FN19	Fitness Counts	675 Main	Oxford	TN	37021	345.00	1,950.00	51		
10	JN34	Just Natural	2200 Lawrence	Ashton	VA	20123	360.00	700.00	49		
11	LB20	Le Beauty	13 Devon	Lowton	TN	37084	200.00	1,250.00	49		
12	NC25	Nancy's Place	1027 Wells	Walburg	NC	28819	240.00	550.00	44		
13	RD03	Rose's Day Spa	787 Monroe	Pineville	VA	22503	0.00	975.00	51		
14	TT21	Tan and Tone	1939 Congress	Ashton	VA	20123	160.00	725.00	44		
15	TW56	The Workout Place	34 Gilham	Granger	NC	27036	680.00	125.00	51		
16	WS34	Woody's Sporting Goods	578 Central	Walburg	NC	28819	1,235.00	0.00	49		
17											

(a) Customer Data (Excel Workbook)

	A	B	C	D	E	F	G	H	I	J
1	Sales Rep Number	Last Name	First Name	Street	City	State	Postal Code	Base Pay YTD	Comm Rate	
2	44	Jones	Pat	43 Third	Oxford	TN	37021	13,000.00	0.05	
3	49	Gupta	Pinn	678 Hillcrest	Georgetown	NC	28794	15,000.00	0.06	
4	51	Ortiz	Gabe	982 Victoria	Ashton	VA	20123	12,500.00	0.05	
5	55	Sinson	Terry	45 Elm	Walburg	NC	28819	500.00	0.04	
6										

(b) Sales Rep Data (Excel Workbook)

Figure 1–93

The primary key for the Sales Rep table is Sales Rep Number. Assign the caption SR # to the Sales Rep Number field. Comm Rate is a Number field, and Base Pay YTD is a Currency data type. The field size for Sales Rep Number is 2. The State field size is 2, and the Postal Code field size is 5. All other text fields have a field size of 15.

5. Open the Sales Rep table in Design view and change the field size for the Comm Rate field to Single, the format to Fixed, and the Decimal Places to 2.

6. Add the data shown in Figure 1–93b to the Sales Rep table. Resize the columns to best fit the data. Save the changes to the layout of the table.

7. Create a query using the Simple Query Wizard for the Customer table that displays the Customer Number, Customer Name, Balance, Amount Paid, and Sales Rep Number fields. Use the name Customer Query.

8. Create and save the report shown in Figure 1–94 for the Customer table. The report should include Customer Number, Customer Name, Balance, and Sales Rep Number fields. Include a total for the Balance field.

9. Change the database properties, as specified by your instructor. Submit the revised database in the format specified by your instructor.

Customer Balance Report   Thursday, April 12, 2012
                                                8:55:32 PM

Customer Number	Customer Name	Balance	Sales Rep Number
AM23	Amy's Store	$195.00	44
BF34	Barbara's Fashions	$150.00	51
BL15	Blondie's on Main	$555.00	49
CM09	Casual by Marie	$295.00	51
CY12	Curlin Yoga Studio	$145.00	49
DG14	Della's Designs	$340.00	44
EC07	Environmentally Casual	$0.00	44
FN19	Fitness Counts	$345.00	51
JN34	Just Natural	$360.00	49
LB20	Le Beauty	$200.00	49
NC25	Nancy's Place	$240.00	44
RD03	Rose's Day Spa	$0.00	51
TT21	Tan and Tone	$160.00	44
TW56	The Workout Place	$680.00	51
WS34	Woody's Sporting Goods	$1,235.00	49
		$4,900.00	

Figure 1–94

In the Lab

Lab 2: Creating the Walburg Energy Alternatives Database

Problem: Walburg Energy Alternatives is a nonprofit organization that promotes the use of energy alternatives such as solar power and wind power. The organization provides a variety of services and funds itself through donations. Recently, the organization decided to sell a small number of items in its education center to help fund programs. The store purchases the items from vendors that deal in energy-saving products. Currently, the information about the items and vendors is stored in the Excel workbook shown in Figure 1–95. Each item is assigned to a single vendor, but each vendor may be assigned many items. You volunteer part-time at the store, and the store manager has asked you to create a database that will store the item and vendor information. You have already determined that you need two tables in which to store the information: an Item table and a Vendor table.

Instructions: Perform the following tasks:
1. Design a new database in which to store all the objects related to the items for sale. Call the database Walburg Energy Alternatives.
2. Use the information shown in the Excel workbook in Figure 1–95 to determine the primary keys and determine additional fields. Then, determine the relationships between tables, the data types, and the field sizes.
3. Create the Item table using the information shown in Figure 1–95.
4. Create the Vendor table using the information shown in Figure 1–95. Be sure that the field size for the Vendor Code in the Item table is identical to the field size for the Vendor Code in the Vendor table. Add the caption, Phone, for the Telephone Number field.

Item Number	Description	On Hand	Cost	Selling Price	Vendor Code	Vendor Name	Telephone Number
3663	Air Deflector	8	$5.45	$5.99	AS	Asterman Industries	803-555-7641
3673	Energy Booklet	25	$2.70	$2.99	JM	JMZ Technologies	517-555-3853
4553	Energy Saving Kit	7	$42.75	$43.25	AS	Asterman Industries	803-555-7641
4573	Faucet Aerator	20	$0.89	$0.99	SD	Scryps Distributors	610-555-8741
4583	Fluorescent Light Bulb	18	$4.50	$4.75	JM	JMZ Technologies	517-555-3853
5923	Low Flow Shower Head	11	$8.75	$8.99	SD	Scryps Distributors	610-555-8741
6185	Luminescent Night Light	12	$3.75	$4.50	JM	JMZ Technologies	517-555-3853
6234	Programmable Thermostat	3	$34.25	$36.99	AS	Asterman Industries	803-555-7641
6345	Rain Gauge	16	$2.89	$3.15	SD	Scryps Distributors	610-555-8741
7123	Retractable Clothesline	10	$13.25	$13.99	JM	JMZ Technologies	517-555-3853
7934	Shower Timer	15	$2.45	$2.99	SD	Scryps Distributors	610-555-8741
8136	Smoke Detector	10	$6.10	$6.50	AS	Asterman Industries	803-555-7641
8344	Toilet Tank Water Saver	18	$3.35	$3.50	SD	Scryps Distributors	610-555-8741
8590	Water Conservation Kit	8	$13.45	$13.99	JM	JMZ Technologies	517-555-3853
9458	Windows Insulator Kit	10	$4.95	$5.25	AS	Asterman Industries	803-555-7641

Figure 1–95

5. Add the appropriate data to the Item table. Resize the columns to best fit the data and save the changes to the layout.

6. Add the appropriate data to the Vendor table. Resize the columns to best fit the data and save the changes to the layout.

7. Create a query for the Item table. Include the Item Number, Description, Cost, Selling Price, and Vendor Code in the query. Save the query as Item Query.

8. Open the Item Query and add a criterion to limit retrieval to those items supplied by Scryps Distributors. Save the query as Item-Scryps Query.

9. Create a simple form for the Item table. Use the name, Item, for the form.

10. Create the report shown in Figure 1–96 for the Item table. Do not add any totals.

11. Change the database properties, as specified by your instructor. Submit the database in the format specified by your instructor.

Inventory Status Report

Thursday, April 12, 2012
8:56:19 PM

Item Number	Description	On Hand	Cost
3663	Air Deflector	8	$5.45
3673	Energy Booklet	25	$2.70
4553	Energy Saving Kit	7	$42.75
4573	Faucet Aerator	20	$0.89
4583	Fluorescent Light Bulb	18	$4.50
5923	Low Flow Shower Head	11	$8.75
6185	Luminescent Night Light	12	$3.75
6234	Programmable Thermostat	3	$34.25
6345	Rain Gauge	16	$2.89
7123	Retractable Clothesline	10	$13.25
7934	Shower Timer	15	$2.45
8136	Smoke Detector	10	$6.10
8344	Toilet Tank Water Saver	18	$3.35
8590	Water Conservation Kit	8	$13.45
9458	Windows Insulator Kit	10	$4.95

Figure 1–96

In the Lab

Lab 3: Creating the Philamar Training Database

Problem: Philamar Training provides business processes and information technology training to various companies and organizations. Philamar employs trainers who work with individual companies to determine training needs and then conduct the training. Currently, Philamar keeps data on clients and trainers in two Word documents and two Excel workbooks. Philamar also keeps track of which clients are assigned to which trainers. Each client is assigned to a single trainer, but each trainer might be assigned many clients. Currently, clients BS27, FI28, and MC28 are assigned to trainer 42, Belinda Perry. Clients CE16, CP27, FL93, HN83, and TE26 are assigned to trainer 48, Michael Stevens. Clients EU28 and PS82 are assigned to trainer 53, Manuel Gonzalez. Philamar has an additional trainer, Marty Danville, who has been assigned trainer number 67, but who has not yet been assigned any clients.

Instructions: Using the data shown in Figure 1–97 and the information in the previous paragraph, design the Philamar Training database. The data shown in Figure 1–97 is included in the Data Files for Students in the following files: Lab 1-3a.docx, Lab 1-3b.docx, Lab 1-3c.xlsx, and Lab 1-3d.xlsx. Use the database design guidelines in this chapter to help you in the design process.

Client Number	Client Name	Address	City	State	Postal Code
BS27	Blant and Sons	4806 Park	Kingston	TX	76653
CE16	Center Services	725 Mitchell	San Rita	TX	78364
CP27	Calder Plastics	7300 Cedar	Kingston	TX	76653
EU28	Elba's Furniture	1445 Hubert	Tallmadge	TX	77231
FI28	Farrow-Idsen	829 Wooster	Cedar Ridge	TX	79342
FL93	Fairland Lawn	143 Pangborn	Kingston	TX	76653
HN83	Hurley National	3827 Burgess	Tallmadge	TX	77231
MC28	Morgan-Alyssa	923 Williams	Crumville	TX	76745
PS82	PRIM Staffing	72 Crestview	San Rita	TX	78364
TE26	Telton-Edwards	5672 Anderson	Dunston	TX	77893

(a) Client Address Information (Word Table)

	A	B	C	D	E
1	Client Number	Client Name	Amount Paid	Current Due	
2	BS27	Blant and Sons	$11,876.00	$892.50	
3	CE16	Center Services	$12,512.00	$1,672.00	
4	CP27	Calder Plastics	$5,725.00	$0.00	
5	EU28	Elba's Furniture	$3,245.00	$202.00	
6	FI28	Farrow-Idsen	$8,287.50	$925.50	
7	FL93	Fairland Lawn	$976.00	$0.00	
8	HN83	Hurley National	$0.00	$0.00	
9	MC28	Morgan-Alyssa	$3,456.00	$572.00	
10	PS82	PRIM Staffing	$7,500.00	$485.00	
11	TE26	Telton-Edwards	$6,775.00	$0.00	
12					

(c) Client Financial Information (Excel Workbook)

Trainer Number	Last Name	First Name	Address	City	State	Postal Code
42	Perry	Belinda	261 Porter	Burdett	TX	76734
48	Stevens	Michael	3135 Gill	Rockwood	TX	78884
53	Gonzalez	Manuel	265 Maxwell	Camino	TX	76574
67	Danville	Marty	1827 Maple	Dunston	TX	77893

(b) Trainer Address Information (Word Table)

	A	B	C	D	E
1	Trainer Number	Last Name	First Name	Hourly Rate	YTD Earnings
2	42	Perry	Belinda	$23.00	$17,620.00
3	48	Stevens	Michael	$21.00	$13,567.50
4	53	Gonzalez	Manuel	$24.00	$19,885.00
5	67	Danville	Marty	$20.00	$0.00
6					

(d) Trainer Financial Information (Excel Workbook)

Figure 1–97

When you have completed the database design, create the database, create the tables, and add the data to the appropriate tables. Be sure to determine the correct data types and field sizes.

Finally, prepare the Client Query shown in Figure 1–98 and the Client Status Report shown in Figure 1–99. The report does not include totals. Change the database properties, as specified by your instructor. Submit the database in the format specified by your instructor.

Figure 1–98

Client Status Report

Thursday, April 12, 2012
8:57:10 PM

Client Number	Client Name	Amount Paid	Current Due	Trainer Number
BS27	Blant and Sons	$11,876.00	$892.50	42
CE16	Center Services	$12,512.00	$1,672.00	48
CP27	Calder Plastics	$5,725.00	$0.00	48
EU28	Elba's Furniture	$3,245.00	$202.00	53
FI28	Farrow-Idsen	$8,287.50	$925.50	42
FL93	Fairland Lawn	$976.00	$0.00	48
HN83	Hurley National	$0.00	$0.00	48
MC28	Morgan-Alyssa	$3,456.00	$572.00	42
PS82	PRIM Staffing	$7,500.00	$485.00	53
TE26	Telton-Edwards	$6,775.00	$0.00	48

Figure 1–99

Cases and Places

Apply your creative thinking and problem solving skills to design and implement a solution.

See the inside back cover of this book for instructions for downloading the Data Files for Students, or see your instructor for information on accessing the files required in this book.

1: Design and Create an Advertising Database

Academic

You are a Marketing major currently doing an internship with the Chamber of Commerce in a local city. The Chamber publishes a Newcomer's Guide that contains advertisements from local businesses. Ad reps contact the businesses to arrange for advertising. Each advertiser is assigned to a single ad rep, but each ad rep may be assigned many advertisers. The Chamber would like your help in creating a database of advertisers and advertising representatives.

Based on the information in the Case 1-1 Chamber of Commerce workbook, use the concepts and techniques presented in this chapter to design and create a database to store the data that the Chamber needs. Submit your assignment in the format specified by your instructor.

2: Design and Create a Consignment Database

Personal

You are involved in a volunteer organization that provides clothing and school supplies to needy children. Recently, the Board of Directors decided to open a consignment shop as a way to raise additional funds. In a consignment shop, individuals bring in unwanted items, and the shop sells the items. Proceeds are split between the seller and the shop. The database must keep track of the items for sale in the shop as well as maintain data on the sellers. Each item is assigned to a single seller, but each seller may be assigned many items. The Board has asked you to create a database to store information about the consignment items.

Use the concepts and techniques presented in this chapter to design and create a database to store the consignment data. Then create the necessary tables and enter the data from the Case 1-2 Consignment workbook. Create an Available Items Report that lists the item number, description, price, and seller code. Submit your assignment in the format specified by your instructor.

3: Design and Create a Senior Care Database

Professional

You are co-owner of a company, Senior Care, that provides nonmedical services to older adults who need assistance with daily living. Helpers will drive individuals to appointments, do the grocery shopping, fill prescriptions, help with personal care, and provide companionship. Each client is assigned to a single helper, but each helper may be assigned many clients. The other owners have asked you to create a database of clients and helpers. Use the concepts and techniques presented in this chapter to design and create a database to meet Senior Care needs. Then create the necessary tables and enter the data from the Case 1-3 Senior Care workbook. Create a Client Report that lists each client's client number, client last name, client first name, balance, and helper number. Submit your assignment in the format specified by your instructor.

2 Querying a Database

Objectives

You will have mastered the material in this chapter when you can:

- Create queries using Design view
- Include fields in the design grid
- Use text and numeric data in criteria
- Save a query and use the saved query
- Create and use parameter queries
- Use compound criteria in queries
- Sort data in queries
- Join tables in queries

- Create a report and a form from a query
- Export data from a query to another application
- Perform calculations and calculate statistics in queries
- Create crosstab queries
- Customize the Navigation Pane

2 | Querying a Database

Introduction

One of the primary benefits of using a database management system such as Access is the ability to find answers to questions related to data stored in the database. When you pose a question to Access, or any other database management system, the question is called a query. A **query** is simply a question presented in a way that Access can process.

Thus, to find the answer to a question, you first create a corresponding query using the techniques illustrated in this chapter. After you have created the query, you instruct Access to display the query results, that is, to perform the steps necessary to obtain the answer. Access then displays the answer in Datasheet view.

Project — Querying a Database

Organizations and individuals achieve several benefits from storing data in a database and using Access to manage the database. One of the most important benefits is the capability of easily finding the answers to questions and requests such as those shown in Figure 2–1 and the following, which concern the data in the Camashaly Design database:

1. What are the number, name, amount paid, and current due for client BC76?
2. What are the number, name, amount paid, and current due for all clients whose name starts with Gr?
3. Give me the number, name, amount paid, current due, and business analyst number for all clients whose amount paid is more than $3,000 and whose business analyst number is 11.
4. List the client number, name, business analyst number, and amount paid for all clients. Sort the results by business analyst number and amount paid.
5. For each business analyst, list the number, last name, and first name. Also, list the client number and name for each of the business analyst's clients.
6. List the client number, client name, amount paid, current due, and the total amount (amount paid plus current due) for each client.
7. Give me the average amount paid by clients of each business analyst.
8. Summarize the total amount paid by city and by business analyst.

In addition to these questions, Camashaly Design managers need to find information about clients located in a specific city, but they want to enter a different city each time they ask the question. The company can use a parameter query to accomplish this task. Camashaly Design managers also want to summarize data in a specific way, and they can use a crosstab query to present the data in the desired form.

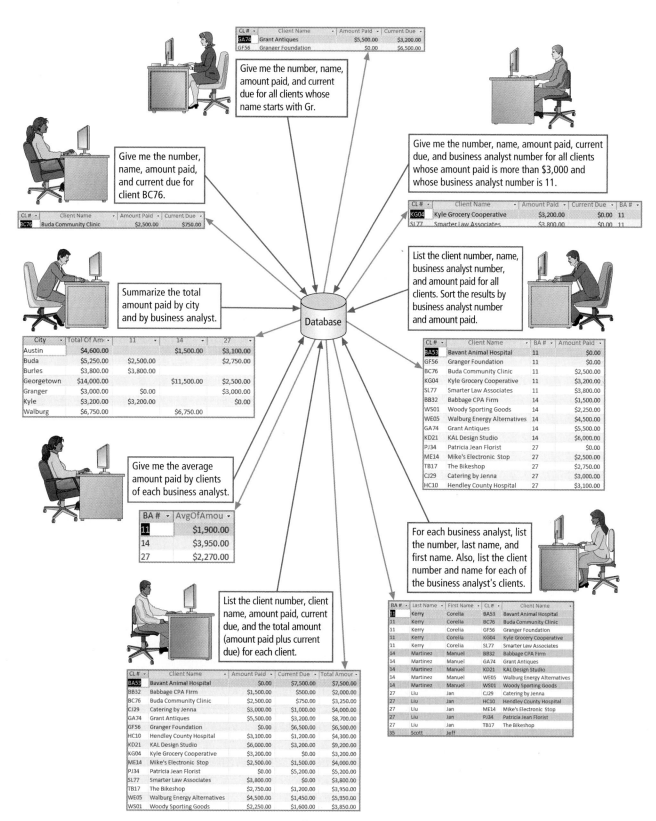

Figure 2–1

Overview

As you read this chapter, you will learn how to query a database by performing these general tasks:

- Create queries using Design view.
- Use criteria in queries.
- Create and use parameter queries.
- Sort data in queries.
- Join tables in queries.
- Create reports and forms from a query.
- Export data from a query.
- Perform calculations in queries.
- Create crosstab queries.

Plan
Ahead

Query Design Decisions

When posing a question to Access, you must design an appropriate query. In the process of designing a query, the decisions you make will determine the fields, tables, criteria, order, and special calculations included in the query. To design a query, you can follow these general guidelines:

1. **Identify the fields.** Examine the question or request to determine which fields from the tables in the database are involved. Examine the contents of these fields to make sure you understand the data type and format for storing the data.

2. **Identify restrictions.** Unless the question or request calls for the inclusion of all records, determine the restrictions or the conditions records must satisfy to be included in the results.

3. **Determine whether special order is required.** Examine the question or request to determine whether the results must appear in some specific order.

4. **Determine whether more than one table is required.** If all the fields identified in Step 1 are in the same table, no special action is required. If this is not the case, identify all tables represented by those fields.

5. **Determine whether calculations are required.** Examine the question or request to determine whether, in addition to the fields determined in Step 1, calculations must be included. Such calculations include individual record calculations (for example, adding the values in two fields) or group calculations (for example, finding the total of the values in a particular field for all the records).

6. **If data is to be summarized, determine whether a crosstab query would be appropriate.** If data is to be grouped by two different types of information, you can use a crosstab query. You will need to identify the two types of information. One of the types will form the row headings and the other will form the column headings in the query results.

When necessary, more specific details concerning the decisions and/or actions are presented at appropriate points in the chapter. The chapter also will identify the use of these guidelines in creating queries such as those shown in Figure 2–1.

BTW

Designing Queries
Before creating queries, examine the contents of the tables involved. You need to know the data type for each field and how the data for the field is stored. If a query includes a state, for example, you need to know whether state is stored as the two-character abbreviation or as the full state name.

To Start Access

The following steps, which assume Windows 7 is running, start Access based on a typical installation. You may need to ask your instructor how to start Access for your computer. For a detailed example of the procedure summarized below, refer to the Office 2010 and Windows 7 chapter at the beginning of this book.

1 Click the Start button on the Windows 7 taskbar to display the Start menu.

2 Type `Microsoft Access` as the search text in the 'Search programs and files' text box and watch the search results appear on the Start menu.

3 Click Microsoft Access 2010 in the search results on the Start menu to start Access.

4 If the Access window is not maximized, click the Maximize button next to the Close button on its title bar to maximize the window.

To Open a Database from Access

In the previous chapter, you saved your database on a USB flash drive using the file name, Camashaly Design. The following steps open the Camashaly Design database from the Access folder in the CIS 101 folder on the USB flash drive. For a detailed example of the procedure summarized below, refer to the Office 2010 and Windows 7 chapter at the beginning of this book.

1 With your USB flash drive connected to one of the computer's USB ports, click File on the Ribbon to open the Backstage view, if necessary.

2 Click Open in the Backstage view to display the Open dialog box.

3 Navigate to the location of the file to be opened (in this case, the USB flash drive, then to the CIS 101 folder [or your class folder], and then to the Access folder).

4 Click Camashaly Design to select the file to be opened.

5 Click the Open button (Open dialog box) to open the selected file and display the opened database in the Access window.

6 If a Security Warning appears, click the Enable Content option button.

Creating Queries

Queries are simply questions, the answers to which are in the database. Access contains a powerful query feature. Through the use of this feature, you can find the answers to a wide variety of complex questions.

For an introduction to Windows 7 and instruction about how to perform basic Windows 7 tasks, read the Office 2010 and Windows 7 chapter at the beginning of this book, where you can learn how to resize windows, change screen resolution, create folders, move and rename files, use Windows Help, and much more.

For an introduction to Office 2010 and instruction about how to perform basic tasks in Office 2010 programs, read the Office 2010 and Windows 7 chapter at the beginning of this book, where you can learn how to start a program, use the Ribbon, save a file, open a file, quit a program, use Help, and much more.

BTW

Q&As
For a complete list of the Q&As found in many of the step-by-step sequences in this book, visit the Access 2010 Q&A Web page (scsite.com/ac2010/qa).

Note: In this chapter, you will save each query example. When you use a query for another task, such as to create a form or report, you will assign a specific name to a query; for example, Analyst-Client Query. In situations in which you will not use the query again, you will assign a name using a convention that includes the chapter number and a query number; for example, Ch2q1. Queries are numbered consecutively.

To Create a Query in Design View

Most of the time, you will use Design view to create queries. Once you have created a new query in Design view, you can specify fields, criteria, sorting, calculations, and so on. The following steps create a new query in Design view.

1
- Close the Navigation Pane.
- Click Create on the Ribbon to display the Create tab.
- Click the Query Design button (Create tab | Queries group) to create a new query (Figure 2–2).

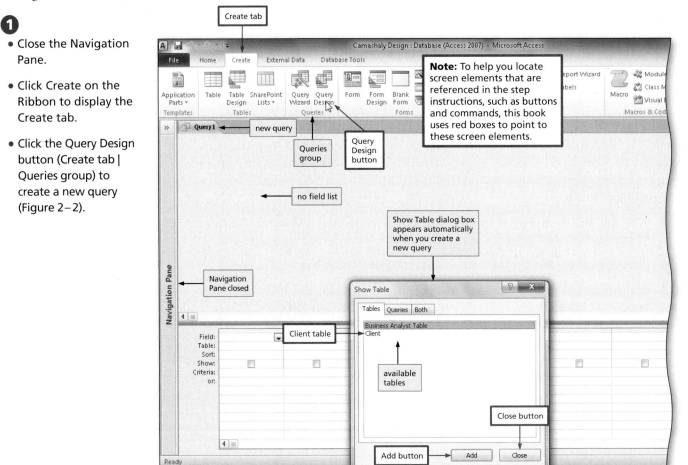

Figure 2–2

2

- Click the Client table (Show Table dialog box) to select the table.

- Click the Add button to add the selected table to the query.

- Click the Close button to remove the dialog box from the screen.

Q&A What if I inadvertently add the wrong table?

Right-click the table that you added in error and click Remove Table on the shortcut menu. You also can just close the query, indicate that you don't want to save it, and then start over.

- Drag the lower edge of the field list down far enough so all fields in the table appear (Figure 2–3).

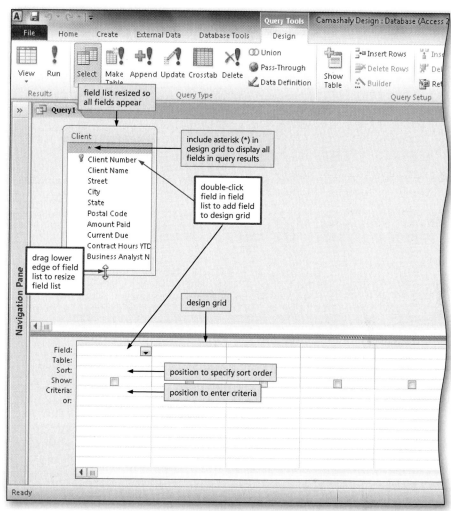

Figure 2–3

Q&A How do I drag the lower edge?

Point to the lower edge, press and hold the left mouse button, move the mouse pointer to the new position for the lower edge, and then release the left mouse button. While the mouse pointer points to the lower edge of the field list, its shape changes to a two-headed arrow.

Q&A Is it essential that I resize the field list?

No. You can always scroll through the list of fields using the scroll bar. It is usually more convenient to resize the field list so all fields appear.

To Add Fields to the Design Grid

Once you have a new query displayed in Design view, you are ready to make entries in the design grid, located in the lower pane of the window. You add the fields you want included in the query to the Field row in the grid. Only the fields that appear in the design grid will be included in the results of the query. The following steps begin the creation of a query that Camashaly Design might use to obtain the client number, client name, amount paid, and current due for a particular client. The following step selects the appropriate fields for the query.

1

- Double-click the Client Number field in the field list to add the field to the query.

Q&A

What if I add the wrong field?

Click just above the field name in the design grid to select the column and then press the DELETE key to remove the field.

- Double-click the Client Name field in the field list to add the field to the query.

- Add the Amount Paid field to the query.

- Add the Current Due field to the query (Figure 2 – 4).

Q&A

What if I want to include all fields? Do I have to add each field individually?

No. Instead of adding individual fields, you can double-click the asterisk (*) to add the asterisk to the design grid. The asterisk is a shortcut indicating all fields are to be included.

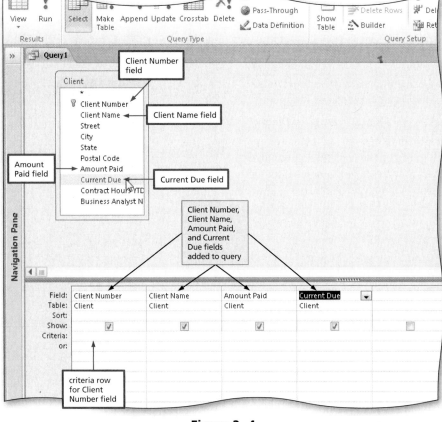

Figure 2–4

BTW

The Ribbon and Screen Resolution

Access may change how the groups and buttons within the groups appear on the Ribbon, depending on the computer's screen resolution. Thus, your Ribbon may look different from the ones in this book if you are using a screen resolution other than 1024 × 768.

Determining Criteria

When you use queries, usually you are looking for those records that satisfy some criterion. In the simple query you created in the previous chapter, for example, you entered a criterion to restrict the records that were included to those on which the business analyst number is 14. In another query, you might want the name, amount paid, and current due amounts of the client whose number is BC76, for example, or of those clients whose names start with the letters, Gr. You enter criteria in the Criteria row in the design grid below the field name to which the criterion applies. For example, to indicate that the client number must be BC76, you first must add the Client Number field to the design grid. You then would type BC76 in the Criteria row below the Client Number field.

To Use Text Data in a Criterion

To use **text data** (data in a field whose data type is Text) in criteria, simply type the text in the Criteria row below the corresponding field name. The following steps finish the creation of a query that Camashaly Design might use to obtain the client number, client name, amount paid, and current due amount of client BC76. These steps add the appropriate criterion so that only the desired client will appear in the results. The steps also save the query.

1

- Click the Criteria row for the Client Number field to produce an insertion point.

- Type **BC76** as the criterion (Figure 2–5).

Figure 2–5

2

- Click the View button (Query Tools Design tab | Results group) to display the query results (Figure 2–6).

Q&A I noticed that there is a View button on both the Home tab and the Design tab. Do they both have the same effect?

Yes. Use whichever one you find most convenient.

Figure 2–6

3
- Click the Save button on the Quick Access Toolbar to display the Save As dialog box.

- Type **Ch2q1** as the name of the query (Figure 2–7).

Q&A

Can I also save from Design view?

Yes. You can save the query when you view it in Design view just as you can save the query when you view the query results in Datasheet view.

Figure 2–7

4
- Click the OK button (Save As dialog box) to save the query (Figure 2–8).

Figure 2–8

Other Ways

1. Right-click query tab, click Save on shortcut menu

Using Saved Queries

After you have created and saved a query, you can use it in a variety of ways:

- To view the results of the query that is not currently open, open it by right-clicking the query in the Navigation Pane and clicking Open on the shortcut menu.

- If you want to change the design of the query that is already open, return to Design view and make the changes.

- If you want to change the design of the query that is not currently open, right-click the query in the Navigation Pane and then click Design View on the shortcut menu to open the query in Design view.

- To print the results with the query open, click File on the Ribbon, click the Print tab in the Backstage view, and then click Quick Print.

- To print the query without first opening it, be sure the query is selected in the Navigation Pane and click File on the Ribbon, click the Print tab in the Backstage view, and then click Quick Print.

- You can switch between views of a query using the View button (Home tab | Views group). Clicking the arrow at the bottom of the button produces the View button menu. You then click the desired view in the menu. The two query views you use in this chapter are Datasheet view (see the results) and Design view (change the design). You can click the top part of the View button, in which case, you will switch to the view identified by the icon on the button. In the figure, the button contains the icon for Design view, so clicking the button would change to Design view. For the most part, the icon on the button represents the view you want, so you can usually simply click the button.

BTW

BTWs

For a complete list of the BTWs found in the margins of this book, visit the Access 2010 BTW Web page (scsite.com/ ac2010/btw).

To Use a Wildcard

Microsoft Access supports wildcards. **Wildcards** are symbols that represent any character or combination of characters. One common wildcard, the **asterisk** (*), represents any collection of characters. Thus Gr* represents the letters, Gr, followed by any collection of characters. Another wildcard symbol is the **question mark** (?), which represents any individual character. Thus T?m represents the letter, T, followed by any single character, followed by the letter, m; a search might return the names Tim or Tom.

The following steps modify the previous query so that Camashaly Design can select only those clients whose names begin with Gr. Because you do not know how many characters will follow the Gr, the asterisk wildcard symbol is appropriate. The steps also save the query with a new name using the Save As command.

1

- Click the View button (Home tab | Views group) to return to Design view.

- If necessary, click the Criteria row below the Client Number field to produce an insertion point.

Q&A

The text I entered now has quotation marks surrounding it. What happened?

Criteria for text data needs to be enclosed in quotation marks. You do not have to type the quotation marks; Access adds them automatically.

- Use the DELETE or BACKSPACE key as necessary to delete the current entry.

- Click the Criteria row below the Client Name field to produce an insertion point.

- Type **Gr*** as the criterion (Figure 2–9).

Figure 2–9

2

- View the query results by clicking the View button (Query Tools Design tab | Results group) (Figure 2–10).

🔍 **Experiment**

- Vary the case of the letters in the criteria and view the results to determine whether case makes a difference when entering a wildcard.

Figure 2–10

3

- Click File on the Ribbon to open the Backstage view (Figure 2–11).

Q&A

Why can't I just click the Save button on the Quick Access Toolbar like I did when I saved the previous query?

If you did, you would replace the previous query with the version you just created. Because you want to save both the previous query and the new one, you need to save the new version with a different name. To do so, you must use Save Object As, which is available through the Backstage view.

Figure 2–11

4

- Click Save Object As in the Backstage view to display the Save As dialog box.

- Type **Ch2q2** as the name for the saved query (Figure 2–12).

Q&A

The current entry in the As text box is Query. Could I save the query as some other type of object?

Although you usually would want to save the query as another query, you also can save it as a form or report by changing the entry in the As text box. If you do, Access would create either a simple form or a simple report for the query.

Figure 2–12

⑤

- Click the OK button (Save As dialog box) to save the query with the new name, and then click File on the Ribbon to close the Backstage view (Figure 2–13).

Q&A

How can I tell that the query was saved with the new name?

The new name will appear on the tab.

Figure 2–13

To Use Criteria for a Field Not Included in the Results

In some cases, you might require criteria for a particular field that should not appear in the results of the query. For example, you may want to see the client number, client name, address, and amount paid for all clients located in Georgetown. The criteria involve the City field, but you do not want to include the City field in the results.

To enter a criterion for the City field, it must be included in the design grid. Normally, this also would mean it would appear in the results. To prevent this from happening, remove the check mark from its Show check box in the Show row of the grid.

The following steps modify the previous query so that Camashaly Design can select only those clients located in Georgetown. Camashaly does not want the city to appear in the results, however. The steps also save the query with a new name.

❶

- Click the View button (Home tab | Views group), shown in Figure 2–13, to return to Design view.

Q&A

The text I entered is now preceded by the word, Like. What happened?

Criteria including wildcards need to be preceded by the word, Like. You do not have to type the word, Like, however. Access adds it automatically to any criterion involving a wildcard.

- Erase the criterion in the Client Name field.

- Add the City field to the query.

- Type **Georgetown** as the criterion for the City field (Figure 2–14).

Figure 2–14

2

- Click the Show check box for the City field to remove the check mark (Figure 2–15).

Q&A

Could I have removed the check mark before entering the criterion?

Yes. The order in which you perform the two operations does not matter.

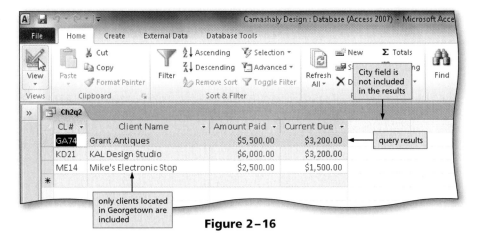

Figure 2–15

3

- View the query results (Figure 2–16).

Experiment

- Click the View button to return to Design view, enter a different city name, and view the results. Repeat this process with a variety of city names, including at least one city name that is not in the database. When finished, change the criterion back to Georgetown.

Figure 2–16

4

- Click File on the Ribbon to open the Backstage view.
- Click Save Object As in the Backstage view to display the Save As dialog box.
- Type **Ch2q3** as the name for the saved query.
- Click the OK button (Save As dialog box) to save the query with the new name.
- Click File on the Ribbon to close the Backstage view.

Creating a Parameter Query

BTW

Queries: Query-by-Example
Query-By-Example, often referred to as QBE, was a query language first proposed in the mid-1970s. In this approach, users asked questions by filling in a table on the screen. The Access approach to queries is based on Query-By-Example.

If you wanted to find clients located in Kyle instead of Georgetown, you would either have to create a new query or modify the existing query by replacing Georgetown with Kyle as the criterion. Rather than giving a specific criterion when you first create the query, on occasion, you may want to be able to enter part of the criterion when you view the query results and then have the appropriate results appear. For example, to include all the clients located in Kyle, you could enter Kyle as a criterion in the City field. From that point on, every time you ran the query, only the clients in Kyle would appear.

A better way is to allow the user to enter the city at the time the user wants to view the results. Thus, a user could view the query results, enter Kyle as the city, and then see all the clients in Kyle. Later, the user could use the same query but enter Georgetown as the city, and then see all the clients in Georgetown.

To enable this flexibility, you create a **parameter query**, which is a query that prompts for input whenever it is used. You enter a parameter (prompt for the user), rather than a specific value as the criterion. You create one by enclosing a value in a criterion in square brackets. It is important that the value in the brackets does not match the name of any field. If you enter a field name in square brackets, Access assumes you want that particular field and does not prompt the user for input. To prompt the user to enter the city name as the input, you could place [Enter City] as the criterion in the City field.

To Create and View a Parameter Query

The following steps create a parameter query that will prompt the users at Camashaly to enter a city, and then display the client number, name, address, and amount paid for all clients located in that city. The steps also save the query with a new name.

1

- Return to Design view.

- Erase the current criterion in the City column, and then type `[Enter City]` as the new criterion (Figure 2–17).

Q&A What is the purpose of the square brackets?

The square brackets indicate that the text entered is not text that the value in the column must match. Without the brackets, Access would search for records on which the city is Enter City.

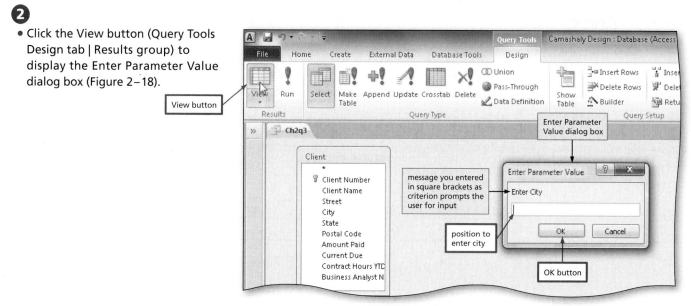

Figure 2–17

Q&A What if I typed a field name in the square brackets?

Access would simply use the value in that field. To create a parameter query, you must not use a field name in the square brackets.

2

- Click the View button (Query Tools Design tab | Results group) to display the Enter Parameter Value dialog box (Figure 2–18).

Figure 2–18

3

- Type `Kyle` as the parameter value in the Enter City text box and then click the OK button (Enter Parameter Value dialog box) to close the dialog box and view the query (Figure 2–19).

Experiment

- Try other characters between the square brackets. In each case, view the results. When finished, change the characters between the square brackets back to Enter City.

Figure 2–19

4

- Click File on the Ribbon to open the Backstage view.

- Click Save Object As in the Backstage view to display the Save As dialog box.

- Type `Client-City Query` as the name for the saved query.

- Click the OK button (Save As dialog box) to save the query with the new name and then click File on the Ribbon (Figure 2–20).

5

- Click the Close button for the Client-City query to close the query.

Figure 2–20

Break Point: If you wish to take a break, this is a good place to do so. You can quit Access now. To resume at a later time, start Access, open the database called Camashaly Design, and continue following the steps from this location forward.

To Use a Parameter Query

You use a parameter query like any other saved query. You can open it or you can print the query results. In either case, Access prompts you to supply a value for the parameter each time you use the query. As with other queries, the query always uses the data that is currently in the table. Thus, if changes have been made to the data since the last time you ran the query, the results of the query may be different, even if you enter the same value for the parameter. The following steps use the parameter query named Client-City Query.

1

- Open the Navigation Pane.

- Right-click the Client-City Query to produce a shortcut menu.

- Click Open on the shortcut menu to open the query and display the Enter Parameter Value dialog box (Figure 2–21).

Q&A The title bar for my Navigation Pane contains Tables and Related Views rather than All Access Objects as it did in Chapter 1. What should I do?

Click the Navigation Pane arrow and then click All Access Objects.

Q&A I do not have the Search bar at the top of the Navigation Pane that I had in Chapter 1. What should I do?

Right-click the Navigation Pane title bar arrow to display a shortcut menu, and then click Search Bar.

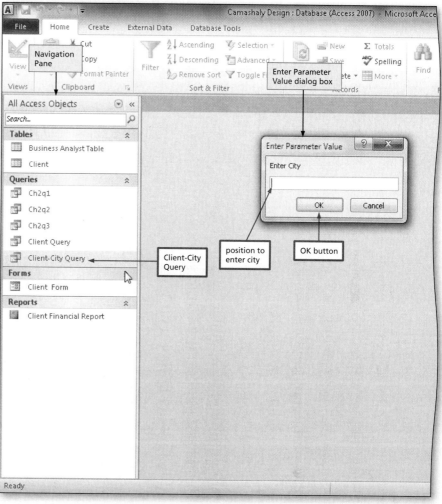

Figure 2–21

2

- Type **Kyle** in the Enter City text box, and then click the OK button (Enter Parameter Value dialog box) to display the results using Kyle as the city, as shown in Figure 2–20.

- Close the query.

To Use a Number in a Criterion

To enter a number in a criterion, type the number without any dollar signs or commas. The following steps create a query that Camashaly Design might use to display all clients whose current due amount is $0. The steps also save the query with a new name.

1

- Close the Navigation Pane.

- Click Create on the Ribbon to display the Create tab.

- Click the Query Design button (Create tab | Queries group) to create a new query.

- Click the Client table (Show Table dialog box) to select the table.

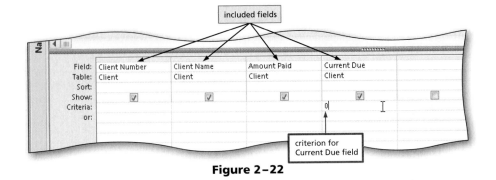

Figure 2–22

- Click the Add button to add the selected table to the query.

- Click the Close button to remove the dialog box from the screen.

- Drag the lower edge of the field list down far enough so all fields in the field list are displayed.

- Include the Client Number, Client Name, Amount Paid, and Current Due fields in the query.

- Type   0   as the criterion for the Current Due field (Figure 2–22).

Q&A Do I need to enter a dollar sign and decimal point?

No. Access will interpret 0 as $0 because the data type for the Current Due field is currency.

2

- View the query results (Figure 2–23).

Q&A Why did Access display the results as $0.00 when I only entered 0?

Access uses the format for the field to determine how to display the result. In this case, the format indicated that Access should include the dollar sign, decimal point, and two decimal places.

Figure 2–23

3

- Save the query as Ch2q4.

Q&A How do I know when to use the Save button to save a query or use the Backstage view to perform a Save As?

If you are saving a new query, the simplest way is to use the Save button on the Quick Access Toolbar. If you are saving changes to a previously saved query but do not want to change the name, use the Save button. If you want to save a previously saved query with a new name, you must use the Backstage view and perform a Save Object As.

To Use a Comparison Operator in a Criterion

Unless you specify otherwise, Access assumes that the criteria you enter involve equality (exact matches). In the last query, for example, you were requesting those clients whose current due amount is equal to 0 (zero). If you want something other than an exact match, you must enter the appropriate **comparison operator**. The comparison operators are > (greater than), < (less than), >= (greater than or equal to), <= (less than or equal to), and NOT (not equal to).

The following steps use the > operator to create a query that Camashaly Design might use to find all clients whose amount paid is more than $3,000. The steps also save the query with a new name.

1
- Return to Design view.
- Erase the 0 in the Current Due column.
- Type >3000 as the criterion for the Amount Paid field (Figure 2–24).

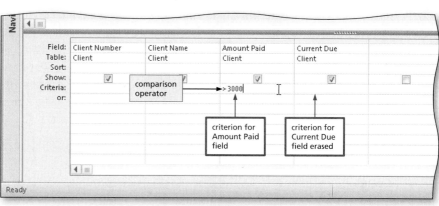

Figure 2–24

2
- View the query results (Figure 2–25).

Experiment
- Return to Design view. Try a different criterion involving a comparison operator in the Amount Paid field and view the results. When finished, return to Design view, enter the original criterion (>3000) in the Amount Paid field, and view the results.

3
- Save the query as Ch2q5.

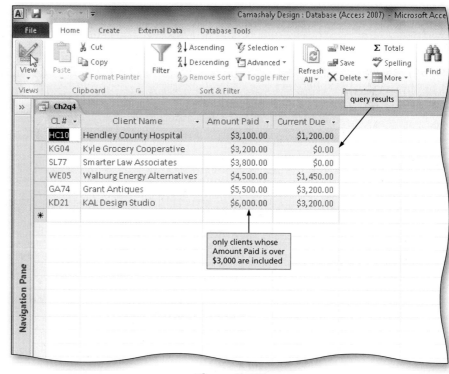

Figure 2–25

Using Compound Criteria

Often you will have more than one criterion that the data for which you are searching must satisfy. This type of criterion is called a **compound criterion**. Two types of compound criteria exist.

In an **AND criterion**, each individual criterion must be true in order for the compound criterion to be true. For example, an AND criterion would allow you to find those clients that have an amount paid greater than $3,000 and whose business analyst is business analyst 11.

Conversely, an **OR criterion** is true provided either individual criterion is true. An OR criterion would allow you to find those clients that have an amount paid greater than $3,000 and also those clients whose business analyst is business analyst 11 — either one criterion or the other is true. In this case, any client whose amount paid is greater than $3,000 would be included in the answer, regardless of whether the client's business analyst is business analyst 11. Likewise, any client whose business analyst is business analyst 11 would be included, regardless of whether the client had an amount paid greater than $3,000.

To Use a Compound Criterion Involving AND

To combine criteria with AND, place the criteria on the same row of the design grid. The following steps use an AND criterion to enable Camashaly to find those clients whose amount paid is greater than $3,000 and whose business analyst is analyst 11. The steps also save the query with a new name.

1
- Return to Design view.

- Include the Business Analyst Number field in the query.

- Type **11** as the criterion for the Business Analyst Number field (Figure 2–26).

Figure 2–26

2
- View the query results (Figure 2–27).

3
- Save the query as Ch2q6.

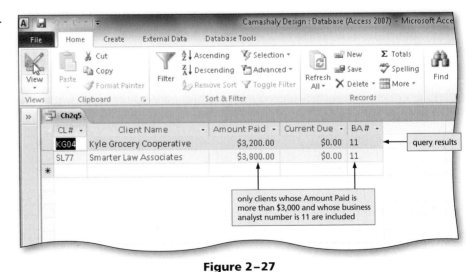

Figure 2–27

To Use a Compound Criterion Involving OR

To combine criteria with OR, the criteria must go on separate rows in the Criteria area of the grid. The following steps use an OR criterion to enable Camashaly to find those clients whose amount paid is greater than $3,000 or whose business analyst is analyst 11 (or both). The steps also save the query with a new name.

1

- Return to Design view.

- If necessary, click the Criteria entry for the Business Analyst Number field and then use the BACKSPACE key or the DELETE key to erase the entry ("11").

- Click the or row (the row below the Criteria row) for the Business Analyst Number field and then type 11 as the entry (Figure 2–28).

Figure 2–28

2

- View the query results (Figure 2–29).

3

- Save the query as Ch2q7.

CL #	Client Name	Amount Paid	Current Due	BA #
BA53	Bavant Animal Hospital	$0.00	$7,500.00	11
BC76	Buda Community Clinic	$2,500.00	$750.00	11
GA74	Grant Antiques	$5,500.00	$3,200.00	14
GF56	Granger Foundation	$0.00	$6,500.00	11
HC10	Hendley County Hospital	$3,100.00	$1,200.00	27
KD21	KAL Design Studio	$6,000.00	$3,200.00	14
KG04	Kyle Grocery Cooperative	$3,200.00	$0.00	11
SL77	Smarter Law Associates	$3,800.00	$0.00	11
WE05	Walburg Energy Alternatives	$4,500.00	$1,450.00	14

only clients whose amount paid is more than $3,000 or whose business analyst number is 11 are included

Figure 2–29

Special Criteria

There are three special criteria you can use in queries:

1. If you want to create a criterion involving a range of values in a single field, you can use the **AND operator**. You place the word AND between the individual conditions. For example, if you wanted to find all clients whose amount paid is >= $1,000 and <= $4,000, you would enter `>= 1000 AND <= 4000` as the criterion in the Amount Paid column.

2. You can select values in a given range by using the **BETWEEN operator**. This is often an alternative to the AND operator. For example, to find all clients whose amount paid is between $1,000 and $4,000, inclusive, you would enter `BETWEEN 1000 AND 4000` as the criterion in the Amount Paid column.

3. You can select values in a list by using the **IN operator**. You follow the word IN with the list of values in parentheses. For example, to find clients whose business analyst number is 11 or 14 using the IN operator, you would enter `IN ("11","14")` as the criterion in the Business Analyst Number column. Unlike when you enter a simple criterion, you must enclose text values in quotation marks.

Sorting

In some queries, the order in which the records appear is irrelevant. All you need to be concerned about are the records that appear in the results. It does not matter which one is first or which one is last.

In other queries, however, the order can be very important. You may want to see the cities in which clients are located and would like them arranged alphabetically. Perhaps you want to see the clients listed by business analyst number. Further, within all the clients of any given business analyst, you might want them to be listed by amount paid from largest amount to smallest.

To order the records in a query result in a particular way, you **sort** the records. The field or fields on which the records are sorted is called the **sort key**. If you are sorting on more than one field (such as sorting by amount paid within business analyst number), the more important field (Business Analyst Number) is called the **major key** (also called the **primary sort key**) and the less important field (Amount Paid) is called the **minor key** (also called the **secondary sort key**).

To sort in Microsoft Access, specify the sort order in the Sort row of the design grid below the field that is the sort key. If you specify more than one sort key, the sort key on the left will be the major sort key, and the one on the right will be the minor key.

The following are guidelines related to sorting in queries.

BTW

Sorting Data in a Query
When sorting data in a query, the records in the underlying tables (the tables on which the query is based) are not actually rearranged. Instead, the DBMS determines the most efficient method of simply displaying the records in the requested order. The records in the underlying tables remain in their original order.

Determine whether special order is required.
Examine the query or request to see if it contains words, such as order or sort, that would
imply that the order of the query results is important. If so, you need to sort the query.

- **Determine the sort key(s).** If sorting is required, identify the field or fields on which the
results are to be sorted. In the request, look for language such as ordered by or sort the
results by, both of which would indicate that the specified field is a sort key.

- **If using two sort keys, determine major and minor key.** If you are using two sort keys,
determine which one is the more important, or the major key. Look for language such as
sort by amount paid within business analyst number, which implies that the overall order
is by business analyst number. Thus, the Business Analyst Number field would be the
major sort key and the Amount Paid field would be the minor sort key.

- **Determine sort order.** Words such as increasing, ascending, or low-to-high imply Ascending
order. Words such as decreasing, descending, or high-to-low imply Descending order.
Sorting in alphabetical order implies Ascending order. If there are no words to imply a
particular order, you would typically use Ascending.

- **Determine restrictions.** Examine the query or request to see if there are any special
restrictions. One common restriction is to exclude duplicates. Another common restriction
is to list only a certain number of records, for example, to list only the first five records.

To Clear the Design Grid

If the fields you want to include in the next query are different from those in the previous query, it is usually
simpler to start with a clear grid, one with no fields already in the design grid. You always can clear the entries in the
design grid by closing the query and then starting over. A simpler approach to clearing the entries is to select all the
entries and then press the DELETE key. The following steps return to Design view and clear the design grid.

1

- Return to Design view.

- Click just above the Client Number
column heading in the grid to select
the column.

Q&A

I clicked above the column heading,
but the column is not selected.
What should I do?

You didn't point to the correct
location. Be sure the mouse pointer
changes into a down-pointing arrow
and then click again.

- Hold the SHIFT key down and click
just above the Business Analyst
Number column heading to select
all the columns (Figure 2–30).

2

- Press the DELETE key to clear the
design grid.

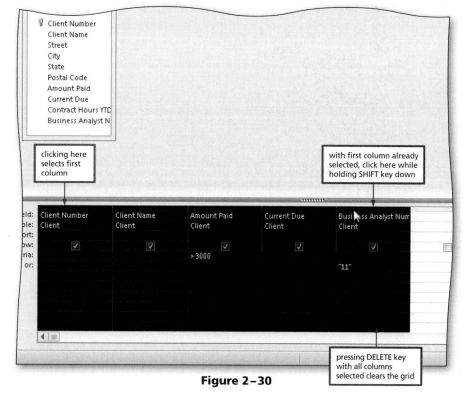

Figure 2–30

To Sort Data in a Query

After determining in the design process that a query is to be sorted, you will need to specify the sort key to Access. The following steps sort the cities in the Client table by indicating that the City field is to be sorted. The steps specify Ascending sort order.

1
- Include the City field in the design grid.
- Click the Sort row below the City field, and then click the Sort row arrow to display a menu of possible sort orders (Figure 2–31).

Figure 2–31

2
- Click Ascending to select the sort order (Figure 2–32).

Figure 2–32

3
- View the query results (Figure 2–33).

🔎 **Experiment**
- Return to Design view and change the sort order to Descending. View the results. Return to Design view and change the sort order back to Ascending. View the results.

Q&A Why do some cities appear more than once?

More than one client is located in those cities.

Figure 2–33

To Omit Duplicates

When you sort data, duplicates normally are included. In Figure 2–33, for example, Austin appeared twice, as did Buda, Burles, Granger, Kyle, and Walburg. Georgetown appeared three times. These duplicates do not add any value, so you should eliminate them from the results. To eliminate duplicates, display the query's property sheet. A **property sheet** is a window containing the various properties of the object. To omit duplicates, you will use the property sheet to change the Unique Values property from No to Yes.

The following steps create a query that Camashaly Design might use to obtain a sorted list of the cities in the Client table in which each city is listed only once. The steps also save the query with a new name.

1

- Return to Design view.

- Click the second field (the empty field to the right of City) in the design grid.

- If necessary, click Design on the Ribbon to display the Design tab.

- Click the Property Sheet button (Query Tools Design tab | Show/Hide group) to display the property sheet (Figure 2–34).

Q&A

My property sheet looks different. What should I do?

If your sheet looks different, you clicked the wrong place and will have to close the property sheet and repeat this step.

Figure 2–34

2

- Click the Unique Values property box, and then click the arrow that appears to produce a list of available choices (Figure 2–35).

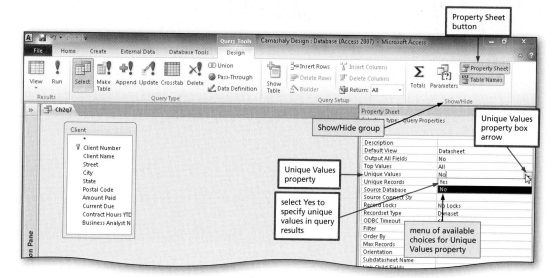

Figure 2–35

3

- Click Yes and then close the Query Properties property sheet by clicking the Property Sheet button (Query Tools Design tab | Show / Hide group) a second time.

- View the query results (Figure 2–36).

4

- Save the query as Ch2q8.

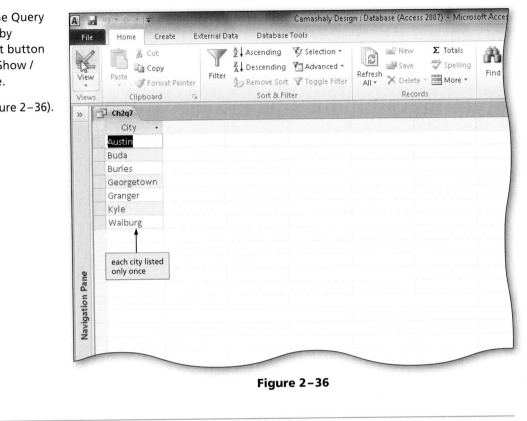

Figure 2–36

Other Ways

1. Right-click second field in design grid, click Properties on shortcut menu

To Sort on Multiple Keys

The following steps sort on multiple keys. Specifically, Camashaly needs the data to be sorted by amount paid (low to high) within business analyst number, which means that the Business Analyst Number field is the major key and the Amount Paid field is the minor key. The steps also save the query with a new name.

1

- Return to Design view. Clear the design grid by clicking the first column in the grid, and then pressing the DELETE key to clear the design grid.

- In the following order, include the Client Number, Client Name, Business Analyst Number, and Amount Paid fields in the query.

- Select Ascending as the sort order for both the Business Analyst Number field and the Amount Paid field (Figure 2–37).

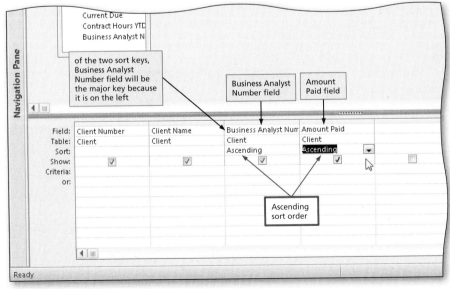

Figure 2–37

2

- View the query results (Figure 2–38).

Experiment

- Return to Design view and try other sort combinations for the Business Analyst Number and Amount Paid fields, such as Ascending for Business Analyst Number and Descending for Amount Paid. In each case, view the results to see the effect of the changes. When finished, select Ascending as the sort order for both fields.

Q&A

What if the Amount Paid field is to the left of the Business Analyst Number field?

It is important to remember that the major sort key must appear to the left of the minor sort key in the design grid. If you attempted to sort by amount paid within business analyst number, but placed the Amount Paid field to the left of the Business Analyst Number field, your results would be incorrect.

within group of clients with the same business analyst number, rows are sorted by amount paid in ascending order

overall order is by business analyst number in ascending order

Figure 2–38

3

- Save the query as Ch2q9.

To Create a Top-Values Query

Rather than show all the results of a query, you may want to show only a specified number of records or a percentage of records. Creating a **top-values query** allows you to quantify the results. When you sort records, you can limit results to those records having the highest (descending sort) or lowest (ascending sort) values. To do so, first create a query that sorts the data in the desired order. Next, use the Return box on the Design tab to change the number of records to be included from All to the desired number or percentage. The following steps create a query for Camashaly Design that shows only the first five records that were included in the results of the previous query. The steps also save the resulting query with a new name.

1

- Return to Design view.

- If necessary, click Design on the Ribbon to display the Design tab.

- Click the Return box arrow (Query Tools Design tab | Query Setup group) to display the Return box menu (Figure 2–39).

Figure 2–39

2

- Click 5 in the Return box menu to specify that the query results should contain the first five rows.

Q&A

Could I have typed the 5? What about other numbers that do not appear in the list?

Yes, you could have typed the 5. For numbers not appearing in the list, you must type the number.

- View the query results (Figure 2–40).

3

- Save the query as Ch2q10.
- Close the query.

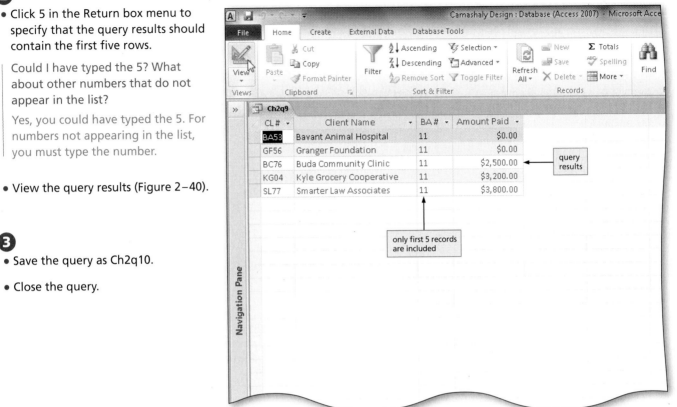

Figure 2–40

Q&A

Do I need to close the query before creating my next query?

Not necessarily. When you use a top-values query, however, it is important to change the value in the Return box back to All. If you do not change the Return value back to All, the previous value will remain in effect. Consequently, you might not get all the records you should in the next query. A good practice whenever you use a top-values query is to close the query as soon as you are done. That way, you will begin your next query from scratch, which guarantees that the value is reset to All.

Break Point: If you wish to take a break, this is a good place to do so. You can quit Access now. To resume at a later time, start Access, open the database called Camashaly Design, and continue following the steps from this location forward.

BTW

Join Line
If you do not get a join line automatically, there may be a problem with one of your table designs. Open each table in Design view and make sure that the data types are the same for the matching field in both tables and that one of the matching fields is the primary key in a table. Correct these errors and create the query again.

Joining Tables

In designing a query, you need to determine whether more than one table is required. If the question being asked involves data from both the Client and Business Analyst tables, for example, both tables are required for the query. For example, a query may require listing the number and name of each client along with the number and name of the client's business analyst. The client's name is in the Client table, whereas the business analyst's name is in the Business Analyst Table. Thus, this query cannot be completed using a single table; both the Client and Business Analyst tables are required. You need to **join** the tables; that is, to find records in the two tables that have identical values in matching fields (Figure 2–41). In this example, you need to find records in the Client table and the Business Analyst table that have the same value in the Business Analyst Number fields.

Client Table

CL #	Client Name	...	BA #
BA53	Bavant Animal Hospital	...	11
BB32	Babbage CPA Firm	...	14
BC76	Buda Community Clinic	...	11
CJ29	Catering by Jenna	...	27
GA74	Grant Antiques	...	14
GF56	Granger Foundation	...	11
HC10	Hendley County Hospital	...	27
KD21	KAL Design Studio	...	14
KG04	Kyle Grocery Cooperative	...	11
ME14	Mike's Electronic Stop	...	27
PJ34	Patricia Jean Florist	...	27
SL77	Smarter Law Associates	...	11
TB17	The Bikeshop	...	27
WE05	Walburg Energy Alternatives	...	14
WS01	Woody Sporting Goods	...	14

Give me the number and name of each client along with the number and name of the client's analyst.

Business Analyst Table

BA #	Last Name	First Name	...
11	Kerry	Cordelia	...
14	Martinez	Manuel	...
27	Liu	Jan	...
35	Scott	Jeff	...

Client Table

CL #	Client Name	...	BA #	Last Name	First Name	...
BA53	Bavant Animal Hospital	...	11	Kerry	Cordelia	...
BB32	Babbage CPA Firm	...	14	Martinez	Manuel	...
BC76	Buda Community Clinic	...	11	Kerry	Cordelia	...
CJ29	Catering by Jenna	...	27	Liu	Jan	...
GA74	Grant Antiques	...	14	Martinez	Manuel	...
GF56	Granger Foundation	...	11	Kerry	Cordelia	...
HC10	Hendley County Hospital	...	27	Liu	Jan	...
KD21	KAL Design Studio	...	14	Martinez	Manuel	...
KG04	Kyle Grocery Cooperative	...	11	Kerry	Cordelia	...
ME14	Mike's Electronic Stop	...	27	Liu	Jan	...
PJ34	Patricia Jean Florist	...	27	Liu	Jan	...
SL77	Smarter Law Associates	...	11	Kerry	Cordelia	...
TB17	The Bikeshop	...	27	Liu	Jan	...
WE05	Walburg Energy Alternatives	...	14	Martinez	Manuel	...
WS01	Woody Sporting Goods	...	14	Martinez	Manuel	...

Figure 2–41

BTW

Join Types
The type of join that finds records from both tables that have identical values in matching fields is called an inner join. An inner join is the default join in Access. Outer joins are used to show all the records in one table as well as the common records; that is, the records that share the same value in the join field. In a left outer join, all rows from the table on the left are included. In a right outer join, all rows from the table on the right are included.

The following are guidelines related to joining tables.

Plan Ahead

Determine whether more than one table is required.
Examine the query or request to see if all the fields involved in the request are in one table. If the fields are in two (or more) tables, you need to join the tables.

- **Determine the matching fields.** If joining is required, identify the matching fields in the two tables that have identical values. Look for the same column name in the two tables or for column names that are similar.

- **Determine whether sorting is required.** Queries that join tables often are used as the basis for a report. If this is the case, it may be necessary to sort the results. For example, the Analyst-Client Report is based on a query that joins the Business Analyst and Client tables. The query is sorted by business analyst number and client number.

- **Determine restrictions.** Examine the query or request to see if there are any special restrictions. For example, the user may only want clients whose current due amount is $0.00.

- **Determine join properties.** Examine the query or request to see if you only want records from both tables that have identical values in matching fields. If you want to see records in one of the tables that do not have identical values, then you need to change the join properties.

To Join Tables

If you have determined in the design process that you need to join tables, you will first bring field lists for both tables to the upper pane of the Query window while working in Design view. Access will draw a line, called a **join line**, between matching fields in the two tables, indicating that the tables are related. You then can select fields from either table. Access joins the tables automatically.

The first step is to create a new query and add the Business Analyst Table to the query. Then, add the Client table to the query. A join line will appear, connecting the Business Analyst Number fields in the two field lists. This join line indicates how the tables are related, that is, linked through these matching fields. If the names of the matching fields differ from one table to the other, Access will not insert the line. You can insert it manually, however, by clicking one of the two matching fields and dragging the mouse pointer to the other matching field.

The following steps create a query that Camashaly Design might use to display information from both the Client table and the Business Analyst Table.

1
- Click Create on the Ribbon to display the Create tab.

- Click the Query Design button (Create tab | Queries group) to create a new query.

- If necessary, click the Business Analyst Table (Show Table dialog box) to select the table.

- Click the Add button (Show Table dialog box) to add a field list for the Business Analyst Table to the query (Figure 2–42).

Figure 2–42

2

- Click the Client table (Show Table dialog box).

- Click the Add button (Show Table dialog box) to add a field list for the Client table.

- Close the Show Table dialog box by clicking the Close button.

- Expand the size of the two field lists so all the fields in the Business Analyst and Client tables appear (Figure 2–43).

Q&A I didn't get a join line. What should I do?

Ensure that the names of the matching fields are exactly the same, the data types are the same, and the matching field is the primary key in one of the two tables. If all of these are true and you still don't have a join line, you can produce one by pointing to one of the matching fields, pressing the left mouse button, dragging to the other matching field, and releasing the left mouse button.

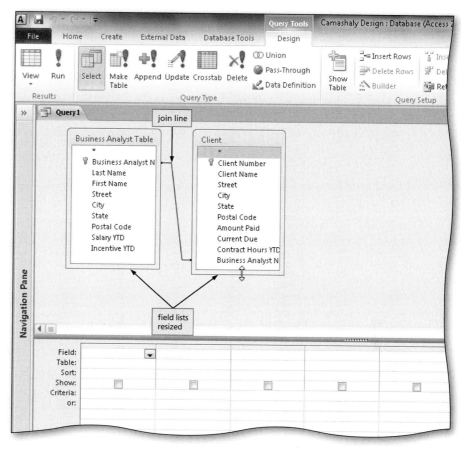

Figure 2–43

3

- In the design grid, include the Business Analyst Number, Last Name, and First Name fields from the Business Analyst Table as well as the Client Number and Client Name fields from the Client table.

- Select Ascending as the sort order for both the Business Analyst Number field and the Client Number field (Figure 2–44).

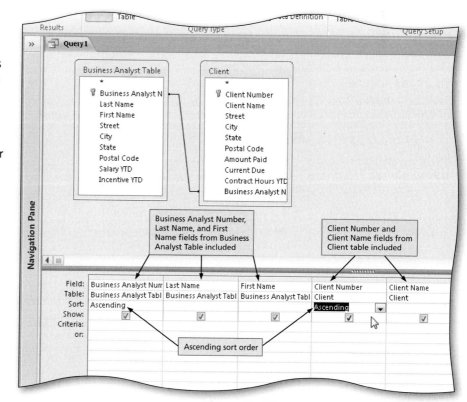

Figure 2–44

4

- View the query results (Figure 2–45).

fields from Business Analyst Table

fields from Client table

Query 1

BA #	Last Name	First Name	CL #	Client Name
11	Kerry	Cordelia	BA53	Bavant Animal Hospital
11	Kerry	Cordelia	BC76	Buda Community Clinic
11	Kerry	Cordelia	GF56	Granger Foundation
11	Kerry	Cordelia	KG04	Kyle Grocery Cooperative
11	Kerry	Cordelia	SL77	Smarter Law Associates
14	Martinez	Manuel	BB32	Babbage CPA Firm
14	Martinez	Manuel	GA74	Grant Antiques
14	Martinez	Manuel	KD21	KAL Design Studio
14	Martinez	Manuel	WE05	Walburg Energy Alternatives
14	Martinez	Manuel	WS01	Woody Sporting Goods
27	Liu	Jan	CJ29	Catering by Jenna
27	Liu	Jan	HC10	Hendley County Hospital
27	Liu	Jan	ME14	Mike's Electronic Stop
27	Liu	Jan	PJ34	Patricia Jean Florist
27	Liu	Jan	TB17	The Bikeshop

within business analyst number, records are further sorted by client number

business analyst 35 not included because he currently has no clients

records are sorted by business analyst number

Figure 2–45

5

- Click the Save button on the Quick Access Toolbar to display the Save As dialog box.

- Type **Analyst-Client Query** as the query name (Figure 2–46).

6

- Click the OK button (Save As dialog box) to save the query.

Save button

Save As dialog box

Query 1

BA #	Last Name	First Name	CL #	Client Name
11	Kerry	Cordelia	BA53	Bavant Animal Hospital
11	Kerry	Cordelia	BC76	Buda Community Clinic
11	Kerry	Cordelia	GF56	Granger Foundation
11	Kerry	Cordelia		Kyle
11	Kerry	Cordelia		Sma
14	Martinez	Manuel	BB32	Bab
14	Martinez	Manuel	GA74	Gra
14	Martinez	Manuel	KD21	KAL Design Studio
14	Martinez	Manuel	WE05	Walburg Energy Alte
14	Martinez	Manuel	WS01	Woody Sporting Goods
27	Liu	Jan	CJ29	Catering by Jenna
		Jan	HC10	H

query name

Save As

Query Name:

Analyst-Client Query

OK   Cancel

OK button

Figure 2–46

To Change Join Properties

Normally, records that do not match do not appear in the results of a join query. For example, a business analyst such as Jeff Scott, for whom no clients currently exist, would not appear in the results. To cause such a record to be displayed, you need to change the **join properties**, which are the properties that indicate which records appear in a join. The following steps change the join properties of the Analyst-Client Query so that Camashaly can include all business analysts in the results, rather than only those analysts who have already been assigned clients.

1

- Return to Design view.

- Right-click the join line to produce a shortcut menu (Figure 2–47).

Q&A

I don't see Join Properties on my shortcut menu. What should I do?

If Join Properties does not appear on your shortcut menu, you did not point to the appropriate portion of the join line. You will need to point to the correct (middle) portion and right-click again.

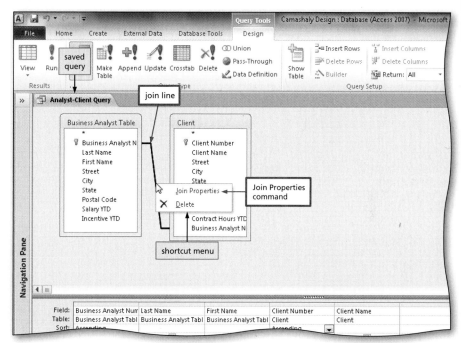

Figure 2–47

2

- Click Join Properties on the shortcut menu to display the Join Properties dialog box (Figure 2–48).

Figure 2–48

❸

- Click option button 2 (Join Properties dialog box) to include all records from the Business Analyst Table regardless of whether they match any clients.

- Click the OK button (Join Properties dialog box) to modify the join properties.

- View the query results (Figure 2–49).

🔍 **Experiment**

- Return to Design view, change the Join properties, and select option button 3. View the results to see the effect of this option. When done, return to Design view, change the Join properties, and once again select option button 2.

❹

- Click the Save button on the Quick Access Toolbar to save the changes to the query.

- Close the Analyst-Client Query.

Q&A

I see a dialog box that asks if I want to save the query. What should I do?

Click the OK button to save the query.

BA #	Last Name	First Name	CL #	Client Name
11	Kerry	Cordelia	BA53	Bavant Animal Hospital
11	Kerry	Cordelia	BC76	Buda Community Clinic
11	Kerry	Cordelia	GF56	Granger Foundation
11	Kerry	Cordelia	KG04	Kyle Grocery Cooperative
11	Kerry	Cordelia	SL77	Smarter Law Associates
14	Martinez	Manuel	BB32	Babbage CPA Firm
14	Martinez	Manuel	GA74	Grant Antiques
14	Martinez	Manuel	KD21	KAL Design Studio
14	Martinez	Manuel	WE05	Walburg Energy Alternatives
14	Martinez	Manuel	WS01	Woody Sporting Goods
27	Liu	Jan	CJ29	Catering by Jenna
27	Liu	Jan	HC10	Hendley County Hospital
27	Liu	Jan	ME14	Mike's Electronic Stop
27	Liu	Jan	PJ34	Patricia Jean Florist
27	Liu	Jan	TB17	The Bikeshop
35	Scott	Jeff		

business analyst 35 included even though he has no clients

client number and name are blank

Figure 2–49

To Create a Report Involving a Join

The following steps use the Report Wizard to create the report for Camashaly Design that is shown in Figure 2–50.

Analyst-Client Report

BA #	Last Name	First Name	CL #	Client Name
11	Kerry	Cordelia	BA53	Bavant Animal Hospital
11	Kerry	Cordelia	BC76	Buda Community Clinic
11	Kerry	Cordelia	GF56	Granger Foundation
11	Kerry	Cordelia	KG04	Kyle Grocery Cooperative
11	Kerry	Cordelia	SL77	Smarter Law Associates
14	Martinez	Manuel	BB32	Babbage CPA Firm
14	Martinez	Manuel	GA74	Grant Antiques
14	Martinez	Manuel	KD21	KAL Design Studio
14	Martinez	Manuel	WE05	Walburg Energy Alternatives
14	Martinez	Manuel	WS01	Woody Sporting Goods
27	Liu	Jan	CJ29	Catering by Jenna
27	Liu	Jan	HC10	Hendley County Hospital
27	Liu	Jan	ME14	Mike's Electronic Stop
27	Liu	Jan	PJ34	Patricia Jean Florist
27	Liu	Jan	TB17	The Bikeshop
35	Scott	Jeff		

Figure 2–50

1

- Open the Navigation Pane, and then select the Analyst-Client Query in the Navigation Pane.

- Click Create on the Ribbon to display the Create tab.

- Click the Report Wizard button (Create tab | Reports group) to display the Report Wizard dialog box (Figure 2–51).

Figure 2–51

2

- Click the Add All Fields button (Report Wizard dialog box) to add all the fields in the Analyst-Client Query.

- Click the Next button to display the next Report Wizard screen (Figure 2–52).

Figure 2–52

3

- Because you will not specify any grouping, click the Next button in the Report Wizard dialog box to display the next Report Wizard screen.

- Because you already specified the sort order in the query, click the Next button again to display the next Report Wizard screen.

- Make sure that Tabular is selected as the Layout and Portrait is selected as the Orientation.

- Click the Next button to display the next Report Wizard screen.

- Erase the current title, and then type **Analyst-Client Report** as the new title.

- Click the Finish button to produce the report (Figure 2–53).

4

- Close the Analyst-Client Report.

Camashaly Design : Database (Access 2007) – Microsoft Access

Portrait | Landscape | Columns | Page Setup | Zoom | One Page | Two Pages | More Pages | Refresh All | Excel | Text File | PDF or XPS | E-mail | More | Close Print Preview

Page Layout | | | | Data | Close Preview

preview of report

lyst-Client Report

Analyst-Client Report

BA #	Last Name	First Name	CL #	Client Name
11	Kerry	Cordelia	BA53	Bavant Animal Hospital
11	Kerry	Cordelia	BC76	Buda Community Clinic
11	Kerry	Cordelia	GF56	Granger Foundation
11	Kerry	Cordelia	KG04	Kyle Grocery Cooperative
11	Kerry	Cordelia	SL77	Smarter Law Associates
14	Martinez	Manuel	BB32	Babbage CPA Firm
14	Martinez	Manuel	GA74	Grant Antiques
14	Martinez	Manuel	KD21	KAL Design Studio
14	Martinez	Manuel	WE05	Walburg Energy Alternatives
14	Martinez	Manuel	WS01	Woody Sporting Goods
27	Liu	Jan	CJ29	Catering by Jenna
27	Liu	Jan	HC10	Hendley County Hospital
27	Liu	Jan	ME14	Mike's Electronic Stop

1 | No Filter | Num Lock | 100%

Figure 2–53

To Print a Report

The following steps print a hard copy of the report.

1 With the Analyst-Client Report selected in the Navigation Pane, click File on the Ribbon to open the Backstage view.

2 Click the Print tab in the Backstage view to display the Print gallery.

3 Click the Quick Print button to print the report.

Creating a Form for a Query

In the previous chapter, you created a form for the Client table. You also can create a form for a query. Recall that a **form** in a database is a formatted document with fields that contain data. Forms allow you to view and maintain data.

To Create a Form for a Query

The following steps create a form and then save the form.

1

- If necessary, select the Analyst-Client Query in the Navigation Pane.

- Click Create on the Ribbon to display the Create tab (Figure 2–54).

Figure 2–54

2

- Click the Form button (Create tab | Forms group) to create a simple form (Figure 2–55).

Figure 2–55

3

- Click the Save button on the Quick Access Toolbar to display the Save As dialog box.

- Type **Analyst-Client Form** as the form name (Figure 2–56).

4

- Click the OK button to save the form.

- Click the Close button for the form to close the form.

Figure 2–56

Exporting Data
You frequently need to export data so that it can be used in other applications and by other users in an organization. For example, the Accounting department might require financial data in an Excel format to perform certain financial functions. Marketing might require a list of client names and addresses in Word or RTF format for sales purposes.

Using a Form

After you have saved a form, you can use it at any time by right-clicking the form in the Navigation Pane and then clicking Open on the shortcut menu. If you plan to use the form to enter data, you must ensure you are viewing the form in Form view.

Exporting Data from Access to Other Applications

You can **export**, or copy, data from an Access database so that another application (for example, Excel or Word) can use the data. The application that will receive the data determines the export process to be used. You can export to text files in a variety of formats. For applications to which you cannot directly export data, you often can export an appropriately formatted text file that the other application can import. Figure 2–57 shows the Analyst-Client Query exported to Excel.

Figure 2–57

To Export Data to Excel

For Camashaly Design to make the Analyst-Client Query available to Excel users, it needs to export the data. To export data to Excel, select the table or query to be exported, and then click the Excel button in the Export group on the External data tab. The following steps export the Analyst-Client Query to Excel and save the export steps. By saving the export steps, you could easily repeat the export process whenever you like without going through all the following steps. You would use the saved steps to export data in the future by clicking the Saved Exports button (External Data tab | Export group) and then selecting the steps you saved.

- Click the Analyst-Client Query in the Navigation Pane to select it.
- Click External Data on the Ribbon to display the External Data tab (Figure 2–58).

Figure 2–58

2

- Click the Excel button (External Data tab | Export group) to display the Export - Excel Spreadsheet dialog box.

- Click the Browse button (Export - Excel Spreadsheet dialog box) to display the File Save dialog box, and select your USB flash drive as the file location.

- Be sure the file name is Analyst-Client Query and then click the Save button (File Save dialog box) (Figure 2–59).

Q&A Did I need to browse?

No. You could type the appropriate file location.

Q&A Could I change the name of the file?

You could change it. Simply replace the current file name with the one you want.

Q&A What if the file I want to export already exists?

Access will indicate that the file already exists and ask if you want to replace it. If you click the Yes button, the file you export will replace the old file. If you click the No button, you must either change the name of the export file or cancel the process.

Export - Excel Spreadsheet dialog box

location of workbook to be created

selected file format (Excel Workbook)

name of workbook to be created

Browse button

check box to include formatting and layout

click arrow if you want to change file format

check box to open destination file after export is complete

check box to only export selected records (only valid if you have selected records prior to the export operation)

OK button

Figure 2–59

3

- Click the OK button (Export - Excel Spreadsheet dialog box) to export the data (Figure 2–60).

message indicates that the export process is complete

Check box to save export steps. You can use these steps to export data in the future by clicking the Saved Exports button (External Data tab | Export group) and then selecting the steps you saved.

Close button

Figure 2–60

4

- Click the 'Save export steps' check box (Export - Excel Spreadsheet dialog box) to display the Save export steps options.

- If necessary, type **Export-Analyst-Client Query** in the Save as text box.

- Type **Export the Analyst-Client Query without formatting** in the Description text box (Figure 2–61).

5

- Click the Save Export button (Export - Excel Spreadsheet dialog box) to save the export steps.

Figure 2–61

To Export Data to Word

It is not possible to export data to the standard Word format. It is possible, however, to export the data as a rich text format (RTF) file, which Word can access. To export data from a query or table to an RTF file, you would use the following steps.

1. With the query or table to be exported selected in the Navigation Pane, click the More button (External Data tab | Export group) and then click Word on the More menu to display the Export - RTF File dialog box.

2. Select the name and location for the file to be created.

3. Click the Save button, and then click the OK button to export the data.

4. Save the export steps if you want, or simply click the Close button in the Export - RTF File dialog box to close the dialog box without saving the export steps.

Text Files

You also can export to text files. Text files contain unformatted characters, including alphanumeric characters, and some special characters, such as tabs, carriage returns, and line feeds.

In **delimited files**, each record is on a separate line, and the fields are separated by a special character, called the **delimiter**. Common delimiters are tabs, semicolons, commas, and spaces. You also can choose any other value that does not appear within the field contents. The comma-separated values (CSV) file often used in Excel is an example of a delimited file.

In **fixed-width files**, the width of any field is the same on every record. For example, if the width of the first field on the first record is 12 characters, the width of the first field on every other record also must be 12 characters.

TO EXPORT DATA TO A TEXT FILE

When exporting data to a text file, you can choose to export the data with formatting and layout. This option preserves much of the formatting and layout in tables, queries, forms, and reports. For forms and reports, this is the only option.

If you do not need to preserve the formatting, you can choose either delimited or fixed-width as the format for the exported file. The most common option, especially if formatting is not an issue, is delimited. You can choose the delimiter and also whether to include field names on the first row. In many cases, delimiting with a comma and including the field names is a good choice.

To export data from a table or query to a comma-delimited file in which the first row contains the column headings, you would use the following steps.

1. With the query or table to be exported selected in the Navigation Pane, click the Text File button (External Data tab | Export group) to display the Export - Text File dialog box.

2. Select the name and location for the file to be created.

3. If you need to preserve formatting and layout, be sure the 'Export data with formatting and layout' check box is checked. If you do not need to preserve formatting and layout, make sure the check box is not checked. Once you have made your selection, click the OK button in the Export - Text File dialog box.

4. To create a delimited file, be sure the Delimited option button is selected in the Export Text Wizard dialog box. To create a fixed-width file, be sure the Fixed Width option button is selected. Once you have made your selection, click the Next button.

5. a. If you are exporting to a delimited file, choose the delimiter that you want to separate your fields, such as a comma. Decide whether to include field names on the first row and, if so, click the Include Field Names on First Row check box. If you want to select a text qualifier, select it in the Text Qualifier list. When you have made your selections, click the Next button.

   b. If you are exporting to a fixed-width file, review the position of the vertical lines that separate your fields. If any lines are not positioned correctly, follow the directions on the screen to reposition them. When you have finished, click the Next button.

6. Click the Finish button to export the data.

7. Save the export steps if you want, or simply click the Close button in the Export - Text File dialog box to close the dialog box without saving the export steps.

Adding Criteria to a Join Query

Sometimes you will want to join tables, but you will not want to include all possible records. For example, you would like to create a report showing only those clients whose amount paid is greater than $3,000. In such cases, you will relate the tables and include fields just as you did before. You also will include criteria. To include only those clients whose amount paid is more than $3,000.00, you will include >3000 as a criterion for the Amount Paid field.

To Restrict the Records in a Join

The following steps modify the Analyst-Client Query so that the results for Camashaly Design only include those clients whose amount paid is more than $3,000.

1
- Open the Analyst-Client Query in Design view and close the Navigation Pane.
- Add the Amount Paid field to the query.
- Type >3000 as the criterion for the Amount Paid field (Figure 2–62).

Figure 2–62

2
- View the query results (Figure 2–63).

3
- Close the query.
- When asked if you want to save your changes, click the No button.

Q&A

What if I saved the changes?

The next time you used this query, you would only see clients whose amount paid is more than $3,000.

Figure 2–63

Calculations

If you have determined that a special calculation is required for a query, you then need to determine whether the calculation is an individual record calculation (for example, adding the values in two fields) or a group calculation (for example, finding the total of the values in a particular field on all the records).

Camashaly Design may want to know the total amount (amount paid and current due) from each client. This would seem to pose a problem because the Client table does not include a field for total amount. You can calculate it, however, because the total amount is equal to the amount paid plus the current due. A field that can be computed from other fields is called a **calculated field** or a **computed field**. A calculated field is an individual record calculation because each calculation only involves fields in a single record.

BTW

Expression Builder
Access includes a tool to help you create complex expressions. If you click Build on the shortcut menu (see Figure 2–64), Access displays the Expression Builder dialog box, which includes an expression box, operator buttons, and expression elements. You can type parts of the expression directly and paste operator buttons and expression elements into the box. You also can use functions in expressions.

Camashaly also may want to calculate the average amount paid for the clients of each business analyst. That is, they may want the average for the clients of business analyst 11, the average for the clients of business analyst 14, and so on. This type of calculation is called a **group calculation** because each calculation involves groups of records. In this example, the clients of business analyst 11 would form one group, the clients of business analyst 14 would be a second group, and the clients of business analyst 27 would form a third group.

The following are guidelines related to calculations in queries.

<table>
<tr>
<td>Plan
Ahead</td>
<td>

Determine whether calculations are required.
Examine the query or request to see if there are special calculations to be included. Look for words such as total, sum, compute, or calculate.

- **Determine a name for the calculated field.** If calculations are required, decide on the name for the field. Assign a name that helps identify the contents of the field. For example, if you are adding the cost of a number of items, the name Total Cost would be appropriate. The name, also called an **alias**, becomes the column name when the query is run.

- **Determine the format for the calculated field.** Determine how the calculated field should appear. If the calculation involves monetary amounts, you would use the currency format. If the calculated value contains decimals, determine how many decimal places to display.

</td>
</tr>
</table>

To Use a Calculated Field in a Query

If you have determined that you need a calculated field in a query, you enter a name, or alias, for the calculated field, a colon, and then the calculation in one of the columns in the Field row of the design grid for the query. Any fields included in the expression must be enclosed in square brackets ([ ]). For example, for the total amount, you will type Total Amount:[Amount Paid]+[Current Due] as the expression.

You can type the expression directly into the Field row. You will not be able to see the entire entry, however, because the Field row is not large enough. The preferred way is to select the column in the Field row and then use the Zoom command on its shortcut menu. When Access displays the Zoom dialog box, you can enter the expression.

You are not restricted to addition in calculations. You can use subtraction (–), multiplication (*), or division (/). You also can include parentheses in your calculations to indicate which calculations should be done first.

The following steps create a query that Camashaly Design might use to obtain financial information on its clients, including the total amount (amount paid + current due), which is a calculated field.

1

- Create a query with a field list for the Client table.

- Add the Client Number, Client Name, Amount Paid, and Current Due fields to the query.

- Right-click the Field row in the first open column in the design grid to display a shortcut menu (Figure 2–64).

Figure 2–64

2

• Click Zoom on the shortcut menu to display the Zoom dialog box.

• Type **Total Amount: [Amount Paid]+ [Current Due]** in the Zoom dialog box (Figure 2–65).

Q&A

Do I always need to put square brackets around field names?

If the field name does not contain spaces, square brackets are technically not necessary, although it is still acceptable to use the brackets. It is a good practice, however, to get in the habit of using the brackets.

Figure 2–65

3

• Click the OK button (Zoom dialog box) to enter the expression (Figure 2–66).

Figure 2–66

4

- View the query results (Figure 2–67).

🔎 **Experiment**

- Return to Design view and try other expressions. In at least one case, omit the Total Amount and the colon. In at least one case, intentionally misspell a field name. In each case, view the results to see the effect of your changes. When finished, reenter the original expression.

CL #	Client Name	Amount Paid	Current Due	Total Amour
BA53	Bavant Animal Hospital	$0.00	$7,500.00	$7,500.00
BB32	Babbage CPA Firm	$1,500.00	$500.00	$2,000.00
BC76	Buda Community Clinic	$2,500.00	$750.00	$3,250.00
CJ29	Catering by Jenna	$3,000.00	$1,000.00	$4,000.00
GA74	Grant Antiques	$5,500.00	$3,200.00	$8,700.00
GF56	Granger Foundation	$0.00	$6,500.00	$6,500.00
HC10	Hendley County Hospital	$3,100.00	$1,200.00	$4,300.00
KD21	KAL Design Studio	$6,000.00	$3,200.00	$9,200.00
KG04	Kyle Grocery Cooperative	$3,200.00	$0.00	$3,200.00
ME14	Mike's Electronic Stop	$2,500.00	$1,500.00	$4,000.00
PJ34	Patricia Jean Florist	$0.00	$5,200.00	$5,200.00
SL77	Smarter Law Associates	$3,800.00	$0.00	$3,800.00
TB17	The Bikeshop	$2,750.00	$1,200.00	$3,950.00
WE05	Walburg Energy Alternatives	$4,500.00	$1,450.00	$5,950.00
WS01	Woody Sporting Goods			$3,850.00

results are calculated by adding the amount paid and the current due

Total Amount field

Figure 2–67

Other Ways

1. Press SHIFT+F2

To Change a Caption

You can change the way items appear in the results of a query by changing their format. You also can change a query result's heading at the top of a column by changing the caption. Just as when you omitted duplicates, you will make this change by using a property sheet. In the property sheet, you can change the desired property, such as the format, the number of decimal places, or the caption. The following steps change the caption of the Amount Paid field to Paid and the caption of the Current Due field to Due. The steps also save the query with a new name.

1

- Return to Design view.

- If necessary, click Design on the Ribbon to display the Design tab.

- Click the Amount Paid field in the design grid, and then click the Property Sheet button (Query Tools Design tab | Show/Hide group) to display the properties for the Amount Paid field.

- Click the Caption box, and then type **Paid** as the caption (Figure 2–68).

Q&A

My property sheet looks different. What should I do?

If your sheet looks different, you clicked the wrong place and will have to close the property sheet and repeat this step.

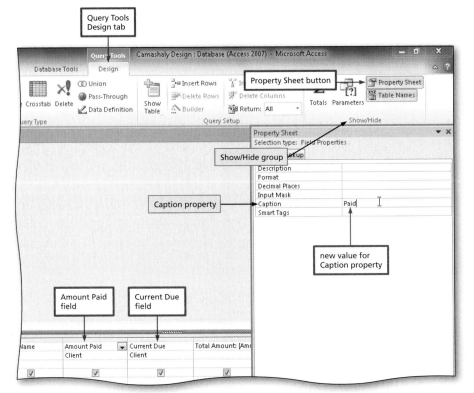

Figure 2–68

2

- Close the property sheet by clicking the Property Sheet button a second time.

- Click the Current Due field in the design grid, and then click the Property Sheet button (Query Tools Design tab | Show/Hide group).

- Click the Caption box, and then type **Due** as the caption.

- Close the Property Sheet by clicking the Property Sheet button a second time.

- View the query results (Figure 2–69).

3

- Save the query as Ch2q11.

- Close the query.

CL #	Client Name	Paid	Due	Total Amoun
BA53	Bavant Animal Hospital	$0.00	$7,500.00	$7,500.00
BB32	Babbage CPA Firm	$1,500.00	$500.00	$2,000.00
BC76	Buda Community Clinic	$2,500.00	$750.00	$3,250.00
CJ29	Catering by Jenna	$3,000.00	$1,000.00	$4,000.00
GA74	Grant Antiques	$5,500.00	$3,200.00	$8,700.00
GF56	Granger Foundation	$0.00	$6,500.00	$6,500.00
HC10	Hendley County Hospital	$3,100.00	$1,200.00	$4,300.00
KD21	KAL Design Studio	$6,000.00	$3,200.00	$9,200.00
KG04	Kyle Grocery Cooperative	$3,200.00	$0.00	$3,200.00
ME14	Mike's Electronic Stop	$2,500.00	$1,500.00	$4,000.00
PJ34	Patricia Jean Florist	$0.00	$5,200.00	$5,200.00
SL77	Smarter Law Associates	$3,800.00	$0.00	$3,800.00
TB17	The Bikeshop	$2,750.00	$1,200.00	$3,950.00
WE05	Walburg Energy Alternatives	$4,500.00	$1,450.00	$5,950.00
WS01	Woody Sporting Goods	$2,250.00	$1,600.00	$3,850.00

captions changed

Figure 2–69

Other Ways

1. Right-click field in design grid, click Properties on shortcut menu

To Calculate Statistics

For group calculations, Microsoft Access supports several built-in statistics: COUNT (count of the number of records), SUM (total), AVG (average), MAX (largest value), MIN (smallest value), STDEV (standard deviation), VAR (variance), FIRST (first value), and LAST (last value). These statistics are called aggregate functions. An **aggregate function** is a function that performs some mathematical function against a group of records. To use any of these aggregate functions in a query, you include it in the Total row in the design grid. The Total row usually does not appear in the grid. To include it, click the Totals button on the Design tab.

The following steps create a new query for the Client table. The steps include the Total row in the design grid, and then calculate the average amount paid for all clients.

1

- Create a new query with a field list for the Client table.

- Click the Totals button (Query Tools Design tab | Show/Hide group) to include the Total row in the design grid.

- Add the Amount Paid field to the query (Figure 2–70).

Figure 2–70

2

- Click the Total row in the Amount Paid column to display the Total box arrow.

- Click the Total box arrow to display the Total list (Figure 2–71).

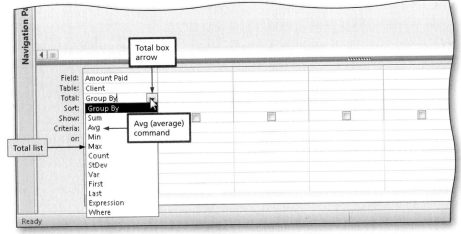

Figure 2–71

3

- Click Avg to select the calculation that Access is to perform (Figure 2–72).

Figure 2–72

4

- View the query results (Figure 2–73).

   Experiment

- Return to Design view and try other aggregate functions. In each case, view the results to see the effect of your selection. When finished, select Avg once again.

Figure 2–73

To Use Criteria in Calculating Statistics

Sometimes calculating statistics for all the records in the table is appropriate. In other cases, however, you will need to calculate the statistics for only those records that satisfy certain criteria. To enter a criterion in a field, first you select Where as the entry in the Total row for the field, and then enter the criterion in the Criteria row. The following steps use this technique to calculate the average amount paid for clients of business analyst 11. The steps also save the query with a new name.

1
- Return to Design view.
- Include the Business Analyst Number field in the design grid.
- Click the Total box arrow in the Business Analyst Number column to produce a Total list (Figure 2–74).

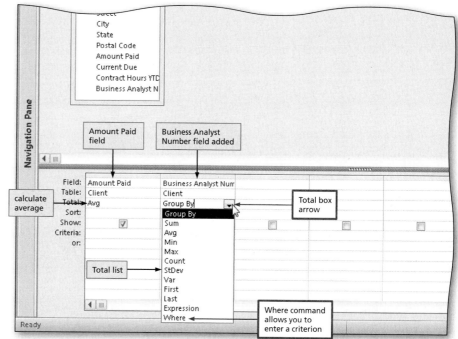

Figure 2–74

2
- Click Where.
- Type 11 as the criterion for the Business Analyst Number field (Figure 2–75).

Figure 2–75

3

- View the query results (Figure 2–76).

4

- Save the query as Ch2q12.

Figure 2–76

To Use Grouping

Another way statistics often are used is in combination with grouping; that is, statistics are calculated for groups of records. You may, for example, need to calculate the average amount paid for the clients of each business analyst. You will want the average for the clients of business analyst 11, the average for clients of business analyst 14, and so on.

Grouping means creating groups of records that share some common characteristic. In grouping by Business Analyst Number, for example, the clients of business analyst 11 would form one group, the clients of business analyst 14 would form a second, and the clients of business analyst 27 would form a third group. The calculations then are made for each group. To indicate grouping in Access, select Group By as the entry in the Total row for the field to be used for grouping.

The following steps create a query that calculates the average amount paid for clients of each business analyst at Camashaly Design. The steps also save the query with a new name.

1

- Return to Design view and clear the design grid.

- Include the Business Analyst Number field in the query.

- Include the Amount Paid field in the query.

- Select Avg as the calculation in the Total row for the Amount Paid field (Figure 2–77).

Q&A | Why didn't I need to change the entry in the Total row for the Business Analyst Number field?

Group By, which is the initial entry in the Total row when you add a field, is correct. Thus, you didn't need to change the entry.

Figure 2–77

②
- View the query results (Figure 2–78).

③
- Save the query as Ch2q13.

- Close the query.

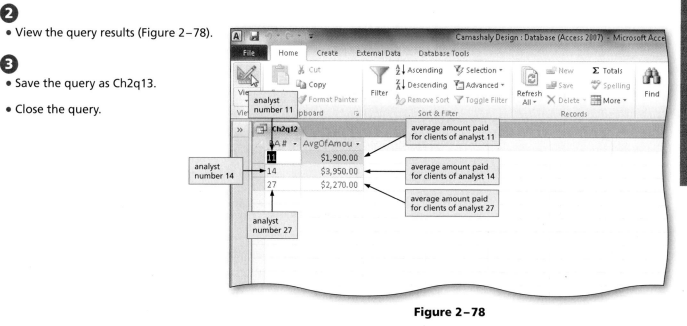

Figure 2–78

Crosstab Queries

A crosstab query calculates a statistic (for example, sum, average, or count) for data that is grouped by two different types of information. One of the types will appear down the side of the resulting datasheet, and the other will appear across the top. Crosstab queries are useful for summarizing data by category or group.

For example, if you have determined that a query must summarize the sum of the amounts paid grouped by both city and business analyst number, you could have cities as the row headings, that is, down the side. You could have business analyst numbers as the column headings, that is, across the top. The entries within the datasheet represent the total of the amounts paid. Figure 2–79 shows a crosstab in which the total of amount paid is grouped by both city and business analyst number with cities down the left side and business analyst numbers across the top. For example, the entry in the row labeled Georgetown and in the column labeled 14 represents the total of the amount paid by all clients of business analyst 14 who are located in Georgetown.

BTW

Certification
The Microsoft Office Specialist (MOS) program provides an opportunity for you to obtain a valuable industry credential — proof that you have the Access 2010 skills required by employers. For more information, visit the Access 2010 Certification Web page (scsite.com/ac2010/cert).

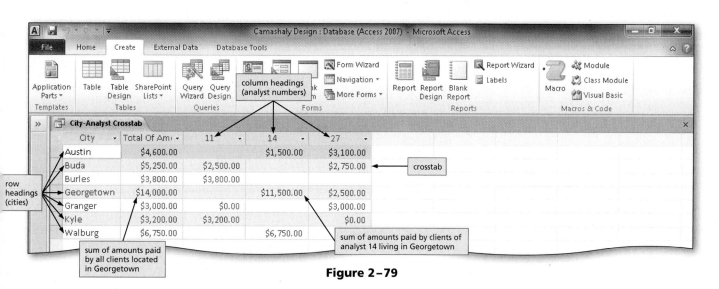

Figure 2–79

To Create a Crosstab Query

The following steps use the Crosstab Query Wizard to create a crosstab query for Camashaly Design that summarizes financial information by city and business analyst.

1

- Click Create on the Ribbon to display the Create tab.

- Click the Query Wizard button (Create tab | Queries group) to display the New Query dialog box (Figure 2–80).

Figure 2–80

2

- Click Crosstab Query Wizard (New Query dialog box).

- Click the OK button to display the Crosstab Query Wizard dialog box (Figure 2–81).

Figure 2–81

3

• With the Tables option button selected, click Table: Client to select the Client table, and then click the Next button to display the next Crosstab Query Wizard screen.

• Click the City field, and then click the Add Field button to select the City field for row headings (Figure 2–82).

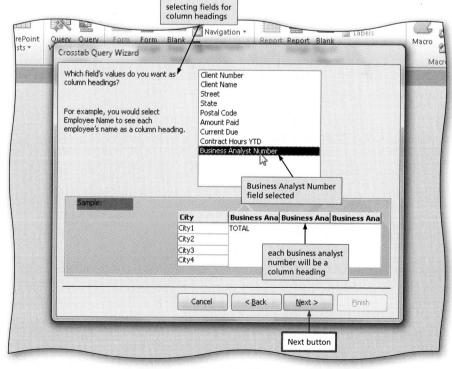

Figure 2–82

4

• Click the Next button to display the next Crosstab Query Wizard screen.

• Click the Business Analyst Number field to select the Business Analyst Number field for column headings (Figure 2–83).

Figure 2–83

5

- Click the Next button to display the next Crosstab Query Wizard screen.

- Click the Amount Paid field to select the Amount Paid field for calculations.

Experiment

- Click other fields. For each field, examine the list of calculations that are available. When finished, click the Amount Paid field again.

- Click Sum to select Sum as the calculation to be performed (Figure 2–84).

Q&A

My list of functions is different. What did I do wrong?

Either you clicked the wrong field, or the Amount Paid field has the wrong data type. For example, if you mistakenly assigned it the Text data type, you would not see Sum in the list of available calculations.

Figure 2–84

6

- Click the Next button to display the next Crosstab Query Wizard screen.

- Type `City-Analyst Crosstab` as the name of the query (Figure 2–85).

7

- Click the Finish button to produce the crosstab shown in Figure 2–79 on Page AC 123.

- Close the query.

Q&A

If I want to view the crosstab at some future date, can I just open the query?

Yes.

Figure 2–85

To Customize the Navigation Pane

Currently, the entries in the Navigation Pane are organized by object type. That is, all the tables are together, all the queries are together, and so on. You might want to change the way the information is organized. For example, you might want to have the Navigation Pane organized by table, with all the queries, forms, and reports associated with a particular table appearing after the name of the table. You also can use the Search bar to restrict the objects that appear to only those that have a certain collection of characters in their name. For example, if you entered the letters, Cl, only those objects containing Cl somewhere within the name will be included.

The following steps change the organization of the Navigation Pane. They also use the Search bar to restrict the objects that appear.

1

- If necessary, click the Shutter Bar Open/Close Button to open the Navigation Pane.

- Click the Navigation Pane arrow to produce the Navigation Pane menu (Figure 2–86).

2

- Click Tables and Related Views to organize the Navigation Pane by table rather than by the type of object (Figure 2–87).

3

- Click the Navigation Pane arrow to produce the Navigation Pane menu.

- Click Object Type to once again organize the Navigation Pane by object type.

Figure 2–86

Figure 2–87

Experiment

- Select different Navigate To Category options to see the effect of the option. With each option you select, select different Filter By Group options to see the effect of the filtering. When you have finished experimenting, select the Object Type Navigate To Category option and the All Access Objects Filter By Group option.

4

- If the Search bar does not appear, right-click the Navigation Pane and click Search Bar on the shortcut menu.

- Click in the Search bar box to produce an insertion point.

- Type **C1** as the search string to restrict the objects displayed to only those containing the desired string (Figure 2–88).

5

- Click the Clear Search String button to remove the search string and redisplay all objects.

Q&A

Did I have to click the button to redisplay all objects? Couldn't I have simply erased the current string to achieve the same result?

You didn't have to click the button. You could have used the DELETE or BACKSPACE keys to erase the current search string.

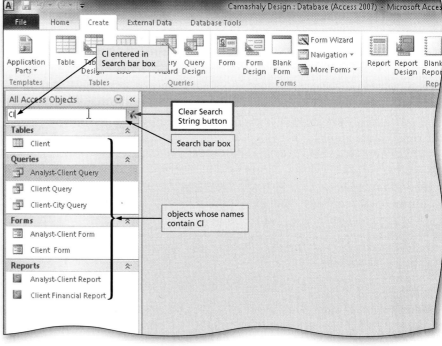

Figure 2–88

BTW

Quick Reference
For a table that lists how to complete the tasks covered in this book using the mouse, Ribbon, shortcut menu, and keyboard, see the Quick Reference Summary at the back of this book, or visit the Access 2010 Quick Reference Web page (scsite.com/ac2010/qr).

To Quit Access

The following steps quit Access.

1 Click the Close button on the right side of the title bar to quit Access.

2 If a Microsoft Access dialog box appears, click the Save button to save any changes made to the object since the last save.

Chapter Summary

In this chapter you have learned to create queries, enter fields, enter criteria, use text and numeric data in queries, use wildcards, use compound criteria, create parameter queries, sort data in queries, join tables in queries, perform calculations in queries, and create crosstab queries. You also learned to create a report and a form that used a query, to export a query, and to customize the Navigation Pane. The items listed below include all the new Access skills you have learned in this chapter.

1. Create a Query in Design View (AC 78)
2. Add Fields to the Design Grid (AC 79)
3. Use Text Data in a Criterion (AC 80)
4. Use a Wildcard (AC 83)
5. Use Criteria for a Field Not Included in the Results (AC 85)
6. Create and View a Parameter Query (AC 87)
7. Use a Parameter Query (AC 89)
8. Use a Number in a Criterion (AC 90)
9. Use a Comparison Operator in a Criterion (AC 91)

10. Use a Compound Criterion Involving AND (AC 92)
11. Use a Compound Criterion Involving OR (AC 93)
12. Clear the Design Grid (AC 95)
13. Sort Data in a Query (AC 96)
14. Omit Duplicates (AC 97)
15. Sort on Multiple Keys (AC 98)
16. Create a Top-Values Query (AC 99)
17. Join Tables (AC 102)
18. Change Join Properties (AC 105)
19. Create a Report Involving a Join (AC 106)

SAM

If you have a SAM 2010 user profile, your instructor may have assigned an autogradable version of this assignment. If so, log into the SAM 2010 Web site at www.cengage.com/sam2010 to download the instruction and start files.

Learn It Online

Test your knowledge of chapter content and key terms.

Instructions: To complete the Learn It Online exercises, start your browser, click the Address bar, and then enter the Web address `scsite.com/ac2010/learn`. When the Access 2010 Learn It Online page is displayed, click the link for the exercise you want to complete and then read the instructions.

Chapter Reinforcement TF, MC, and SA
A series of true/false, multiple choice, and short answer questions that test your knowledge of the chapter content.

Flash Cards
An interactive learning environment where you identify chapter key terms associated with displayed definitions.

Practice Test
A series of multiple choice questions that test your knowledge of chapter content and key terms.

Who Wants To Be a Computer Genius?
An interactive game that challenges your knowledge of chapter content in the style of a television quiz show.

Wheel of Terms
An interactive game that challenges your knowledge of chapter key terms in the style of the television show *Wheel of Fortune*.

Crossword Puzzle Challenge
A crossword puzzle that challenges your knowledge of key terms presented in the chapter.

Apply Your Knowledge

Reinforce the skills and apply the concepts you learned in this chapter.

Using Wildcards in a Query, Creating a Parameter Query, Joining Tables, and Creating a Report

Instructions: Start Access. Open the Babbage CPA Firm database that you modified in Apply Your Knowledge in Chapter 1 on page AC 64. (If you did not complete this exercise, see your instructor for a copy of the modified database.)

Perform the following tasks:
1. Create a query for the Client table and add the Client Number, Client Name, City, and Amount Paid fields to the design grid. Find all clients who live in cities that start with Bu. Save the query as Apply 2 Step 1 Query.

Continued >

Apply Your Knowledge *continued*

2. Create a query for the Client table and add the Client Number, Client Name, Bookkeeper Number, and Balance Due fields to the design grid. Sort the records in descending order by Balance Due. Add a criterion for the Bookkeeper Number field that allows the user to enter a different bookkeeper each time the query is run. Save the query as Apply 2 Step 2 Query.

3. Create a query that joins the Bookkeeper and the Client tables. Add the Bookkeeper Number, First Name, and Last Name fields from the Bookkeeper table and the Client Number and Client Name fields from the Client table. Sort the records in ascending order by Bookkeeper Number and Client Number. All bookkeepers should appear in the result, even if they currently have no clients. Save the query as Bookkeeper-Client Query.

4. Create the report shown in Figure 2–89. The report uses the Bookkeeper-Client Query.

Bookkeeper-Client Report

BKR #	First Name	Last Name	CL #	Client Name
22	Johanna	Lewes	A54	Afton Mills
22	Johanna	Lewes	D76	Dege Grocery
22	Johanna	Lewes	J77	Jones Plumbing
22	Johanna	Lewes	S56	SeeSaw Industries
24	Mario	Rodriguez	A62	Atlas Suppliers
24	Mario	Rodriguez	B26	Blake-Scripps
24	Mario	Rodriguez	G56	Grand Cleaners
24	Mario	Rodriguez	M26	Mohr Crafts
34	Choi	Wong	C29	Catering by Jenna
34	Choi	Wong	H21	Hill Shoes
34	Choi	Wong	T45	Tate Repair
34	Choi	Wong	W24	Woody Sporting Goods
38	Theresa	Sinthin		

Figure 2–89

5. Submit the revised database in the format specified by your instructor.

Extend Your Knowledge

Extend the skills you learned in this chapter and experiment with new skills. You may need to use Help to complete the assignment.

Creating Crosstab Queries, Creating Queries Using Criteria, and Exporting a Query

Instructions: Start Access. Open the Natural Earthscapes database. See the inside back cover of this book for instructions for downloading the Data Files for Students, or see your instructor for information on accessing the files required in this book.

Natural Earthscapes is a small landscaping company that specializes in landscaping with native plants. The owners have created an Access database in which to store information about the customers they serve and the workers they employ. You will create the crosstab shown in Figure 2–90. You also will query the database using specified criteria.

Figure 2–90

Perform the following tasks:

1. Create the crosstab query shown in Figure 2–90. The crosstab query groups the total of customers' balances by city and worker number.
2. Create a query to find all customers who do not live in Kingston. Include the Customer Number, Last Name, Balance, and Amount Paid fields in the design grid. Save the query as Extend 2 Step 2 Query.
3. Create a query to find all customers where the customer's first name is either Frances or Francis. Include the Customer Number, Last Name, First Name, Street, and City fields in the query results. Save the query as Extend 2 Step 3 Query.
4. Create a query to find all customers where the worker number is 303 or 305 and the balance is greater than $40.00. Include the Customer Number, Last Name, First Name, Balance, and Worker Number fields in the design grid. Use the IN operator in your query design. Save the query as Extend 2 Step 4 Query.
5. Export the City-Worker Crosstab as a Word file with the name City-Worker Crosstab.rtf and save the export steps.
6. Open the Customer table and change the balance for AB10 to $90.
7. Use the saved export steps to export the City-Worker Crosstab again. When asked if you want to replace the existing file, click Yes.
8. Change the database properties, as specified by your instructor. Submit the revised database and the exported RTF file in the format specified by your instructor.

Make It Right

Analyze a database and correct all errors and/or improve the design.

Correcting Errors in the Query Design

Instructions: Start Access. Open the Retired Pet Sitters database. See the inside back cover of this book for instructions for downloading the Data Files for Students, or see your instructor for information on accessing the files required in this book.

Continued >

Make It Right *continued*

Retired Pet Sitters is a database maintained by a small pet-sitting business. The queries shown in Figure 2–91 contain a number of errors that need to be corrected before the queries run properly. The query shown in Figure 2–91a displays the query results in the proper order (Last Name, First Name, Balance, Sitter Number), but it is sorted incorrectly. The query results should be sorted by last name within sitter number in ascending order. Also, the caption for the Balance field should be Owed. Save the query with your changes.

When you try to run the query shown in Figure 2–91b, you get 0 results. You are trying to find all customers who live on Magee. Correct the error and save the query with your changes.

Last Name	First Name	Balance	Sitter Numb
Alvarez	Frances	$45.00	103
Breaton	Alex	$80.00	105
Ferdon	Jean	$0.00	107
Gammort	Frank	$70.00	105
Heijer	Bill	$29.00	103
Klinger	Cynthia	$60.00	103
Manston	Lisa	$0.00	107
Prestz	Martin	$95.00	105
Santoro	Maria	$0.00	107
Trent	Gerry	$40.00	105

Figure 2–91 (a) Incorrect Sort Query

Field:	Customer Numb	First Name	Last Name	Street	City		
Table:	Customer	Customer	Customer	Customer	Customer		
Sort:							
Show:	✓	✓	✓	✓	✓	☐	☐
Criteria:				"Magee"			
or:							

Figure 2–91 (b) Incorrect Criteria Query

Change the database properties, as specified by your instructor. Submit the revised database in the format specified by your instructor.

In the Lab

Design, create, modify, and/or use a database following the guidelines, concepts, and skills presented in this chapter. The assignments are listed in order of increasing difficulty.

Lab 1: Querying the ECO Clothesline Database

Problem: The management of ECO Clothesline has determined a number of questions it wants the database management system to answer. You must obtain answers to the questions posed by management.

Instructions: Use the database modified in the In the Lab 1 of Chapter 1 on page AC 66 for this assignment, or see your instructor for information on accessing the files required for this book.

Perform the following tasks:

1. Open the ECO Clothesline database and create a new query for the Customer table that includes the Customer Number, Customer Name, Amount Paid, and Sales Rep Number fields in the design grid for all customers where the sales rep number is 49. Save the query as Lab 2-1 Step 1 Query.

2. Create a query that includes the Customer Number, Customer Name, and Amount Paid fields for all customers located in Virginia (VA) with a paid amount greater than $1,000.00. Save the query as Lab 2-1 Step 2 Query.

3. Create a query that includes the Customer Number, Customer Name, Street, and City fields for all customers whose names begin with T. Save the query as Lab 2-1 Step 3 Query.

4. Create a query that lists all cities in ascending order. Each city should appear only once. Save the query as Lab 2-1 Step 4 Query.

5. Create a query that allows the user to enter the city to search when the query is run. The query results should display the Customer Number, Customer Name, Balance, and Amount Paid fields. Test the query by searching for those records where the client is located in Ashton. Save the query as Lab 2-1 Step 5 Query.

6. Include the Customer Number, Customer Name, and Balance fields in the design grid. Sort the records in descending order by the Balance field. Display only the top 25 percent of the records in the query result. Save the query as Lab 2-1 Step 6 Query.

7. Join the Sales Rep and the Customer table. Include the Sales Rep Number, First Name, and Last Name fields from the Sales Rep table. Include the Customer Number, Customer Name, and Balance from the Customer table. Sort the records in ascending order by sales rep's last name and customer name. All sales reps should appear in the result even if they currently have no customers. Save the query as Lab 2-1 Step 7 Query.

8. Open the Lab 2-1 Step 7 Query in Design view and remove the Sales Rep table. Add the Amount Paid field to the design grid. Calculate the total of the balance and amount paid amounts. Assign the alias Total Amount to the calculated field. Change the caption for the Balance field to Due. Save the query as Lab 2-1 Step 8 Query.

9. Create a query to display the average balance amount for all customers. Save the query as Lab 2-1 Step 9 Query.

10. Create a query to display the average balance amount for sales rep 51. Save the query as Lab 2-1 Step 10 Query.

11. Create a query to display the average balance amount for each sales rep. Save the query as Lab 2-1 Step 11 Query.

12. Create the crosstab shown in Figure 2–92. The crosstab groups the total of customers' amount paid amounts by state and sales rep number. Save the crosstab as State-Sales Rep Crosstab.

13. Submit the revised database in the format specified by your instructor.

State	Total Of Am	44	49	51
NC	$2,235.00	$1,400.00	$710.00	$125.00
TN	$6,245.00	$1,695.00	$2,600.00	$1,950.00
VA	$5,180.00	$2,425.00	$700.00	$2,055.00

Figure 2–92

In the Lab

Lab 2: Querying the Walburg Energy Alternatives Database

Problem: The manager of the Walburg Energy Alternatives store has determined a number of questions he wants the database management system to answer. You must obtain answers to the questions posed by the manager.

Instructions: Use the database created in the In the Lab 2 of Chapter 1 on page AC 67 for this assignment, or see your instructor for information on accessing the files required for this book.

Perform the following tasks:

1. Open the Walburg Energy Alternatives database and create a query that includes all fields and all records in the Item table. There should be only one column in the design grid. Name the query Lab 2-2 Step 1 Query.

2. Create a query that includes the Item Number, Description, Cost, and Vendor Code fields for all items where the vendor code is JM. Save the query as Lab 2-2 Step 2 Query.

3. Create a query that includes the Item Number and Description fields for all items where the description starts with the letters, En. Save the query as Lab 2-2 Step 3 Query.

4. Create a query that includes the Item Number and Description fields for all items with a cost less than $4.00. Save the query as Lab 2-2 Step 4 Query.

5. Create a query that includes the Item Number and Description fields for all items with a selling price greater than $20.00. Save the query as Lab 2-2 Step 5 Query.

6. Create a query that includes all fields for all items with a vendor code of AS and where the number on hand is fewer than 10. Save the query as Lab 2-2 Step 6 Query.

7. Create a query that includes all fields for all items that have a selling price greater than $10.00 or a vendor code of JM. Save the query as Lab 2-2 Step 7 Query.

8. Join the Vendor table and the Item table. Include the Vendor Code and Vendor Name fields from the Vendor table and the Item Number, Description, On Hand, and Cost fields from the Item table. Sort the records in ascending order by item number within vendor code. Save the query as Vendor-Item Query.

9. Create the form shown in Figure 2–93. The form uses the Vendor-Item Query.

Figure 2–93

10. Create a query that includes the Item Number, Description, On Hand, and Cost fields. Calculate the inventory value (on hand*cost) for all records in the table. Assign the alias Inventory Value to the calculated field. Change the caption for the On Hand column to In Stock. Format the Inventory Value field as currency with two decimal places. Sort the records in descending order by inventory value. Save the query as Lab 2-2 Step 10 Query.

11. Create a query that calculates and displays the average cost of all items. Save the query as Lab 2-2 Step 11 Query.

12. Create a query that calculates and displays the average cost of items grouped by vendor code. Save the query as Lab 2-2 Step 12 Query.

13. Submit the revised database in the format specified by your instructor.

In the Lab

Lab 3: Querying the Philamar Training Database

Problem: The management of Philamar Training has determined a number of questions it wants the database management system to answer. You must obtain answers to the questions posed by management.

Instructions: Use the database created in the In the Lab 3 of Chapter 1 on page AC 70 for this assignment, or see your instructor for information on accessing the files required for this book. For Part 1 and Part 3, save each query using a format similar to the following: Lab 2-3 Part 1a Query, Lab 2-3 Part 3a Query, and so on. Submit the revised database and the Trainer-Client Query.xlsx file in the format specified by your instructor.

Instructions Part 1: Create a new query for the Client table and include the Client Number, Client Name, Amount Paid, and Current Due fields in the design grid. Create queries that answer the following questions: (a) Which clients' names begin with F? (b) Which clients are located in Kingston? (c) Which clients have a current due amount of $0.00? (d) Which clients have an amount paid amount between $5,000.00 and $10,000.00? (e) Which two clients have the highest current due amounts? (f) For each client, what is the total of the current due and amount paid?

Instructions Part 2: Join the Trainer and the Client table. In the design grid, include the Trainer Number, First Name, and Last Name from the Trainer table and the Client Number, Client Name, and Amount Paid from the Client table. Sort the records in ascending order by trainer number and client number. All trainers should appear in the result, even if they currently have no clients. Save the query as Trainer-Client Query. Export the query to Excel and save the export steps.

Instructions Part 3: Create queries to calculate the following statistics: (a) What is the average current due amount for clients assigned to trainer 42? (b) What is the total current due amount for all clients? (c) What is the total amount paid for each trainer?

Cases and Places

Apply your creative thinking and problem solving skills to design and implement a solution.

Note: To complete these assignments, you may be required to use the Data Files for Students. See the inside back cover of this book for instructions on downloading the Data Files for Students, or contact your instructor for information about accessing the required files.

1: Querying the Chamber of Commerce Database

Academic

Use the Chamber of Commerce database you created in Cases and Places 1 in Chapter 1 on page AC 72 for this assignment. Use the concepts and techniques presented in this chapter to create queries for the following:

a. Find the advertiser name and address of all advertisers located on Main.

Continued >

Cases and Places *continued*

b. Find the advertiser number, advertiser name, balance, and amount paid for all advertisers whose balance is greater than $300 or whose amount paid is $0.00.

c. Find the total of the balance and amount paid amounts for each advertiser. Show the advertiser number, advertiser name, and total amount. Sort the results in descending order by total.

d. Find the advertiser number, advertiser name, balance, and amount paid for all advertisers whose balance is between $200 and $500.

e. Create a parameter query for the Advertiser table that will allow the user to enter a different postal code each time the query is run. The user should see all fields in the query result.

f. Find the ad rep for each advertiser. List the ad rep number, last name, first name, advertiser number, advertiser name, and balance. Sort the results in ascending order by ad rep number and advertiser number.

g. Determine the total of the balance amounts and amount paid amounts for all advertisers.

Submit the revised database in the format specified by your instructor.

2: Querying the Consignment Database

Personal

Use the Consignment database you created in Cases and Places 2 in Chapter 1 on page AC 72 for this assignment. Use the concepts and techniques presented in this chapter to create queries for the following:

a. Find the item number and description of all items that contain the word, Table.

b. Find the item number, description, condition, and date of the item that has the earliest posting date.

c. Find the total price (price*quantity) of each item available for sale. Show the item number, item description, and total price.

d. Find the seller of each item. Show the seller's first name and last name as well as the item description, price, quantity, and date posted. Sort the results by item description within seller last name.

e. Create a report based on the query you created in Step d. Include all fields in the report.

f. Modify the query you created in Step d to restrict retrieval to those items with a price greater than $50.00.

g. Find all items posted between March 1, 2012, and March 4, 2012. The user should see all fields in the query result.

Submit the revised database in the format specified by your instructor.

3: Querying the Senior Care Database

Professional

Use the Senior Care database you created in Cases and Places 3 in Chapter 1 on page AC 72 for this assignment. Use the concepts and techniques presented in this chapter to create queries for the following:

a. Find the first name, last name, and address of all clients where the street name begins with the letter U.

b. Find the client number, last name, first name, balance, and amount paid for all clients whose balance is $0.00 or whose amount paid is $0.00.

c. Find the total of the balance and amount paid amounts for each client. Show the client number, client last name, client first name, and total amount. Sort the results in descending order by total.

d. Find the helper for each client. List the helper number, helper last name, helper first name, client number, client last name, and client first name. Sort the results in ascending order by helper number and client number.

e. Create a report for the query created in Step d. Include all fields except the helper first name in the report. Create a form for the query created in Step d.

f. Export the query created in Step d as a text file.

g. Find the highest and lowest balances.

Submit the exported text file and revised database in the format specified by your instructor.

3 Maintaining a Database

Objectives

You will have mastered the material in this chapter when you can:

- Add, change, and delete records
- Search for records
- Filter records
- Update a table design
- Use action queries to update records
- Use delete queries to delete records
- Specify validation rules, default values, and formats

- Create and use single-valued lookup fields
- Create and use multivalued lookup fields
- Add new fields to an existing report
- Format a datasheet
- Specify referential integrity
- Use a subdatasheet
- Sort records

3 | Maintaining a Database

Introduction

Once a database has been created and loaded with data, it must be maintained. **Maintaining the database** means modifying the data to keep it up to date by adding new records, changing the data for existing records, and deleting records. Updating can include mass updates or mass deletions, that is, updates to, or deletions of, many records at the same time.

Maintenance of a database also can involve the need to **restructure the database** periodically, that is, to change the database structure. Restructuring can include adding new fields to a table, changing the characteristics of existing fields, and removing existing fields. Restructuring also includes the creation of validation rules and referential integrity. Validation rules ensure the validity of the data in the database, whereas referential integrity ensures the validity of the relationships. Maintaining a database also can include filtering records, a process that ensures that only the records that satisfy some criterion appear when viewing and updating the data in a table. Changing the appearance of a datasheet is a maintenance activity.

BTW

Database Backup
If you are doing mass changes to a database, be sure to back up the database prior to doing the updates.

Project — Maintaining a Database

Camashaly Design faces the task of keeping its database up to date. As the company takes on new clients and business analysts, it will need to add new records, make changes to existing records, and delete records. Camashaly believes that it can serve its clients better by changing the structure of the database to categorize the clients by type. The company will do this by adding a Client Type field to the Client table. Business analysts believe they can maintain better client relationships if the database includes the services that are of interest to clients. The company will do so by adding a Services Needed field to the Client table. Because clients may need more than one service, this field will be a multivalued field, which is a field that can store multiple values or entries. Along with these changes, Camashaly staff wants to change the appearance of a datasheet when displaying data.

Camashaly would like the ability to make mass updates, that is, to update or delete many records in a single operation. It wants rules that make sure users can enter only valid, or appropriate, data into the database. Camashaly also wants to ensure that the database cannot contain the name of a client who is not associated with a specific business analyst. A final goal for Camashaly is to improve the efficiency of certain types of processing, specifically, sorting and retrieving data.

BTW

The Ribbon and Screen Resolution
Access may change how the groups and buttons within the groups appear on the Ribbon, depending on the computer's screen resolution. Thus, your Ribbon may look different from the ones in this book if you are using a screen resolution other than 1024 × 768.

Figure 3–1 summarizes some of the various types of activities involved in maintaining the Camashaly Design database.

Figure 3–1

Overview

As you read through this chapter, you will learn how to maintain a database by performing these general tasks:

- Add, change, and delete records.
- Filter records so that only those records that satisfy some criterion appear in a datasheet or form.
- Change the structure of a table.
- Make mass changes to a table.
- Create validation rules to ensure that the database contains only valid data.
- Use single-valued and multivalued lookup fields.
- Update forms and reports to reflect changes to the table structure.
- Change the appearance of a datasheet.
- Enforce relationships by creating referential integrity.
- Order records.

Plan
Ahead

Database Maintenance Decisions

When maintaining a database in Access, you must consider how the database is being used and how it could be improved. The decisions you make will affect the modification of records, fields, default settings, formatting, and table relationships. To maintain a database, you should follow these general guidelines:

1. **Determine when it is necessary to add, change, or delete records in a database.** Decide how often updates are necessary. You might need to update the database on a regular schedule, or only as needed, depending on your needs. Also determine whether to make the updates to individual records or whether mass updates would be more efficient.

2. **Determine whether you should filter records.** For each situation where a user will be working with a table in the database, examine whether it might be desirable to have the records filtered, that is, to have only those records that satisfy some criterion appear.

3. **Determine whether additional fields are necessary or whether existing fields should be deleted.** Have there been any changes to the initial requirements that would require the addition of a field (or fields) to one of the tables? If so, you will need to add the field to the appropriate table. Also, now that the database has been in operation for a period of time, determine whether all the fields actually are being used. If some fields are not in use, verify that they are, in fact, no longer needed. If so, you can delete the field from the table.

4. **Determine whether validation rules, default values, and formats are necessary.** Can you improve the accuracy of the data entry process by enforcing data validation? What values are allowed for a particular field? For example, client name data should not be allowed in a city field. Are there some fields in which one particular value is used more than another? You can control the values that are entered in a field by modifying the table design to include default values, formats, and validation rules.

5. **Determine whether changes to the format of a datasheet are desirable.** Do you want to modify the appearance of the Datasheet view of your tables? It is a good idea to be consistent throughout all your tables except in special circumstances.

6. **Identify related tables in order to implement relationships between the tables.** Examine the database design you created earlier to identify related tables. Is there a one-to-many relationship between the tables? If so, which table is the one table? Which table is the many table? For each pair of related tables, you will need to make decisions about the implementation of the relationship between the tables.

When necessary, more specific details concerning the above decisions and/or actions are presented at appropriate points in the chapter. The chapter also will identify the use of these guidelines in database maintenance tasks such as those shown in Figure 3–1.

To Start Access

For an introduction to Windows 7 and instruction about how to perform basic Windows 7 tasks, read the Office 2010 and Windows 7 chapter at the beginning of this book, where you can learn how to resize windows, change screen resolution, create folders, move and rename files, use Windows Help, and much more.

The following steps, which assume Windows 7 is running, start Access based on a typical installation. You may need to ask your instructor how to start Access for your computer. For a detailed example of the procedure summarized below, refer to the Office 2010 and Windows 7 chapter at the beginning of this book.

1 Click the Start button on the Windows 7 taskbar to display the Start menu.

2 Type `Microsoft Access` as the search text in the 'Search programs and files' text box and watch the search results appear on the Start menu.

3 Click Microsoft Access 2010 in the search results on the Start menu to start Access.

4 If the Access window is not maximized, click the Maximize button next to the Close button on its title bar to maximize the window.

To Open a Database from Access

In Chapter 1, you created and saved your database on a USB flash drive using the file name, Camashaly Design. The following steps open the Camashaly Design database from the Access folder in the CIS 101 folder on the USB flash drive. For a detailed example of the procedure summarized below, refer to the Office 2010 and Windows 7 chapter at the beginning of this book.

1 With your USB flash drive connected to one of the computer's USB ports, click File on the Ribbon to open the Backstage view.

2 Click Open in the Backstage view to display the Open dialog box.

3 Navigate to the location of the file to be opened (in this case, the USB flash drive, then to the CIS 101 folder [or your class folder], and then to the Access folder).

4 Click Camashaly Design to select the file to be opened.

5 Click the Open button (Open dialog box) to open the selected file and display the opened database in the Access window.

6 If a Security Warning appears, click the Enable Content option button.

For an introduction to Office 2010 and instruction about how to perform basic tasks in Office 2010 programs, read the Office 2010 and Windows 7 chapter at the beginning of this book, where you can learn how to start a program, use the Ribbon, save a file, open a file, quit a program, use Help, and much more.

Updating Records

Keeping the data in a database up to date requires updating records in three ways: adding new records, changing the data in existing records, and deleting existing records.

Adding Records

In Chapter 1, you added records to a database using Datasheet view; that is, as you added records, the records appeared on the screen in a datasheet. The data looked like a table. When you need to add additional records, you can use the same techniques.

In Chapter 1, you used a simple form to view records. You also can use a **split form**, a form that allows you to simultaneously view both simple form and datasheet views of the data. You can use either portion of a split form to add or update records. To add new records, change existing records, or delete records, you use the same techniques you used in Datasheet view.

BTW

Q&As
For a complete list of the Q&As found in many of the step-by-step sequences in this book, visit the Access 2010 Q&A Web page (scsite.com/ac2010/qa).

To Create a Split Form

The following steps create a split form.

1

- Open the Navigation Pane if it is currently closed.

- If necessary, click the Client table in the Navigation Pane to select it.

- Click Create on the Ribbon to display the Create tab.

- Click the More Forms button (Create tab | Forms group) to display the More Forms menu (Figure 3–2).

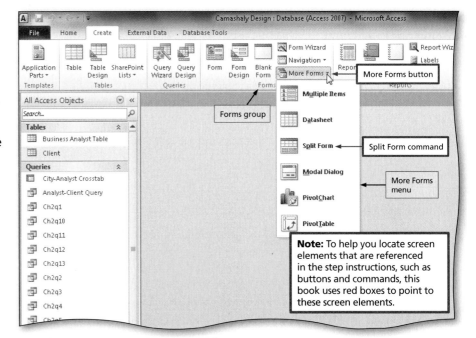

Figure 3–2

2

- Click Split Form to create a split form.

- Close the Navigation Pane (Figure 3–3).

Q&A Is the form automatically saved the way the report was created when I used the Report Wizard?

No. You will need to take specific actions if you want to save the form.

Figure 3–3

❸

- If the form appears in Layout view, click the Form View button on the Access Status bar to display the form in Form view (Figure 3–4).

🔍 **Experiment**

- Click the various Navigation buttons (First record, Next record, Previous record, Last record, and New (blank) record) to see each button's effect. Click the Current Record box, change the record number, and press the ENTER key to see how to move to a specific record.

Figure 3–4

❹

- Click the Save button on the Quick Access Toolbar to display the Save As dialog box.

- Type **Client Split Form** as the form name (Figure 3–5).

❺

- Click the OK button (Save As dialog box) to save the form.

Figure 3–5

To Use a Form to Add Records

Once a form or split form is open in Form view, you can add records using the same techniques you used to add records in Datasheet view. The changes you make on the form are automatically made on the datasheet. You do not need to take any special action. The following steps use the split form that you just created to add records.

1

- Click the 'New (blank) record' button on the Navigation bar to enter a new record, and then type the data for the new record, as shown in Figure 3–6. Press the TAB key after typing the data in each field, except after typing the data for the final field (Business Analyst Number).

Figure 3–6

2

- Press the TAB key to complete the entry of the record.

- Close the form.

Other Ways

1. Click New button (Home tab | Records group)
2. Press CTRL+PLUS SIGN (+)

To Search for a Record

In the database environment, **searching** means looking for records that satisfy some criteria. Looking for the client whose number is GF56 is an example of searching. The queries in Chapter 2 also were examples of searching. Access had to locate those records that satisfied the criteria.

However, you can perform a search in Form view or Datasheet view without creating a query. To update client GF56, for example, first you need to find the client.

The following steps show how to search for the client whose number is GF56.

1

• Open the Navigation Pane.

• Scroll down in the Navigation Pane, if necessary, so that Client Split Form appears on your screen, right-click Client Split Form to display a shortcut menu, and then click Open on the shortcut menu to open the form in Form view.

Q&A Which command on the shortcut menu gives me Form view? I see both Layout View and Design View, but no option for Form View.

The Open command opens the form in Form view.

• Close the Navigation Pane (Figure 3–7).

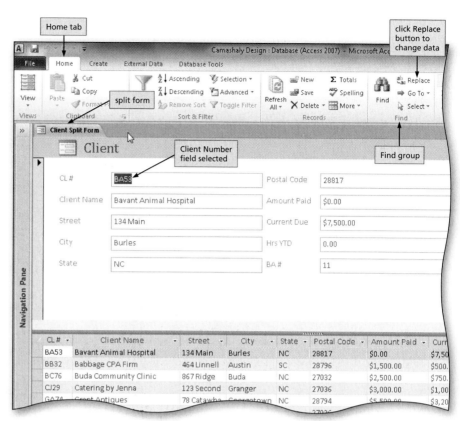

Figure 3–7

2

• Click the Find button (Home tab | Find group) to display the Find and Replace dialog box.

• Type **GF56** in the Find What text box (Find and Replace dialog box).

• Click the Find Next button to find client GF56 (Figure 3–8).

Q&A Can I find records in Datasheet view or in Form view?

Yes. You use the same process to find records whether you are viewing the data with a split form, in Datasheet view, or in Form view.

Experiment

• Find records using other client numbers. Try to find a record using a client number that does not exist. Click in a different field and try to find records based on the value in that field. Try to use wildcards just as you did in queries. When done, once again locate client GF56.

Figure 3–8

❸

- Click the Cancel button (Find and Replace dialog box) to remove the dialog box from the screen.

Q&A Why does the button in the dialog box read, Find Next, rather than simply Find?

In some cases, after locating a record that satisfies a criterion, you might need to find the next record that satisfies the same criterion. For example, if you just found the first client whose business analyst number is 14, you then may want to find the second such client, then the third, and so on. To do so, click the Find Next button. You will not need to retype the value each time.

Q&A Can I replace one value with another using this dialog box?

Yes. Either click the Replace button (Home tab | Find group) or click the Replace tab in the Find and Replace dialog box. You then can enter both the value to find and the new value.

BTW

BTWs
For a complete list of the BTWs found in the margins of this book, visit the Access 2010 BTW Web page (scsite.com/ac2010/btw).

Other Ways
1. Press CTRL+F

To Update the Contents of a Record

After locating the record to be changed, select the field to be changed by clicking the field. You also can press the TAB key repeatedly until the desired field is selected. Then make the appropriate changes. (Clicking the field automatically produces an insertion point. If you use the TAB key, you will need to press F2 to produce an insertion point.)

The following step uses Form view to change the name of client GF56 from Granger Foundation to Granger Family Foundation.

❶

- Click in the Client Name field in the form for client GF56 immediately to the left of the F in the word, Foundation.

- Type the word **Family** before the word, Foundation, and then press the SPACEBAR to insert a space.

- Press the TAB key to complete the change and move to the next field (Figure 3–9).

Q&A Could I have changed the contents of the field in the datasheet portion of the split form?

Yes. You will first need to ensure the record to be changed appears in the datasheet. You then can change the value just as in the form.

Q&A Do I need to save my change?

No. Once you move to another record or close this form, the change to the name will become permanent.

Figure 3–9

To Delete a Record

When records no longer are needed, delete the records (remove them) from the table. If client GA74 no longer is served by Camashaly Design and its final payment has been received, the record can be deleted. The following steps delete client GA74.

1

• With the Client Split Form open, click the record selector in the datasheet, the small box that appears to the left of the first field of the record on which the client number is GA74 to select the record (Figure 3–10).

Q&A That technique works in the datasheet portion. How do I select the record in the form portion?

With the desired record appearing in the form, click the record selector (the triangle in front of the record) to select the entire record.

Figure 3–10

2

• Press the DELETE key to delete the record (Figure 3–11).

3

• Click the Yes button to complete the deletion.

• Close the Client Split Form.

Figure 3–11

Filtering Records

You can use the Find button in either Datasheet view or Form view to locate a record quickly that satisfies some criterion (for example, the client number is GF56). All records appear, however, not just the record or records that satisfy the criterion. To have only the record or records that satisfy the criterion appear, use a **filter**. Four types of filters are available: Filter By Selection, Common Filters, Filter By Form, and Advanced Filter/Sort. You can use a filter in either Datasheet view or Form view.

BTW

**Plan
Ahead**

Filter By Selection
If you want to search a
field for a collection of
characters, select the
characters, and then click
the Selection button
arrow. For example, to
find all cities in the Client
table that contain the
characters, ge, select the
characters in the City field,
click the Selection button
arrow, then click Contains
"ge" on the Selection
button menu. Access
filters the Client table and
returns records where the
city is either Georgetown
or Granger.

Determine whether to filter records.
If you determine that it is desirable to have only those records that satisfy some criterion
appear, you have two choices: You can create a query or create a filter. The following guidelines apply to this decision.

- If you think that you will frequently want to display records that satisfy precisely this same
criterion, you should consider creating a query whose results only contain the records that
satisfy the criterion. To display those records in the future, simply open the query.

- If you are viewing data in a datasheet or form and decide you want to restrict the records
to be included, it is easier to create a filter than a query. You can create and use the filter
while you are viewing the data.

- If you have created a filter that you would like to be able to use again, you can save the
filter as a query.

Once you have decided to use a filter, you need to decide which type of filter to use.

- If your criterion for filtering is that the value in a particular field matches or does not
match a certain specific value, you can use Filter By Selection.

- If your criterion only involves a single field but is more complex (for example, the
criterion specifies that the value in the field begins with a certain collection of letters)
you can use a common filter.

- If your criterion involves more than one field, use Filter By Form.

- If your criterion involves more than a single And or Or, or if it involves sorting, you will
probably find it simpler to use Advanced Filter/Sort.

To Use Filter By Selection

The simplest type of filter is called Filter By Selection. To use Filter By Selection, you give Access an example
of the data you want by selecting the data within the table. You then choose the option you want on the Selection
menu. For example, if you only want to display those clients located in Burles, Filter By Selection is appropriate.
The following steps use Filter By Selection in Datasheet view to display only the records for clients in Burles.

1
- Open the Navigation Pane.

- Open the Client table, and close the
Navigation Pane.

- Click the City field on the first record
to select the city on that record as
the city (Figure 3–12).

Q&A

Could I have selected the City field
on another record where the city is
also Burles to select the same city?

Yes. It does not matter which record
you select as long as the city is Burles.

Figure 3–12

2

- Click the Selection button (Home tab | Sort & Filter group) to display the Selection menu (Figure 3–13).

Figure 3–13

3

- Click Equals "Burles" to select only those clients whose city is Burles (Figure 3–14).

Q&A Can I also filter in Form view?

Yes. Filtering works the same whether you are viewing the data with split form, in Datasheet view, or in Form view.

Experiment

- Try each of the other values in the Selection menu to see their effect. When done, once again select those clients whose city is Burles.

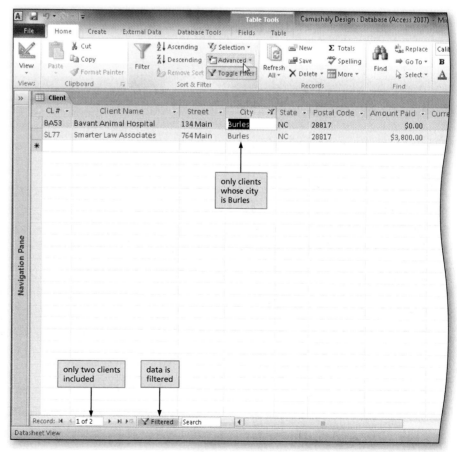

Figure 3–14

To Toggle a Filter

The Toggle Filter button toggles between filtered and unfiltered displays of the records in the table. That is, if only filtered records currently appear, clicking the Toggle Filter button will redisplay all records. If all records are currently displayed and there is a filter that is in effect, clicking the Toggle Filter button will display only the filtered records. If no filter is active, the Toggle Filter button will be dimmed, so clicking it would have no effect.

The following step toggles the filter to redisplay all records.

1

• Click the Toggle Filter button (Home tab | Sort & Filter group) to toggle the filter and redisplay all records (Figure 3–15).

Q&A

Does that action clear the filter?

No. The filter is still in place. If you click the Toggle Filter button a second time, you will again see only the filtered records.

Figure 3–15

To Clear a Filter

Once you have finished using a filter, you can clear the filter. After doing so, you no longer will be able to use the filter by clicking the Toggle Filter button. The following steps clear the filter.

1 Click the Advanced button (Home tab | Sort & Filter group) to display the Advanced menu.

2 Click Clear All Filters on the Advanced menu.

To Use a Common Filter

You can filter individual fields by clicking the arrow to the right of the field name and using one of the common filters that are available for the field. If you have determined you want to include those clients whose city begins with G, Filter By Selection would not be appropriate. You could instead use the common filter for the field that would include only those records whose city begins with a particular value. The following steps use this common filter to include only those clients whose city begins with G.

1

- Click the City arrow to display the common filter menu.

- Point to the Text Filters command to display the custom text filters (Figure 3–16).

Q&A

I selected the City field and then clicked the Filter button on the Home tab | Sort & Filter group. My screen looks the same. Is this right?

Yes. That is another legitimate way to display the common filter menu.

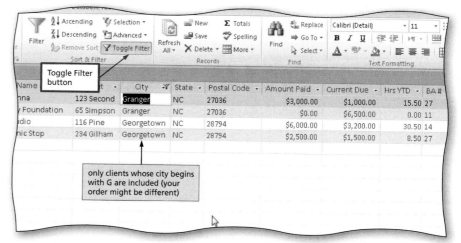

Figure 3–16

2

- Click Begins With to display the Custom Filter dialog box.

- Type G as the 'City begins with' value (Figure 3–17).

Q&A

If I wanted certain cities included, could I use the check boxes?

Yes. Be sure the cities you want are the only ones checked.

Experiment

- Try other options in the common filter menu to see their effects. When done, once again select those clients whose city begins with G.

Figure 3–17

3

- Click the OK button to filter the records (Figure 3–18).

Q&A

Can I use the same technique in Form view?

In Form view, you would need to click the field and then click the Filter button to display the Common Filter menu. The rest of the process would be the same.

4

- Click the Toggle Filter button (Home tab | Sort & Filter group) to toggle the filter and redisplay all records.

Figure 3–18

To Use Filter By Form

Filter By Selection and the common filter method you just used are quick and easy ways to filter by the value in a single field. For more complex criteria, however, these methods are not appropriate. Filter by Form allows you to filter based on multiple criteria, for example, to find only those clients whose postal code is 27036 and whose amount paid is 0. The following steps use Filter by Form to restrict the records that appear.

1

- Click the Advanced button (Home tab | Sort & Filter group) to display the Advanced menu (Figure 3–19).

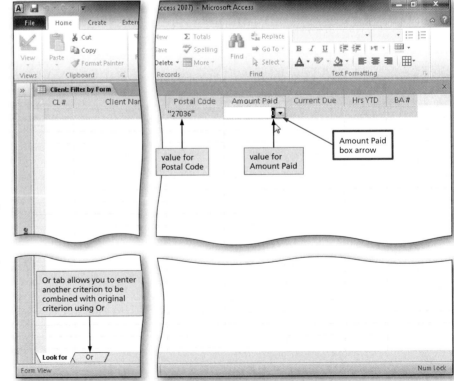

Figure 3–19

2

- Click Clear All Filters on the Advanced menu to clear the existing filter.

- Click the Advanced button again to display the Advanced menu a second time.

- Click Filter By Form on the Advanced menu.

- Click the blank row in the Postal Code field, click the arrow that appears, and then click 27036.

- Click the Amount Paid field, click the arrow that appears, and then click 0 (Figure 3–20).

Q&A Is there any difference in the process if I am viewing a table in Form view rather than in Datasheet view?

In Form view, you will make your entries in a form rather than a datasheet. Otherwise, the process is the same.

Figure 3–20

- Click the Toggle Filter button (Home tab | Sort & Filter group) to apply the filter (Figure 3–21).

Experiment

- Select Filter by Form again and enter different criteria. In each case, toggle the filter to see the effect of your selection. When done, once again select those clients whose postal code is 27036 and whose amount paid is $0.

Figure 3–21

To Use Advanced Filter/Sort

In some cases, your criteria may be too complex even for Filter By Form. You might decide you want to include any client for which the postal code is 27036 and the amount paid is $0. Additionally, you might want to include any client whose amount paid is greater than $4,000, no matter where the client is located. Further, you might want to have the results sorted by name. To filter records using complex criteria, you need to use Advanced Filter/Sort, as in the following steps.

1

- Click the Advanced button (Home tab | Sort & Filter group) to display the Advanced menu, and then click Clear All Filters on the Advanced menu to clear the existing filter.

- Click the Advanced button to display the Advanced menu a second time.

- Click Advanced Filter/Sort on the Advanced menu.

- Expand the size of the field list so all the fields in the Client table appear.

- Include the Client Name field and select Ascending as the sort order to specify the order in which the filtered records will appear.

- Include the Postal Code field and enter 27036 as the criterion.

- Include the Amount Paid field and enter 0 as the criterion in the Criteria row and >4000 as the criterion in the or row (Figure 3–22).

Figure 3–22

2

- Click the Toggle Filter button (Home tab | Sort & Filter group) to toggle the filter so that only records that satisfy the criteria will appear (Figure 3–23).

Q&A

Why are those particular records included?

The first record is included because the postal code is 27036 and the amount paid is $0.00. The other two records are included because the amount paid is over $4,000.

Figure 3–23

Experiment

- Select Advanced Filter/Sort again and enter different sorting options and criteria. In each case, toggle the filter to see the effect of your selection. When done, change back to the sorting options and criteria you entered in Step 1.

3

- Close the Client table. When asked if you want to save your changes, click the No button.

Q&A

Shouldn't I have cleared all filters before closing the table?

If you are closing a table and not saving the changes, it is not necessary to clear the filter. No filter will be active when you next open the table.

Filters and Queries

BTW

Using Wildcards in Filters
Both the question mark (?) and the asterisk (*) wildcards can be used in filters created using Advanced Filter/Sort.

Now that you are familiar with how filters work, you might notice similarities between filters and queries. Filters and queries are related in three ways.

1. You can apply a filter to the results of a query just as you can apply a filter to a table.
2. When you have created a filter using Advanced Filter/Sort, you can save the filter settings as a query by using the Save as Query command on the Advanced menu.
3. You can restore filter settings that you previously saved in a query by using the Load from Query command on the Advanced menu.

Break Point: If you wish to take a break, this is a good place to do so. You can quit Access now. To resume at a later time, start Access, open the database called Camashaly Design, and continue following the steps from this location forward.

Changing the Database Structure

BTW

Moving a Field in a Table Structure
If you add a field to a table and later realize the field is in the wrong location, you can move the field. To do so, click the row selector for the field and then drag the field to the new location.

When you initially create a database, you define its **structure**; that is, you assign names and types to all the fields. In many cases, the structure you first define will not continue to be appropriate as you use the database.

Perhaps a field currently in the table no longer is necessary. If no one ever uses a particular field, it is not needed in the table. Because it is occupying space and serving no useful purpose, you should remove it from the table. You also would need to delete the field from any forms, reports, or queries that include it.

More commonly, an organization will find that it needs to maintain additional information that was not anticipated at the time the database was first designed. The organization's own requirements may have changed. In addition, outside regulations that the organization must satisfy may change as well. Either case requires the addition of fields to an existing table.

Although you can make some changes to the database structure in Datasheet view, it is usually easier and better to make these changes in Design view.

TO DELETE A FIELD

If a field in one of your tables no longer is needed, you should delete the field; for example, it may serve no useful purpose, or it may have been included by mistake. To delete a field, you would use the following steps.

1. Open the table in Design view.
2. Click the row selector for the field to be deleted.
3. Press the DELETE key.
4. When Access displays the dialog box requesting confirmation that you want to delete the field, click the Yes button.

BTW

Changing Data Types
It is possible to change the data type for a field that already contains data. Before you change a data type, however, you should consider what effect the change will have on other database objects, such as forms, queries, and reports. For example, you could convert a Text field to a Memo field if you find that you do not have enough space to store the data that you need. You also could convert a Number field to a Currency field or vice versa.

To Add a New Field

You can add fields to a table in a database. Camashaly Design has decided that it needs to categorize its clients. To do so requires an additional field, Client Type. The possible values for Client Type are NON (which indicates the client is a nonprofit organization), RET (which indicates the client is a retail organization), or SER (which indicates the client is a service organization). The following steps add the Client Type field to the Client table immediately after the Postal Code field.

1
- If necessary, open the Navigation Pane.
- Open the Client table in Design view.
- Click the row selector for the Amount Paid field, and then press the INSERT key to insert a blank row above the selected field (Figure 3–24).

2
- Click the Field Name column for the new field.
- Type `Client Type` as the field name and then press the TAB key.

Figure 3–24

Other Ways
1. Click Insert Rows button (Table Tools Design tab | Tools group)

To Create a Lookup Field

Because there are only three possible values for the Client Type field, you should make it easy for users to enter the appropriate value. A **lookup field** allows the user to select from a list of values when updating the contents of the field.

The following steps make the Client Type field a lookup field.

- Click the Data Type column for the Client Type field, and then click the Data Type box arrow to display the menu of available data types (Figure 3–25).

Figure 3–25

- Click Lookup Wizard, and then click the 'I will type in the values that I want.' option button (Lookup Wizard dialog box) to indicate that you will type in the values (Figure 3–26).

Q&A When would I use the other option button?

You would use the other option button if the data to be entered in this field is found in another table or query.

Figure 3–26

❸

- Click the Next button to display the next Lookup Wizard screen (Figure 3–27).

Figure 3–27

❹

- Click the first row of the table (below Col1), and then type **NON** as the value in the first row.

- Press the DOWN ARROW key, and then type **RET** as the value in the second row.

- Press the TAB key, and then type **SER** as the value in the third row (Figure 3–28).

Q&A

I notice you can press either the DOWN ARROW or the TAB key to move to the second row. Can you also press the ENTER key?

No. Pressing the ENTER key will exit the Lookup Wizard without finishing the process of adding a Lookup field.

Figure 3–28

5
- Click the Next button to display the next Lookup Wizard screen.
- Ensure Client Type is entered as the label for the lookup field and that the Allow Multiple Values check box is NOT checked (Figure 3–29).

6
- Click the Finish button to complete the definition of the lookup field.

Q&A

Why does the data type for the Client Type field still show Text?

The data type is still Text because the values entered in the wizard were entered as text.

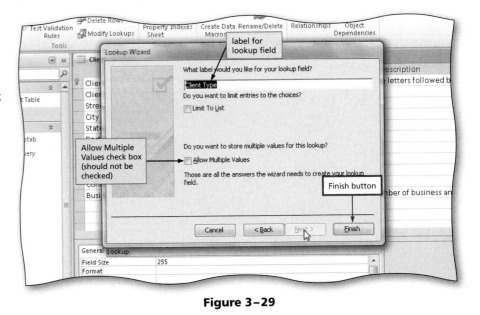

Figure 3–29

To Add a Multivalued Field

Normally, fields contain only a single value. In Access, it is possible to have **multivalued fields**, that is, fields that can contain more than one value. Camashaly Design wants to use such a field to store the abbreviations of the various services its clients need (see Table 3–1 for the service abbreviations and descriptions). Unlike the Client Type, where each client only had one type, clients can require multiple service descriptions. One client might need Ad, Ban, Bill, and Logo (Ad Design, Banners, Billboards, and Logo Design). Another client might only need Host (Web Site Hosting).

Table 3–1 Service Abbreviations and Descriptions

Service Abbreviation	Description
Ad	Ad Design
Ban	Banners
Bill	Billboards
Bus	Business Cards
ENews	Email Newsletter
Host	Web Site Hosting
Logo	Logo Design
Mkt	Marketing Research
News	Printed Newsletters
Pod	Podcasting
SE	Search Engine Visibility
Shop	Shopping Cart
Soc	Social Networking

Creating a multivalued field uses the same process as creating a lookup field, with the exception that you check the Allow Multiple Values check box. The following steps create a multivalued field.

Click the row selector for the Amount Paid field, and then press the INSERT key to insert a blank row.

② Click the Field Name column for the new field, type `Services Needed` as the field name, and then press the TAB key.

③ Click the Data Type arrow to display the menu of available data types for the Services Needed field, and then click Lookup Wizard in the menu of available data types to start the Lookup Wizard.

④ Click the 'I will type in the values that I want.' option button to indicate that you will type in the values.

⑤ Click the Next button to display the next Lookup Wizard screen.

⑥ Click the first row of the table (below Col1), and then type `Ad` as the value in the first row.

⑦ Enter the remaining values from the first column in Table 3–1. Before typing each value, press the TAB key to move to a new row.

⑧ Click the Next button to display the next Lookup Wizard screen.

⑨ Ensure that Services Needed is entered as the label for the lookup field.

⑩ Click the Allow Multiple Values check box to allow the user to enter multiple values.

⑪ Click the Finish button to complete the definition of the Lookup Wizard field.

To Add a Calculated Field

A field that can be computed from other fields is called a **calculated field** or a **computed field**. In Chapter 2, you created a calculated field in a query that provided total amount data. With Access 2010, it is now possible to also include a calculated field in a table. Users will not be able to update this field. Instead, Access will automatically perform the necessary calculation whenever you display or use this field in any way. The following steps add a calculated field in the table.

①

- Click the row selector for the Contract Hours YTD field, and then press the INSERT key to insert a blank row above the selected field.

- Click the Field Name column for the new field.

- Type `Total Amount` as the field name and then press the TAB key.

- Click the Data Type box arrow to display the menu of available data types (Figure 3–30).

Figure 3–30

2

- Click Calculated to select the Calculated data type and display the Expression Builder dialog box (Figure 3–31).

Figure 3–31

3

- Double-click the Amount Paid field in the Expression Categories area (Expression Builder dialog box) to add the field to the expression.

Q&A

I don't have the list of fields in the Expression Categories area. What should I do?

Click Client in the Expression Elements area.

- Type a plus sign (+).

Q&A

Could I select the plus sign from a list rather than typing it?

Yes. Double-click Operators in the Expression Elements area to display available operators and then click the plus sign.

- Double-click the Current Due field in the Expression Categories area (Expression Builder dialog box) to add the field to the expression (Figure 3–32).

Figure 3–32

4

- Click the OK button (Expression Builder dialog box) to enter the expression in the Expression property of the selected field (Figure 3–33).

Q&A
Could I have simply typed the expression in the Expression Builder dialog box rather than selecting the fields from a list?

Yes. You can use whichever technique you find more convenient.

Q&A
When I entered a calculated field in a query, I typed the expression in the Zoom dialog box. Could I have used the Expression Builder instead?

Yes. To do so, you would click Build rather than Zoom on the shortcut menu.

Figure 3–33

To Save the Changes and Close the Table

The following steps save the changes; that is, they save the addition of the new fields and close the table.

1 Click the Save button on the Quick Access Toolbar to save the changes.

2 Close the Client table.

TO MODIFY SINGLE OR MULTIVALUED LOOKUP FIELDS

You may find that you later want to change the list of choices in a lookup field. If you find you need to modify a single or multivalued lookup field, you can use the following steps.

1. Open the table in Design view and select the field to be modified.
2. Click the Lookup tab in the Field Properties pane.
3. Change the list in the Row Source property to change the desired list of values.

BTW

Calculated Fields
Do not add a calculated field to a table if you plan to also use the database with Access 2007. Access 2007 does not recognize calculated fields. Also, if you modify the expression used to create the calculated field, the field may not update correctly.

Mass Changes

In some cases, rather than making individual changes to records, you will want to make mass changes. That is, you will want to add, change, or delete many records in a single operation. You can do this with action queries. Unlike the queries that you created in Chapter 2, which simply presented data in specific ways, an **action query** adds, deletes, or changes data in a table. An **update query** allows you to make the same change to all records satisfying some criterion. If you omit the criterion, you will make the same changes to all records in the table. A **delete query** allows you to delete all the records satisfying some criterion. You can add the results of a query to an existing table by using an **append query**. You also can add the query results to a new table by using a **make-table query**.

To Use an Update Query

The new Client Type field is blank on every record in the Client table. One approach to entering the information for the field would be to step through the entire table, assigning each record its appropriate value. If most of the clients have the same type, a simpler approach is available.

In the Camashaly Design database, for example, more clients are type NON. Initially, you can set all the values to NON. To accomplish this quickly and easily, you can use an **update query**, which is a query that makes the same change to all the records satisfying a criterion. Later, you can change the type for retail organizations and service organizations.

The following steps use an update query to change the value in the Client Type field to NON for all the records. Because all records are to be updated, criteria are not required.

1

- Create a new query for the Client table, and close the Navigation Pane.

- Click the Update button (Query Tools Design tab | Query Type group), double-click the Client Type field to select the field, click the Update To row in the first column of the design grid, and then type **NON** as the new value (Figure 3–34).

Q&A Don't I have to enter a criterion?

If you only want the change to be made on some of the records, you would need to enter a criterion to identify those records. Without a criterion, the change will be made on all records, which is what you want in this update.

Figure 3–34

②

- Click the Run button (Query Tools Design tab | Results group) to run the query and update the records (Figure 3–35).

Q&A Why don't I click the View button to update the records?

The purpose of the View button is to simply view results. The Run button causes the updates specified by the query to take place.

Q&A Why doesn't the dialog box appear on my screen when I click the Run button?

If the dialog box does not appear, it means that you did not click the Enable Content button when you first opened the database. Close the database, open it again, and enable the content. Then, create and run the query again.

Figure 3–35

Experiment

- Create an update query to change the client type to RET. Enter a criterion to restrict the records to be updated, and then run the query. Open the table to view your changes. When finished, create and run an update query to change the client type to NON on all records.

③

- Click the Yes button to make the changes.

Q&A Is there any way to see the records that will be updated before performing the update, in case you are not sure you are updating the correct records?

Yes. Click the Select button (Query Tools Design tab | Query Type group) to convert the query to a select query, add any additional fields that would help you identify the records, and then view the results. Return to Design view and make any necessary corrections to the query. When you are satisfied, click the Update button to once again convert the query to an update query.

Other Ways

1. Right-click any open area in upper pane, point to Query Type on shortcut menu, click Update Query on Query Type submenu

To Use a Delete Query

In some cases, you may need to delete several records at a time. If, for example, all clients in a particular postal code are to be serviced by another firm, the clients with this postal code can be deleted from the Camashaly Design database. Instead of deleting these clients individually, which could be very time consuming in a large database, you can delete them in one operation by using a **delete query**, which is a query that will delete all the records satisfying the criteria entered in the query.

The following steps use a delete query to delete any client whose postal code is 28819. (Two such clients currently exist in the database.)

1

- Click the column heading for the Client Type field and then press the DELETE key to clear the grid.

- Click the Delete button (Query Tools Design tab | Query Type group) to make the query a delete query.

- Double-click the Postal Code field to select the field.

- Click the Criteria row for the Postal Code field and type 28819 as the criterion (Figure 3–36).

2

- Run the query by clicking the Run button.

- Click the Yes button when Access displays a message indicating that there are two records which will be deleted to complete the deletion.

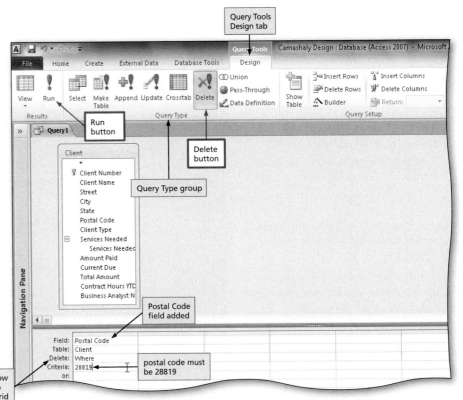

Figure 3–36

Q&A

Is there any way to see the records that will be deleted before performing the deletion, in case you are not sure you are deleting the correct records?

Yes. Prior to running the query, you would click the Select button (Query Tools Design tab | Query Type group) to convert the query to a select query, add any additional fields that would help you identify the records, and then view the results. You would then return to Design view and make any corrections to the query. When you are satisfied, click the Delete button to once again convert the query to a delete query.

- Close the Query window. Because you do not need to use this delete query again, do not save the query.

Other Ways

1. Right-click any open area in upper pane, point to Query Type on shortcut menu, click Delete Query on Query Type submenu

To Use an Append Query

An **append query** adds a group of records from one table to the end of another table. For example, suppose that Camashaly Design acquires some new clients and a database containing a table with those clients. To avoid entering all this information manually, you can append it to the Client table in the Camashaly Design database using the append query. To create an append query, you would use the following steps.

1. Create a query for the table containing the records to append.

2. In Design view, indicate the fields to include, and then enter any necessary criteria.

3. View the query results to be sure you have specified the correct data, and then return to Design view.

4. Click the Append button (Query Tools Design tab | Query Type group).

5. When Access displays the Append dialog box, specify the name of the table to receive the new records and its location. Run the query by clicking the Run button (Query Tools Design tab | Results group).

6. When Access indicates the number of records to be appended, click the OK button.

BTW

Delete Queries
If you do not specify any criteria in a delete query, Access will delete all the records in the table.

To Use a Make-Table Query

In some cases, you might want to copy the records from an existing table to a new table, that is, a table that has not yet been created. If so, use a **make-table query** to add the records to a new table. To create a make-table query, you would use the following steps.

1. Create a query for the table containing the records to add.

2. In Design view, indicate the fields to include, and then enter any necessary criteria.

3. View the query results to be sure you have specified the correct data, and then return to Design view.

4. Click the Make Table button (Query Tools Design tab | Query Type group).

5. When Access displays the Make Table dialog box, specify the name of the table to receive the new records and its location. Run the query by clicking the Run button (Query Tools Design tab | Results group).

6. When Access indicates the number of records to be inserted, click the OK button.

Break Point: If you wish to take a break, this is a good place to do so. You can quit Access now. To resume at a later time, start Access, open the database called Camashaly Design, and continue following the steps from this location forward.

BTW

Archive Tables
You can use a make table query to create an archive table. An **archive table** is a table that contains data that is no longer used in operations but that might still be needed by the organization.

Validation Rules

You now have created, loaded, queried, and updated a database. Nothing you have done so far, however, restricts users to entering only valid data, that is, data that follows the rules established for data in the database. An example of such a rule would be that client types can only be NON, RET, or SER. To ensure the entry of valid data, you create these **validation rules,** that is, rules that a user must follow when entering the data. As you will see, Access will prevent users from entering data that does not follow the rules. The steps also specify **validation text**, which is the message that will appear if a user violates the validation rule.

Validation rules can indicate a **required field**, a field in which the user actually must enter data. Validation rules can restrict a user's entry to a certain **range of values**; for example, the values in the Amount Paid field must be between $0 and $30,000. They can specify a **default value**, that is, a value that Access will display on the screen in a particular field before the user begins adding a record. To make data entry of client numbers more convenient, you also can have lowercase letters appear automatically as uppercase letters. Finally, validation rules can specify a collection of acceptable values.

BTW

Database Design: Validation
In most organization, decisions about what is valid and what is invalid data are made during the requirements gathering process and the database design process.

To Change a Field Size

The Field Size property for text fields represents the maximum number of characters a user can enter in the field. Because the field size for the Client Number field is 4, for example, a user would not be able to enter a fifth character in the field. Occasionally, you may find that the field size that seemed appropriate when you first created a table is no longer appropriate. In the Client table, there is now a name that is longer than 30 characters. To allow this name in the table, you need to change the field size for the Client Name field to a number that is large enough to accommodate the new name. The following step changes the field size for the Client Name field from 30 to 35.

1 Ensure that the Client table is open in Design view and that the Navigation Pane is closed.

2 Select the Client Name field by clicking its row selector.

3 Click the Field Size property to select it, delete the current entry (30), and then type **3 5** as the new field size.

To Specify a Required Field

To specify that a field is to be required, change the value for the Required property from No to Yes. The following step specifies that the Client Name field is to be a required field.

1

• Ensure that the Client Name field is still selected.

• Click the Required property box in the Field Properties pane, and then click the down arrow that appears.

• Click Yes in the list (Figure 3–37).

Q&A What is the effect of this change?

Users cannot leave the Client Name field blank when entering or editing records.

Figure 3–37

To Specify a Range

The following step specifies that entries in the Current Due field must be between $0 and $30,000. To indicate this range, the criterion specifies that the amount paid amount must be both >= 0 (greater than or equal to 0) and <= 30000 (less than or equal to 30,000).

1

• Select the Current Due field by clicking its row selector, click the Validation Rule property box to produce an insertion point, and then type >=0 and <=30000 as the rule.

• Click the Validation Text property box to produce an insertion point, and then type **Must be at least $0.00 and at most $30,000.00** as the text (Figure 3–38).

Q&A What is the effect of this change?

Users now will be prohibited from entering a current due amount that either is less than $0.00 or greater than $30,000.00 when they add records or change the value in the Current Due field.

Figure 3–38

To Specify a Default Value

To specify a default value, enter the value in the Default Value property box. The following step specifies NON as the default value for the Client Type field. This simply means that if users do not enter a client type, the type will be NON.

1

- With the Client Type field selected, click the Default Value property box to produce an insertion point, and then type =NON as the value (Figure 3–39).

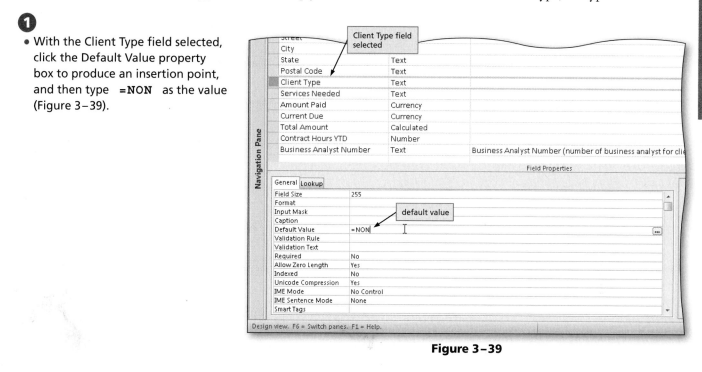

Figure 3–39

To Specify a Collection of Legal Values

The only **legal values**, **or allowable values**, for the Client Type field are NON, RET, and SER. An appropriate validation rule for this field prevents Access from accepting any entry other than these three possibilities. The following step specifies the legal values for the Client Type field.

1

- With the Client Type field selected, click the Validation Rule property box to produce an insertion point and then type =NON or =RET or =SER as the validation rule.

- Click the Validation Text property box and then type **Must be NON, RET, or SER** as the validation text (Figure 3–40).

Q&A What is the effect of this change?

Users now will be allowed to enter only NON, RET, or SER in the Client Type field when they add records or make changes to this field.

Figure 3–40

To Specify a Format

To affect the way data appears in a field, you can use a **format**. To use a format with a Text field, you enter a special symbol, called a **format symbol**, in the field's Format property box. The Format property uses different settings for different data types. The following step specifies a format for the Client Number field in the Client table and illustrates the way you enter a format. The format symbol used in the example is >, which causes Access to display lowercase letters automatically as uppercase letters. The format symbol < causes Access to display uppercase letters automatically as lowercase letters.

1

- Select the Client Number field.

- Click the Format property box and then type > (Figure 3–41).

Q&A

What is the effect of this change?

From this point on, any lowercase letters will appear automatically as uppercase when users add records or change the value in the Client Number field.

Figure 3–41

To Save the Validation Rules, Default Values, and Formats

The following steps save the validation rules, default values, and formats.

1 Click the Save button on the Quick Access Toolbar to save the changes (Figure 3–42).

2 Click the No button to save the changes without testing current data.

3 Close the Client table.

Q&A

Should I always click the No button when saving validation rules?

If this were a database used to run a business or to solve some other critical need, you would click Yes. You would want to be sure that the data already in the database does not violate the rules.

Figure 3–42

Updating a Table that Contains Validation Rules

When updating a table that contains validation rules, Access provides assistance in making sure the data entered is valid. It helps in making sure that data is formatted correctly. Entering a number that is out of the required range, for example, or entering a value that is not one of the possible choices, will produce an error message in the form of a dialog box. The database will not be updated until the error is corrected.

If the client number entered contains lowercase letters, such as wi12 (Figure 3–43), Access will display the data automatically as WI12 (Figure 3–44).

Figure 3–43

Figure 3–44

BTW

Modifying Table Properties
You can change the properties of a table by opening the table in Design view and then clicking the Propery Sheet button. To display the records in a table in an order other than primary key (the default sort order), use the Order By property. For example, to display the Client table automatically in Client Name order, change the the Order By property box setting to `Client.Client Name.` in the property box, close the property sheet, and save the change to the table design. When you open the Client table in Datasheet view, the records will be sorted in Client Name order.

If the client type is not valid, such as xxx, Access will display the text message you specified (Figure 3–45) and prevent the data from entering the database.

Figure 3–45

If the amount paid value is not valid, such as 50000, which is too large, Access also displays the appropriate message (Figure 3–46) and refuses to accept the data.

Figure 3–46

If a required field contains no data, Access indicates this by displaying an error message as soon as you attempt to leave the record (Figure 3–47). The field must contain a valid entry before Access will move to a different record.

Figure 3–47

When entering data into a field with a validation rule, you may find that Access displays the error message and you are unable to make the necessary correction. It may be that you cannot remember the validation rule you created or it was created incorrectly. In such a case, you neither can leave the field nor close the table because you have entered data into a field that violates the validation rule.

If this happens, first try again to type an acceptable entry. If this does not work, repeatedly press the BACKSPACE key to erase the contents of the field and then try to leave the field. If you are unsuccessful using this procedure, press the ESC key until the record is removed from the screen. The record will not be added to the database.

Should the need arise to take this drastic action, you probably have a faulty validation rule. Use the techniques of the previous sections to correct the existing validation rules for the field.

To Change the Contents of a Field

Now that the size for the Client Name field has been increased, you can change the name for client HC10 to Hendley County Regional Hospital. Changing the field size for the field does not automatically increase the width of the corresponding column in the datasheet, however. You need to take the necessary action to resize the column, just as you resized columns in Chapter 1 on page AC 29. The following steps change the name and resize the column in the datasheet to accommodate the new name.

1

- Open the Client table in Datasheet view and ensure the Navigation Pane is closed.

- Click in the Client Name field for client HC10 immediately before the word, Hospital, to produce an insertion point.

- Change the name from Hendley County Hospital to Hendley County Regional Hospital by typing the word **Regional** and pressing the SPACEBAR.

2

- Resize the Client Name column to best fit the new data by double-clicking the right boundary of the field selector, that is, the column heading (Figure 3–48).

3

- Save the changes to the layout by clicking the Save button on the Quick Access Toolbar.

- Close the Client table.

Figure 3–48

To Use a Lookup Field

Earlier, you changed all the entries in the Client Type field to NON. Thus, you have created a rule that will ensure that only legitimate values (NON, RET, or SER) can be entered in the field. You also made Client Type a lookup field for all clients using a mass change. You can make changes to a lookup field for individual records by clicking the field to be changed, clicking the arrow that appears in the field, and then selecting the desired value from the list.

The following steps change the Client Type values to the correct values.

1

- Open the Client table in Datasheet view and ensure the Navigation Pane is closed.

- Click in the Client Type field on the first record to display an arrow.

- Click the arrow to display the drop-down list of available choices for the Client Type field (Figure 3–49).

Q&A

I got the drop-down list as soon as I clicked. I didn't need to click the arrow. What happened?

If you click in the position where the arrow would appear, you will get the drop-down list. If you click anywhere else, you would need to click the arrow.

Figure 3–49

Q&A

Could I type the value instead of selecting it from the list?

Yes. Once you have either deleted the previous value or selected the entire previous value, you can begin typing. You do not have to type the full entry. When you begin with the letter, R, for example, Access will automatically add the ET.

Experiment

- Select the Client Type field on the first record. Try to change the client type by typing various values. Try to type an invalid client type (like MAN). When finished, change the value on the record to SER.

2

- Click SER to change the value.

- In a similar fashion, change the values on the other records to match those shown in Figure 3–50.

Figure 3–50

To Use a Multivalued Lookup Field

Using a multivalued lookup field is similar to using a regular lookup field. The difference is that when you drop down the list, the entries all will be preceded by check boxes. You then can check all the entries that you want. The appropriate entries are shown in Figure 3–51. As indicated in the figure, the services needed for client BA53 are Ad, Ban, Bill, and Logo.

CL #	Client Name	Services Needed
BA53	Bavant Animal Hospital	Ad, Ban, Bill, Logo
BB32	Babbage CPA Firm	Ad, Bus, ENews
BC76	Buda Community Clinic	Ban, Host, News
CJ29	Catering by Jenna	Bus, Host, Logo
GF56	Granger Family Foundation	Host
HC10	Hendley County Regional Hospital	ENews, News, Soc
KD21	KAL Design Studio	Host, Mkt, SE
KG04	Kyle Grocery Cooperative	Ad, Bill, Soc
KM03	Kyle Museum of Art	ENews, Host, Pod, Shop
ME14	Mike's Electronic Stop	Ad, Ban, Logo
PJ34	Patricia Jean Florist	Bus, Mkt, Shop
SL77	Smarter Law Associates	ENews, Pod
TB17	The Bikeshop	Ad, SE

Figure 3–51

The following steps make the appropriate entries for the Services Needed field.

1

- Click the Services Needed field on the first record to display the arrow.

- Click the arrow to display the list of available services (Figure 3–52).

All the services currently appear in the box. What if there were too many services to fit?

Access would automatically include a scroll bar that you could use to scroll through all the choices.

Figure 3–52

2

- Click the Ad, Ban, Bill, and Logo check boxes to select the services for the first client (Figure 3–53).

Figure 3–53

3

- Click the OK button to complete the selection.

- Using the same technique, enter the services given in Figure 3–51 on page AC 172 for the remaining clients.

- Double-click the right boundary of the field selector for the Services Needed field to resize the field so that it best fits the data (Figure 3–54).

4

- Save the changes to the layout by clicking the Save button on the Quick Access Toolbar.

- Close the Client table.

Q&A What if I closed the table without saving the layout changes?

You would be asked if you want to save the changes.

Figure 3–54

To Update a Form to Reflect the Changes in the Table

In the first chapter, on page AC 48, you clicked the Form button (Create tab | Forms group) to create a simple form that contained all the fields in the Client table. Now that you have added additional fields, the form you created, Client Form, no longer contains all the fields in the table. Because creating the form required only clicking a single button, the simplest way to include all the fields from the Client table in the form is to delete the form and create it once again. The following steps delete the Client Form and then create it a second time. The form then will contain all the fields.

1

- Open the Navigation Pane, and then right-click the Client Form in the Navigation Pane to display a shortcut menu.

- Click Delete on the shortcut menu to delete the selected form, and then click the Yes button in the Microsoft Access dialog box to confirm the deletion.

- Click the Client table in the Navigation Pane to select the table.

- Click Create on the Ribbon to display the Create tab.

- Click the Form button (Create tab | Forms group) to create a simple form (Figure 3–55).

Figure 3–55

2

- Click the Save button on the Quick Access Toolbar to save the form.

- Type **Client Form** as the form name, and then click the OK button to save the form.

- Close the form.

To Update a Report to Reflect the Changes in the Table

You also may want to include the new fields in the Client Financial Report you created earlier. Just as you did with the form, you could delete the current version of the report and then create it all over again. There are several steps involved in creating a report, however, so it is more complicated than the process of re-creating the form. An easier way is to modify the report in Layout view. In Layout view, you easily can resize columns and add new fields. The following steps modify the Client Financial Report by resizing the Client Name field so that the entire name of Hendley County Regional Hospital appears. They also add the Client Type and Total Amount fields. Finally, to accommodate the extra fields, the steps change the orientation of the report from Portrait to Landscape.

1

- Open the Navigation Pane, if necessary, and then right-click the Client Financial Report in the Navigation Pane to display a shortcut menu.

- Click Layout View on the shortcut menu to open the report in Layout view.

- Close the Navigation Pane.

- Click the column heading for the Client Name column, point to the right-hand border of the column heading so that the mouse pointer becomes a two-headed arrow, and then drag the pointer to the approximate position shown in Figure 3–56 to resize the column.

Q&A Do I have to be exact?

No. Make sure, however, that you can see all the data in the client name for client HC10. If not, you need to drag the border further to the right.

Figure 3–56

Q&A Did I have to select the column heading or could I have selected one of the entries in the column?

You could have selected any of the entries in the column.

2

- Click the Add Existing Fields button (Report Layout Tools Design tab | Tools group) to display a field list (Figure 3-57).

Q&A

Why are there two Services Needed fields in the list?

They serve different purposes. If you were to select Services Needed, you would get all the services for a given client on one line. If you were to select Services Needed.Value, each service would be on a separate line. You are not selecting either one for this report.

Figure 3-57

3

- Point to the Client Type field in the field list, press and hold the left mouse button, and then drag the mouse pointer until the line to the left of the mouse pointer is between the Client Name and Amount Paid fields (Figure 3-58).

- Release the left mouse button to place the field.

Q&A

What if I make a mistake?

You can delete the field by clicking the field and then pressing the DELETE key. You can move the field by dragging it to the correct position.

Figure 3-58

4

- Using the same technique, add the Total Amount field between the Current Due and Hrs YTD fields.

- Click the Add Existing Fields button (Report Layout Tools Design tab | Tools group) to remove the field list from the screen (Figure 3–59).

Q&A What would I do if the field list covered the portion of the report where I wanted to insert a new field?

You can move the field list to a different position on the screen by dragging its title bar.

Figure 3–59

- Scroll the report, if necessary, so that the entire width of the report appears on the screen.

5

- Click Page Setup on the Ribbon to display the Page Setup tab.

- Click the Landscape button (Report Layout Tools Page Setup tab | Page Layout group) to change the orientation of the report to Landscape.

- Click the Save button on the Quick Access Toolbar to save your changes.

- Close the report.

To Include Totals in a Datasheet

It is possible to include totals and other statistics at the bottom of a datasheet in a special row called the Total row. The following steps display the total of the salary YTD and Incentive YTD for analysts in the Total row.

1

- Open the Business Analyst Table in Datasheet view and close the Navigation Pane.

- Click the Totals button (Home tab | Records group) to include the Total row in the datasheet.

- Click the Total row in the Salary YTD column to display an arrow.

- Click the arrow to display a menu of available calculations (Figure 3–60).

Q&A

Will I always get the same list?

No. You will only get the items that are applicable to the type of data in the column. You cannot calculate the sum of text data, for example.

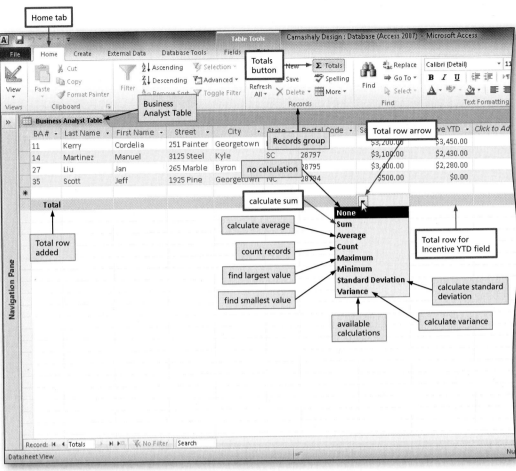

Figure 3–60

2

- Click Sum to calculate the total of the salary YTD amounts.

- Click the Total row in the Incentive YTD column to display an arrow, click the arrow to display a menu of available calculations, and then click Sum to calculate the total of the incentive YTD amounts (Figure 3–61).

Experiment

- Experiment with other statistics. When finished, once again select the sum in both columns.

Figure 3–61

To Remove Totals from a Datasheet

If you no longer want the totals to appear as part of the datasheet, you can remove the Total row. The following step removes the Total row.

1
- Click the Totals button (Home tab | Records group), which is shown in Figure 3–60, to remove the Total row from the datasheet.

Changing the Appearance of a Datasheet

You can change the appearance of a datasheet in a variety of ways. For example, you can change the appearance of gridlines or change the text colors and font. Figure 3–62 shows the various buttons, found in the Text Formatting group on the Home tab, that are available to change the datasheet appearance.

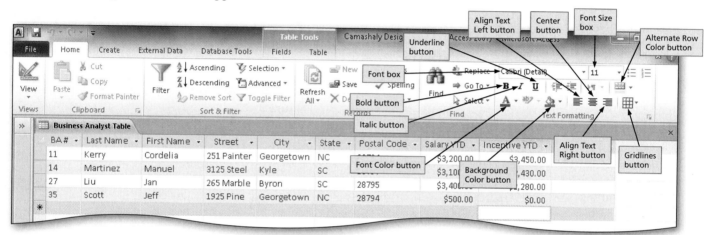

Figure 3–62

The changes to the datasheet will be reflected not only on the screen, but also when you print or preview the datasheet.

Determine whether changes to the format of a datasheet are desirable.
You need to decide if changes to the format of a datasheet would improve its appearance and/or its usefulness. The following are the decisions you would make.

- Would totals or other calculations be useful in the datasheet? If so, include the Total row and select the appropriate computations.

- Would different gridlines make the datasheet more useful? If so, change to the desired gridlines.

- Would alternating colors in the rows make them easier to read? If so, change the alternate fill color.

- Would a different font and/or font color make the text stand out better? If so, change the font color and/or the font.

- Is the font size appropriate? Can you see enough data at one time on the screen and yet have the data be readable? If not, change the font size to an appropriate value.

- Is the column spacing appropriate? Are some columns wider than they need to be? Do some columns not display all the data? Change the column sizes as necessary.

As a general guideline, once you have decided on a particular look for a datasheet, all your datasheets should have the same look, unless there is a compelling reason for one of your datasheets to differ.

Plan
Ahead

To Change Gridlines in a Datasheet

One of the changes you can make to a datasheet is which gridlines appear. You may feel that the appearance would be improved by having only horizontal gridlines. The following steps change the datasheet so that only horizontal gridlines are included.

1

- Open the Business Analyst Table in Datasheet view, if it is not already open.

- If necessary, close the Navigation Pane.

- Click the box in the upper-left corner of the Datasheet selector to select the entire datasheet (Figure 3–63).

Figure 3–63

2

- Click the Gridlines button (Home tab | Text Formatting group) to display the Gridlines gallery (Figure 3–64).

Q&A Does it matter whether I click the button or the arrow?

In this case, it does not matter. Either one will produce the same result.

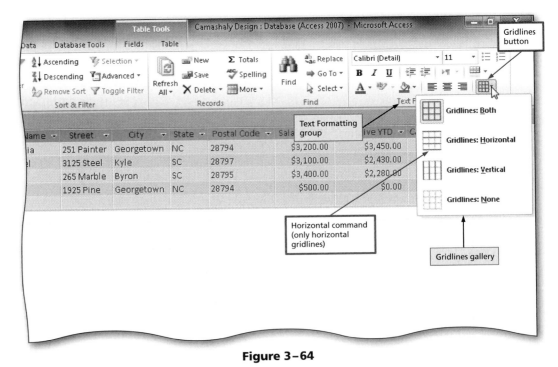

Figure 3–64

3

- Click the Gridlines: Horizontal command in the Gridlines gallery to include only horizontal gridlines.

Experiment

- Experiment with other gridline options. When finished, once again select horizontal gridlines.

To Change the Colors and Font in a Datasheet

You may also decide to modify the appearance of the datasheet by changing the colors and the font. The following steps change the Alternate Fill color, a color that appears on every other row in the datasheet. They also change the font color, the font, and the font size.

1

• With the datasheet for the Business Analyst Table selected, click the Alternate Row Color button arrow (Home tab | Text Formatting group) to display the color palette (Figure 3–65).

Q&A Does it matter whether I click the button or the arrow?

Yes. Clicking the arrow produces a color palette. Clicking the button applies the currently selected color. When in doubt, you should click the arrow.

Figure 3–65

2

• Click Brown in the upper-right corner of Standard Colors to select brown as the alternate color.

• Click the Font Color button arrow, and then click Red (the second color in the bottom row) in the lower-left corner of Standard Colors to select Red as the font color.

• Click the Font box arrow, scroll down in the list until Bodoni MT appears, and then select Bodoni MT as the font. (If it is not available, select any font of your choice.)

• Click the Font Size box arrow, and select 10 as the font size (Figure 3–66).

Q&A Does the order in which I make these selections make a difference?

No. You could have made these selections in any order.

Experiment

• Experiment with other colors, fonts, and font sizes. When finished, return to the options selected in this step.

Figure 3–66

Using the Datasheet Formatting Dialog Box

As an alternative to using the individual buttons, you can click the Datasheet Formatting dialog box launcher to display the Datasheet Formatting dialog box (Figure 3–67). You can use the various options within the dialog box to make changes to the datasheet format. Once you are finished, click the OK button to apply your changes.

Figure 3–67

To Close the Datasheet without Saving the Format Changes

The following steps close the datasheet without saving the changes to the format. Because the changes are not saved, the next time you open the Business Analyst Table in Datasheet view, it will appear in the original format. If you had saved the changes, the changes would be reflected in its appearance.

1 Close the Business Analyst Table.

2 Click the No button in the Microsoft Access dialog box when asked if you want to save your changes.

Multivalued Fields in Queries

You can use multivalued fields in queries just as you can use other fields. You have a choice concerning how the multiple values appear. You can choose to have them on a single row or on multiple rows.

To Query a Multivalued Field Showing Multiple Values on a Single Row

To include a multivalued field in the results of a query, place the field in the query design grid just like any other field. The results will list all of the values for the multivalued field on a single row, just as in a datasheet. The following steps create a query to display the client number, client name, client type, and services needed for all clients.

1

- Create a query for the Client table and close the Navigation Pane.

- Include the Client Number, Client Name, Client Type, and Services Needed fields (Figure 3–68).

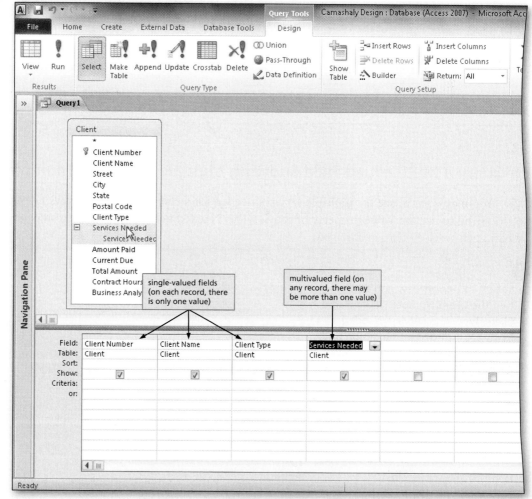

Figure 3–68

BTW

Using Criteria with Multivalued Fields
To enter criteria in a multivalued field, simply enter the criteria in the Criteria row. For example, to find all clients who need banners, enter **BAN** in the Criteria row.

2

- View the results (Figure 3–69).

Q&A
Can I include criteria for the multivalued field?

Yes. You can include criteria for the multivalued field.

Experiment

- Return to Design view and enter various criteria in the Services Needed field. Run the queries. When finished, return to the options selected in this step.

Figure 3–69

To Query a Multivalued Field Showing Multiple Values on Multiple Rows

You may want to see the multiple services needed for a client on separate rows rather than a single row. To do so, you need to use the Value property of the Services Needed field. The following steps use the Value property to display each service on a separate row.

1

- Return to Design view and ensure that the Client Number, Client Name, Client Type, and Services Needed fields are included in the design grid.

- Click the Services Needed field to produce an insertion point, press the RIGHT ARROW key as necessary to move the insertion point to the end of the field name, and then type a period and the word **Value** after the word, Needed, to use the Value property (Figure 3–70).

Q&A
I don't see the word, Services. Did I do something wrong?

No. There is not enough room to display the entire name. If you wanted to see it, you could point to the right boundary of the column selector and then either drag or double-click.

Figure 3–70

2

- View the results (Figure 3–71).

Q&A Can I now include criteria for the multivalued field?

Yes. You could enter a criterion just like in any other query.

3

- Close the query.

- When asked if you want to save the query, click the No button.

Figure 3–71

Break Point: If you wish to take a break, this is a good place to do so. You can quit Access now. To resume at a later time, start Access, open the database called Camashaly Design, and continue following the steps from this location forward.

Referential Integrity

When you have two related tables in a database, it is essential that the data in the common fields match. There should not be a client in the Client table whose business analyst number is 11, for example, unless there is a record in the Business Analyst Table whose number is 11. This restriction is enforced through **referential integrity**, which is the property that ensures that the value in a foreign key must match that of another table's primary key.

A **foreign key** is a field in one table whose values are required to match the *primary key* of another table. In the Client table, the Business Analyst Number field is a foreign key that must match the primary key of the Business Analyst Table; that is, the business analyst number for any client must be a business analyst currently in the Business Analyst Table. A client whose business analyst number is 92, for example, should not be stored because no such business analyst exists.

In Access, to specify referential integrity, you must define a relationship between the tables by using the Relationships button. Access then prohibits any updates to the database that would violate the referential integrity.

The type of relationship between two tables specified by the Relationships command is referred to as a **one-to-many relationship**. This means that *one* record in the first table is related to, or matches, *many* records in the second table, but each record in the second table is related to only *one* record in the first. In the Camashaly Design database, for example, a one-to-many relationship exists between the Business Analyst Table and the Client table. *One* business analyst is associated with *many* clients, but each client is associated with only a single business analyst. In general, the table containing the foreign key will be the *many* part of the relationship.

Plan Ahead

BTW

Relationships
You also can use the Relationships window to specify a one-to-one relationship. In a one-to-one relationship, the matching fields are both primary keys. If Camashaly maintained a company car for each analyst, the data concerning the cars might be kept in a Car table, in which the primary key is Business Analyst Number — the same primary key as the Business Analyst Table. Thus, there would be a one-to-one relationship between analysts and cars.

Identify related tables in order to implement relationships between the tables.
When specifying referential integrity, you need to decide how to handle deletions. In the relationship between clients and business analysts, for example, deletion of a business analyst for whom clients exist, such as business analyst number 14, would violate referential integrity. Any clients for business analyst 14 no longer would relate to any business analyst in the database. You can handle this in two ways. For each relationship, you need to decide which of the approaches is appropriate.

- The normal way to avoid this problem is to prohibit such a deletion.
- The other option is to **cascade the delete.** This means that Access would allow the deletion but then delete all related records. For example, it would allow the deletion of the business analyst from the Client table but then automatically delete any clients related to the deleted business analyst.

You also need to decide how to handle the update of the primary key. In the relationship between business analysts and clients, for example, changing the business analyst number for business analyst 14 to 41 in the Business Analyst Table would cause a problem because some clients in the Client table have business analyst number 14. These clients no longer would relate to any business analyst. You can handle this in two ways. For each relationship, you need to decide which of the approaches is appropriate.

- The normal way to avoid this problem is to prohibit this type of update.
- The other option is to **cascade the update.** This means to allow the change, but make the corresponding change in the foreign key on all related records. In the relationship between clients and business analysts, for example, Access would allow the update but then automatically make the corresponding change for any client whose business analyst number was 14. It now will be 41.

To Specify Referential Integrity

The following steps use the Relationships button on the Database Tools tab to specify referential integrity by specifying a relationship between the Business Analyst and Client tables. The steps also ensure that update will cascade, but that delete will not.

1

- Click Database Tools on the Ribbon to display the Database Tools tab. (Figure 3–72).

Figure 3–72

2

- Click the Relationships button (Database Tools tab | Relationships group) to open the Relationships window and display the Show Table dialog box (Figure 3–73).

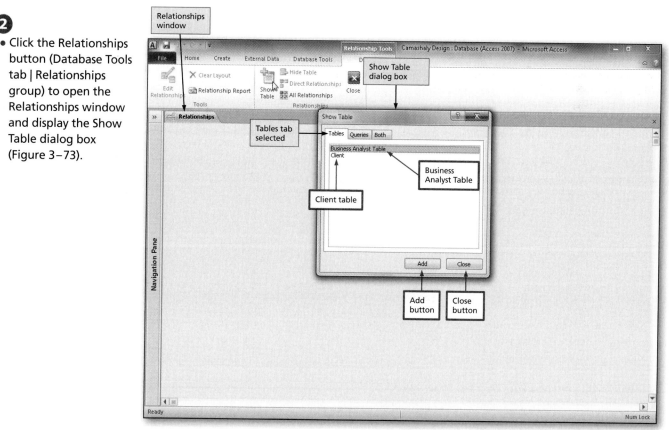

Figure 3–73

❸

• If necessary, click the Business Analyst Table (Show Table dialog box) and then click the Add button to add the Business Analyst Table.

• Click the Client table and then click the Add button to add the Client table.

• Click the Close button (Show Table dialog box) to close the dialog box.

• Resize the field lists that appear so all fields are visible (Figure 3–74).

Q&A Do I need to resize the field lists?

No. You can use the scroll bars. Before completing the next step, however, you would need to make sure the Business Analyst Number fields in both tables appear on the screen.

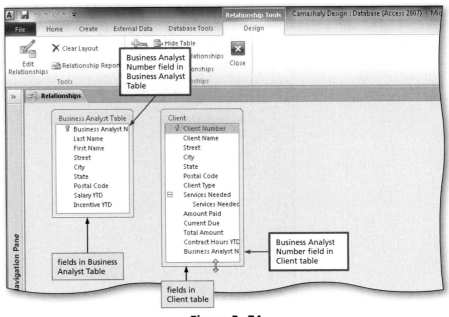

Figure 3–74

❹

• Drag the Business Analyst Number field in the Business Analyst Table field list to the Business Analyst Number field in the Client table field list to display the Edit Relationships dialog box to create a relationship.

Q&A Do I actually move the field from the Business Analyst Table to the Client table?

No. The mouse pointer will change shape to indicate you are in the process of dragging, but the field does not move.

• Click the Enforce Referential Integrity check box (Edit Relationships dialog box).

• Click the Cascade Update Related Fields check box (Figure 3–75).

Q&A The Cascade check boxes were dim until I clicked the Enforce Referential Integrity check box. Is that correct?

Yes. Until you have chosen to enforce referential integrity, the cascade options are not applicable.

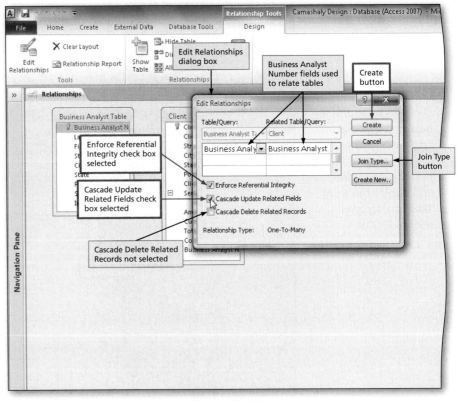

Figure 3–75

Q&A Can I change the join type like I can in queries?

Yes. Click the Join Type button in the Edit Relationships dialog box. Just as with queries, option button 1 creates an INNER join, option button 2 creates a LEFT join, and option button 3 creates a RIGHT join.

5

• Click the Create button (Edit Relationships dialog box) to complete the creation of the relationship (Figure 3–76).

Q&A
What is the symbol at the lower end of the join line?

It is the mathematical symbol for infinity. It is used here to denote the "many" end of the relationship.

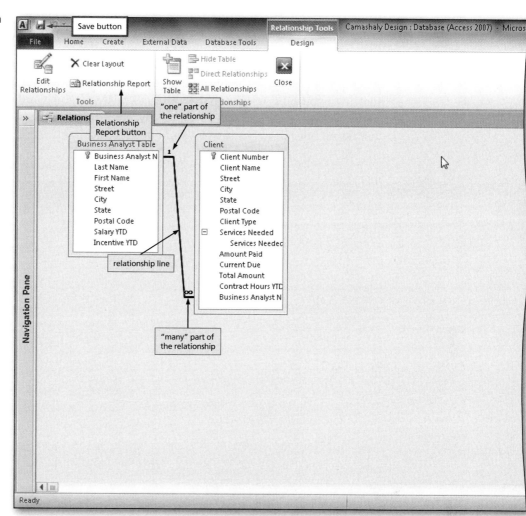

Figure 3–76

Q&A
Can I print a copy of the relationship?

Yes. Click the Relationship Report button (Relationship Tools Design tab | Tools group) to produce a report of the relationship. You can print the report. You also can save it as a report in the database for future use. If you do not want to save it, close the report after you have printed it and do not save the changes.

6

• Click the Save button on the Quick Access Toolbar to save the relationship you created.

• Close the Relationships window.

Q&A
Can I later modify the relationship if I want to change it in some way?

Yes. Click Database Tools on the Ribbon to display the Database Tools tab, and then click the Relationships button (Database Tools tab | Relationships group) to open the Relationships window. To add another table, click the Show Table button on the Design tab. To remove a table, click the Hide Table button. To edit a relationship, select the relationship and click the Edit Relationships button.

Effect of Referential Integrity

Referential integrity now exists between the Business Analyst and Client tables. Access now will reject any number in the Business Analyst Number field in the Client table that does not match a business analyst number in the Business Analyst Table. Attempting to change the business analyst number for a client to one that does not match any business analyst in the Business Analyst Table would result in the error message shown in Figure 3–77. Similarly, attempting to add a client whose business analyst number does not match would produce the same error message.

Figure 3–77

Access also will reject the deletion of a business analyst for whom related clients exist. Attempting to delete business analyst 11 from the Business Analyst Table, for example, would result in the message shown in Figure 3–78.

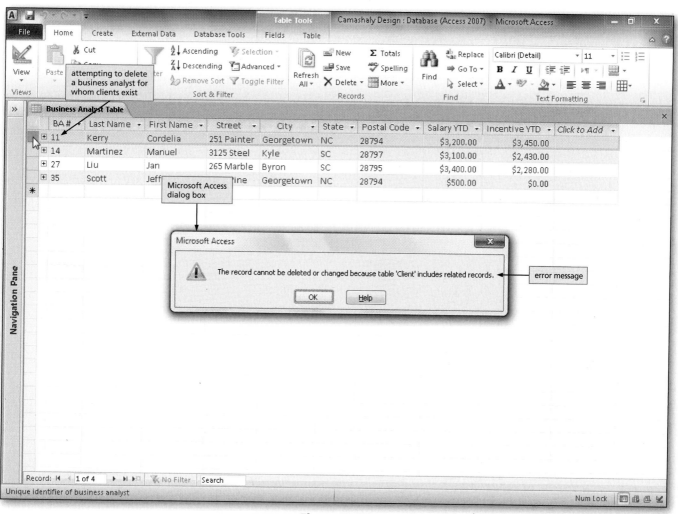

Figure 3–78

Access would, however, allow the change of a business analyst number in the Business Analyst Table. Then it automatically makes the corresponding change to the business analyst number for all the business analyst's clients. For example, if you changed the business analyst number of business analyst 14 to 41, the same 41 would appear in the business analyst number field for clients whose business analyst number had been 14.

To Use a Subdatasheet

Now that the Business Analyst Table is related to the Client table, it is possible to view the clients of a given business analyst when you are viewing the datasheet for the Business Analyst Table. The clients for the business analyst will appear below the business analyst in a **subdatasheet**. The availability of such a subdatasheet is indicated by a plus sign that appears in front of the rows in the Business Analyst Table. The following steps display the subdatasheet for business analyst 14.

1

- Open the Business Analyst Table in Datasheet view and close the Navigation Pane (Figure 3–79).

+ sign indicates subdatasheet available

click to display subdatasheet for analyst 14

Figure 3–79

2

- Click the plus sign in front of the row for business analyst 14 to display the subdatasheet (Figure 3–80).

Q&A

How do I hide the subdatasheet when I no longer want it to appear?

When you clicked the plus sign, it changed to a minus sign. Click the minus sign.

Experiment

- Display subdatasheets for other business analysts. Display more than one subdatasheet at a time. Remove the subdatasheets from the screen.

+ sign changed to - sign

subdatasheet for business analyst 14

click to hide subdatasheet

Figure 3–80

3

- Close the datasheet for the Business Analyst Table.

Handling Data Inconsistency

In many organizations, databases evolve and change over time. One department may create a database for its own internal use. Employees in another department may decide they need their own database containing much of the same information. For example, the Purchasing department may create a database of products that it buys and the Receiving department may create a database of products that it receives. Each department is keeping track of the same products. When the organization eventually merges the databases, they may find inconsistencies and duplication. The Find Duplicates Query Wizard and the Find Unmatched Query Wizard can assist in clearing the resulting database of duplication and errors.

TO FIND DUPLICATE RECORDS

One reason to include a primary key for a table is to eliminate duplicate records. A possibility still exists, however, that duplicate records can get into your database. The following steps illustrate how to use the Find Duplicates Query Wizard to find duplicate records.

1. Click Create on the Ribbon, and then click the Query Wizard button (Create tab | Queries group).
2. When Access displays the New Query dialog box, click the Find Duplicates Query Wizard and then click the OK button.
3. Identify the table and field or fields that might contain duplicate information.
4. Indicate any other fields you want displayed.
5. Finish the wizard to see any duplicate records.

TO FIND UNMATCHED RECORDS

Occasionally, you may want to find records in one table that have no matching records in another table. For example, you may want to determine which business analysts currently have no clients. The following steps illustrate how to find unmatched records using the Find Unmatched Query Wizard.

1. Click Create on the Ribbon, and then click the Query Wizard button (Create tab | Queries group).
2. When Access displays the New Query dialog box, click the Find Unmatched Query Wizard and then click the OK button.
3. Identify the table that might contain unmatched records and then identify the related table.
4. Indicate the fields you want displayed.
5. Finish the wizard to see any duplicate records.

Ordering Records

Normally, Access sequences the records in the Client table by client number whenever listing them because the Client Number field is the primary key. You can change this order, if desired.

To Use the Ascending Button to Order Records

To change the order in which records appear, use the Ascending or Descending buttons. Either button reorders the records based on the field in which the insertion point is located.

The following steps order the records by city using the Ascending button.

1

- Open the Client table in Datasheet view and close the Navigation Pane.

- Click the City field on the first record to select the field (Figure 3–81).

Q&A

Did I have to click the field on the first record?

No. Any other record would have worked as well.

Figure 3–81

BTW

Certification
The Microsoft Office Specialist (MOS) program provides an opportunity for you to obtain a valuable industry credential — proof that you have the Access 2010 skills required by employers. For more information, visit the Access 2010 Certification Web page (scsite.com/ac2010/cert).

2

- Click the Ascending button (Home tab | Sort & Filter group) to sort the records by City (Figure 3–82).

Q&A What if I wanted the cities to appear in reverse alphabetical order?

Click the Descending button.

Experiment

- Sort the records by city in reverse order. When done, sort the records by city in the original order.

Figure 3–82

- Close the Client table.

- Click the No button (Microsoft Access dialog box) when asked if you want to save your changes.

TO USE THE ASCENDING BUTTON TO ORDER RECORDS ON MULTIPLE FIELDS

Just as you are able to sort the answer to a query on multiple fields, you also can sort the data that appears in a datasheet on multiple fields. To do so, the major and minor keys must be next to each other in the datasheet with the major key on the left. (If this is not the case, you can drag the columns into the correct position. Instead of dragging, however, usually it will be easier to use a query that has the data sorted in the desired order.)

To sort on a combination of fields where the major key is just to the left of the minor key, you would use the following steps.

1. Click the field selector at the top of the major key column to select the entire column.

2. Hold down the SHIFT key and then click the field selector for the minor key column to select both columns.

3. Click the Ascending button to sort the records.

To Quit Access

The following steps quit Access.

1 Click the Close button on the right side of the title bar to quit Access.

2 If a Microsoft Access dialog box appears, click the Save button to save any changes made to the object since the last save.

Chapter Summary

In this chapter you have learned how to use a form to add records to a table, search for records, delete records, filter records, create and use lookup fields, create calculated fields, create and use multivalued fields, make mass changes, create validation rules, change the appearance of a datasheet, specify referential integrity, and use subdatasheets. The items listed below include all the new Access skills you have learned in this chapter.

1. Create a Split Form (AC 142)
2. Use a Form to Add Records (AC 144)
3. Search for a Record (AC 144)
4. Update the Contents of a Record (AC 146)
5. Delete a Record (AC 147)
6. Use Filter By Selection (AC 148)
7. Toggle a Filter (AC 150)
8. Use a Common Filter (AC 150)
9. Use Filter By Form (AC 152)
10. Use Advanced Filter/Sort (AC 153)
11. Delete a Field (AC 155)
12. Add a New Field (AC 155)
13. Create a Lookup Field (AC 156)
14. Add a Calculated Field (AC 159)
15. Modify Single or Multivalued Lookup Fields (AC 161)
16. Use an Update Query (AC 162)
17. Use a Delete Query (AC 163)
18. Use an Append Query (AC 164)
19. Use a Make-Table Query (AC 165)
20. Specify a Required Field (AC 166)
21. Specify a Range (AC 166)
22. Specify a Default Value (AC 167)
23. Specify a Collection of Legal Values (AC 167)
24. Specify a Format (AC 168)
25. Change the Contents of a Field (AC 170)
26. Use a Lookup Field (AC 171)
27. Use a Multivalued Lookup Field (AC 172)
28. Update a Form to Reflect the Changes in the Table (AC 174)
29. Update a Report to Reflect the Changes in the Table (AC 175)
30. Include Totals in a Datasheet (AC 177)
31. Remove Totals from a Datasheet (AC 179)
32. Change Gridlines in a Datasheet (AC 180)
33. Change the Colors and Font in a Datasheet (AC 181)
34. Query a Multivalued Field Showing Multiple Values on a Single Row (AC 183)
35. Query a Multivalued Field Showing Multiple Values on Multiple Rows (AC 184)
36. Specify Referential Integrity (AC 186)
37. Use a Subdatasheet (AC 191)
38. Find Duplicate Records (AC 193)
39. Find Unmatched Records (AC 193)
40. Use the Ascending Button to Order Records (AC 194)
41. Use the Ascending Button to Order Records on Multiple Fields (AC 195)

Learn It Online

Test your knowledge of chapter content and key terms.

Instructions: To complete the Learn It Online exercises, start your browser, click the Address bar, and then enter the Web address **scsite.com/ac2010/learn**. When the Access 2010 Learn It Online page is displayed, click the link for the exercise you want to complete and then read the instructions.

Chapter Reinforcement TF, MC, and SA
A series of true/false, multiple choice, and short answer questions that test your knowledge of the chapter content.

Flash Cards
An interactive learning environment where you identify chapter key terms associated with displayed definitions.

Practice Test
A series of multiple choice questions that test your knowledge of chapter content and key terms.

Who Wants To Be a Computer Genius?
An interactive game that challenges your knowledge of chapter content in the style of a television quiz show.

Wheel of Terms
An interactive game that challenges your knowledge of chapter key terms in the style of the television show *Wheel of Fortune*.

Crossword Puzzle Challenge
A crossword puzzle that challenges your knowledge of key terms presented in the chapter.

Apply Your Knowledge

Reinforce the skills and apply the concepts you learned in this chapter.

Specifying Validation Rules, Updating Records, Formatting a Datasheet, and Creating Relationships

Instructions: Start Access. Open the Babbage CPA Firm database that you modified in Apply Your Knowledge in Chapter 2 on page AC 129. (If you did not complete this exercise, see your instructor for a copy of the modified database.)

Perform the following tasks:

1. Open the Client table in Design view, as shown in Figure 3–83 on page AC 198.

2. Format the Client Number field so any lowercase letters appear in uppercase and make the Client Name field a required field.

3. Specify that balance due amounts must be between $0 and $1,200. Include validation text.

4. Save the changes to the Client table.

5. Create a split form for the Client table and find the record for M26 and change the customer name to Mohr Craft Supplies.

6. Use the form to add the following record:

L50	Lou's Salon	124 Fulton	Granger	27036	$0.00	$325.00	38

Continued >

Apply Your Knowledge *continued*

Figure 3–83

7. Save the form as Client Split Form and close the form.

8. Open the Client table in Datasheet view and use Filter By Selection to find the record for H21. Delete the record. Remove the filter.

9. Add totals to the datasheet for the Amount Paid and Balance Due fields. Remove the gridlines from the datasheet.

10. Save the changes to the layout of the table. Close the Client table.

11. Establish referential integrity between the Bookkeeper table (the one table) and the Client table (the many table). Cascade the update but do not cascade the delete. Create a relationship report for the relationship. Save the report with the default report name Relationships for Babbage CPA Firm.

12. Submit the revised database in the format specified by your instructor.

Extend Your Knowledge

Extend the skills you learned in this chapter and experiment with new skills. You may need to use Help to complete the assignment.

Creating Action Queries and Changing Table Properties

Instructions: See the inside back cover of this book for instructions for downloading the Data Files for Students, or see your instructor for information on accessing the required files.

Generic Temp Services is a company that specializes in placing temporary workers in various administrative positions. Philamar Training has been approached about buying Generic Temp Services. Philamar is interested in knowing how many clients the companies have in common. Generic also needs to do some database maintenance by finding duplicates and finding unmatched records.

Perform the following tasks:

1. Open the Generic Temp Services database. Create and run a make-table query to create the Potential Clients table in the Generic Temp Services database shown in Figure 3–84. Save the query as Make Table Query.

Client Name	Street	City	Postal Code
Afton Manufac	612 Revere	Granger	27036
Atlas Distribute	227 Dandelion	Burles	28817
Blake-Scryps	557 Maum	Georgetown	28794
Dege Grocery C	446 Linton	Burles	28817
Grandston Clea	337 Abelard	Buda	27032
Hill Country Sh	247 Fulton	Granger	27036
Jones Plumbin	75 Getty	Buda	27032
Mohr Art Suppl	665 Maum	Georgetown	28794
SeeSaw Indust	31 Liatris	Walburg	28819
Tate Repair	824 Revere	Granger	27036
Woody Sportin	578 Central	Walburg	28819
Catering by Jer	123 Second	Granger	27036

Figure 3–84

2. Open the Potential Clients table, change the font size to 14, and resize the columns to best fit the data.

3. Save the changes to the layout of the table. Close the table.

4. Use the Find Duplicates Query Wizard to find duplicate information in the City field. Include the Client Name field in the query. Name the query City Duplicates Query. Close the query.

5. Use the Find Unmatched Query Wizard to find all records in the Worker table that do not match records in the Client table. Worker Number is the common field in both tables. Include the Worker Number, Last Name, and First Name in the query. Name the query Worker Unmatched Query. Close the query.

6. Submit the revised database in the format specified by your instructor.

Make It Right

Analyze a database and correct all errors and/or improve the design.

Correcting Table Design Errors

Instructions: Start Access. Open the Senior Jobbers database. See the inside back cover of this book for instructions for downloading the Data Files for Students, or see your instructor for information on accessing the required files.

Perform the following tasks:

Senior Jobbers provides a variety of small repairs and maintenance to homeowners. The owner of Senior Jobbers has decided that he could better manage the business if he added a multivalued field that lists the various types of repairs and maintenance that customers request. He created the field shown in Figure 3–85 but forgot to add Clean Gutters as one of the job types. Modify the multivalued lookup field to include Clean Gutters as a job type. By mistake, the owner also added the contact number field shown in Figure 3–85 to the Customer table. That field should be deleted.

Figure 3–85

Finally, he wanted to add referential integrity between the Worker table and the Customer table. The relationship shown in Figure 3–86 is not correct and must be fixed. The owner does not want to cascade the update or the delete.

Figure 3–86

Submit the revised database in the format specified by your instructor.

In the Lab

Design, create, modify, and/or use a database following the guidelines, concepts, and skills presented in this chapter. Labs 1, 2, and 3 are listed in order of increasing difficulty.

Lab 1: Maintaining the ECO Clothesline Database

Problem: ECO Clothesline is expanding rapidly and needs to make some database changes to handle the expansion. The company needs to know more about its customers, such as the type of business, and it needs to ensure that data that is entered is valid. It also needs to update the records in the database.

Use the database modified in the In the Lab 1 of Chapter 2 on page AC 132 for this assignment, or see your instructor for information on accessing the files required for this book.

Perform the following tasks:

1. Open the ECO Clothesline database and then open the Customer table in Design view.

2. Add a Lookup field, Customer Type, to the Customer table. The field should appear after the Postal Code field. The field will contain data on the type of customer. The customer types are SAL (Salons, Studios, Fitness Clubs), SPG (Sporting Goods), and WMN (Women's Wear). Save these changes to the structure.

Continued >

3. Using a query, change all the entries in the Customer Type column to WMN. Save the query as Customer Type Update Query.

4. Open the Customer table and make the following changes. You can use either the Find button or Filter By Selection to locate the records to change:

    a. Change the customer type for customers CY12, FN19, LB20, RD03, TT21, and TW56 to SAL.

    b. Change the customer type for customer WS34 to SPG.

    c. Change the name of customer LB20 to Le Beauty Salon & Spa.

5. Change the alternate background color on the datasheet to white and remove the vertical gridlines. Save the changes to the layout of the table.

6. Create the following validation rules for the Customer table and save the changes.

    a. Specify the legal values SAL, SPT, and WMN for the Customer Type field. Include validation text.

    b. Assign a default value of WMN to the Customer Type field.

    c. Ensure that any letters entered in the Customer Number field appear as uppercase.

    d. Make Customer Name a required field.

7. Open the Customer table and use Filter By Form to find all records where the customer is located in Lowton and has a customer type of WMN, and then delete these records.

8. ECO Clothesline has signed up a sporting goods store, Ralph's (Customer Number RA21) and needs to add the record to the Customer table. Ralph's is at 72 Main in Lowton, TN 37084. Terry Sinson is the sales rep assigned to the account. To date, Ralph's has not been billed nor does the company owe for any services. Create a split form for the Customer table and use this split form to add the record. Save the split form as Customer Split Form.

9. Specify referential integrity between the Sales Rep table (the one table) and the Customer table (the many table). Cascade the update but not the delete.

10. Add the Customer Type field to the Customer Balance Report. The field should follow the Customer Name field. Save the changes to the report.

11. Submit the revised database in the format specified by your instructor.

In the Lab

Lab 2: Maintaining the Walburg Energy Alternatives Database

Problem: The management of the Walburg Energy Alternatives recently acquired some items from a store that is going out of business. You now need to append these new items to the current item table. You also need to change the database structure and add some validation rules to the database.

Use the database modified in the In the Lab 2 of Chapter 2 on page AC 134 for this assignment. You also will use the More Items database from the Data Files for Students. See the inside back cover of this book for instructions for downloading the Data Files for Students, or see your instructor for information on accessing the required files.

Perform the following tasks:

1. Open the More Items database from the Data Files for Students.

2. Create a new query for the Item table and add all fields to the query.

3. Using an append query, append all records in the More Items database to the Item table in the Walburg Energy Alternatives database, as shown in Figure 3–87.

Figure 3–87

4. Save the append query as Walburg Append Query and close the More Items database.

5. Open the Walburg Energy Alternatives database and then open the Item table in Datasheet view. There should be 20 records in the table.

6. The items added from the More Items database do not have a vendor assigned to them. Assign items 1234 and 2234 to vendor JM. Assign item 2216 to vendor AS. Assign items 2310 and 2789 to vendor SD.

7. Create an advanced filter for the Item table. The filter should display records with fewer than 10 items on hand and be sorted in ascending order by Description. Save the filter settings as a query and name the filter Reorder Filter.

8. Make the following changes to the Item table:

   a. Change the field size for the On Hand field to Integer. The Format should be fixed and the decimal places should be 0.

   b. Make Description a required field.

   c. Specify that the number on hand must be between 0 and 50. Include validation text.

   d. Add a calculated field Inventory Value (On Hand*Cost) following the Cost field. Format the field as currency.

9. Save the changes to the table design. If a dialog box appears indicating that some data may be lost, click the Yes button.

10. Add the Inventory Value field to the Inventory Status Report. Place the field after the Cost field. Save the changes to the report.

11. Specify referential integrity between the Vendor table (the one table) and the Item table (the many table). Cascade the update but not the delete.

12. Submit the revised More Items database and the Walburg Energy Alternatives database in the format specified by your instructor.

In the Lab

Lab 3: Maintaining the Philamar Training Database

Problem: Philamar Training is expanding rapidly and needs to make some database changes to handle the expansion. The company needs to know more about its clients, such as the type of business and the training services needed. You also are to add validation rules and update records in the database.

Use the Philamar Training database modified in the In the Lab 3 of Chapter 2 on page AC 135 for this assignment, or see your instructor for information on accessing the files required for this book. Submit the revised database in the format specified by your instructor.

Instructions Part 1: Several changes must be made to the database structure. For example, management would like a lookup field, Client Type, added to the Client table. The field should appear after the Postal Code field. The field will contain data on the type of client. The client types are MAN (Manufacturing), RET (Retail), and SER (Service). Philamar also needs a multivalued field that lists the general type of computer training of interest to each client. This knowledge can help Philamar better meet the needs of their clients. Add the field following the Client Type field. Table 3–2 lists the training abbreviations and descriptions that management would like in a Training Needed multivalued field.

Table 3–2 Training Abbreviations and Descriptions

Training Abbreviation	Description
APP	Application Software
HRD	Hardware
LAN	Local Area Networks
SEC	Security
WEB	Internet and World Wide Web
WIN	Windows

Management wants to ensure that an entry always appears in the Client Name field and that any letters entered in the Client Number field appear in uppercase. It also requires that the amount in the Current Due field is never less than 0 or greater than $5,000. The only values in the Client Type field are MAN, SER, and RET. Most clients are manufacturing organizations. Make the changes to the database structure.

Instructions Part 2: Use a query to assign the client type MAN to all records in the Client table. Save the query as Update Query. Clients EU28 and FI28 are retail organizations. Clients CE16, HN83, and PS82 are service organizations. The data for the Training Needed field shown in Figure 3–88 must be added to the database. The address for PRIM Staffing is incorrect. It should be 727 Crestview. Hurley National is really Hurley National Bank. A new retail organization, Ralph's, just became a Philamar client. The address for the store is 42 Main, Crumville, TX 76745. Ralph's is interested in application software and Windows training.

Management wants to use RA10 as the client number and Marty Danville as the trainer. The new client has not yet received any training and does not owe any money to Philamar.

CL # ▾	Client Name ▾	Training Needed ▾
BS27	Blant and Sons	HRD, LAN, SEC
CE16	Center Services	APP, WEB, WIN
CP27	Calder Plastics	LAN, SEC, WEB
EU28	Elba's Furniture	APP, SEC, WEB
FI28	Farrow-Idsen	APP, WEB
FL93	Fairland Lawn	LAN, SEC, WEB
HN83	Hurley National Bank	APP, WIN
MC28	Morgan-Alyssa	HRD, LAN
PS82	PRIM Staffing	APP, WEB, WIN
RA10	Ralph's	APP, WIN
TE26	Telton-Edwards	SEC

Figure 3–88

Instructions Part 3:   Management wants to make sure that clients are not assigned to a trainer who is not in the database. It also wants the ability to change a trainer number in the Trainer table and have the change applied to the Client table. Create the appropriate relationship that would satisfy management's needs.

Cases and Places

Apply your creative thinking and problem solving skills to design and implement a solution.

See the inside back cover of this book for instructions for downloading the Data Files for Students, or see your instructor for information on accessing the required files.

1: Maintaining the Chamber of Commerce Database

Academic

Use the Chamber of Commerce database you modified in Cases and Places 1 in Chapter 2 on page AC 135 for this assignment. Use the concepts and techniques presented in this chapter to modify the database as follows:

1. The chamber would like to categorize the businesses that advertise in the guide as retail, dining, or service establishments. These three types are the only valid category types. Most businesses are retail businesses.

2. Advertisers A228, C135, G346, H123, K109, M321, T167, and W456 are retail establishments. Advertisers C048, C234, D217, N007, and P124 are service establishments. The remaining advertisers are dining establishments.

3. An entry should always appear in the Advertiser Name field and any letters in the Advertiser Number field should appear in uppercase.

4. Chloe's Salon has changed its name to Chloe's Salon and Spa.

Continued >

5. AAA Diner is a new restaurant in town and wants to advertise in the guide. Assign the Advertiser Number A245 to AAA Diner. The restaurant is located at 23 Berton, the postal code is 19363, and the telephone number is 555-0998. It has not yet made a payment and the balance is $75.00. Lars Tolbert is the ad rep.

6. Specify referential integrity. Cascade the update but not the delete.

7. Change the ad rep number for ad rep 26 to 22.

Submit the revised database in the format specified by your instructor.

2: Maintaining the Consignment Database

Personal

Use the Consignment database you modified in Cases and Places 2 in Chapter 2 on page AC 136 for this assignment. Use the concepts and techniques presented in this chapter to modify the database as follows:

1. Make the Condition field a lookup field. Only the current values in the database should be legal values. Most items are in good condition.

2. Update descriptions: A better description for the recliner is Leather Recliner. A better description for the bar stools is Kitchen Counter Stools.

3. The clothes hamper has been sold.

4. The minimum price of any item is $2.

5. The Description field always should contain data.

6. It would be easier to find items for sale if the default sort order for the Items table was by Description rather than by Item Number. Also, all descriptions should be displayed completely in Datasheet view.

7. Add the Condition field to the Available Items Report you created in Chapter 1. The field should follow the Description field. All descriptions should display completely.

8. Specify referential integrity. Cascade the delete but not the update.

Submit the revised database in the format specified by your instructor.

3: Maintaining the Senior Care Database

Professional

Use the Senior Care database you modified in Cases and Places 3 in Chapter 2 on page AC 136 for this assignment. Use the concepts and techniques presented in this chapter to modify the database as follows:

1. Senior Care could better serve its clients by adding a field that would list the type of services each client needs. Table 3–3 lists the service abbreviations and descriptions that should appear in the field.

Table 3–3 Service Abbreviations and Descriptions	
Service Abbreviation	**Description**
Bill	Bill/Mail/Correspondence Help
Cmp	Companionship
Hskp	Light Housekeeping
Hyg	Hygiene Assistance
Meal	Meal Planning/Preparation
Tran	Transportation/Errands

2. Add the data for this multivalued field shown in Figure 3-89 to the database.

3. This multivalued field also should appear in the Client Report you created in Chapter 1.

4. Senior Care is having trouble finding helpers willing to help with hygiene. Query the Client table to find all clients who require hygiene assistance. Save the query as Hygiene Needs Query.

5. Mike Preston has moved to assisted living and is no longer a client of Senior Care. Use Find or Filter By Selection to delete this record.

6. An entry should always appear in the client first and last name fields. Any letters in the Client Number field should appear in uppercase.

7. Specify referential integrity. Cascade the update but not the delete.

Client Number	Last Name	First Name	Services Needed
AB10	Alvarez	Francine	Bill, Cmp, Meal
BR18	Breeton	Alex	Hskp, Hyg
CH21	Chalmer	Ben	Cmp, Tran
FE47	Ferber	Jane	Cmp
GM50	Gammon	Fred	Hskp
HA15	Hammond	Lois	Bill, Hskp, Meal
HJ05	Heijer	Bill	Hyg, Tran
KL10	Klinger	Cynthia	Hskp, Meal
LA75	Last	Bill	Hyg, Tran
MA24	Manchester	Liz	Cmp, Tran
SA23	Santoro	Maria	Bill, Meal, Tran
TH41	Thomas	Albert	Bill, Tran
TR35	Trent	Jerry	Hskp, Hyg
WI87	Width	Evelyn	Cmp, Meal

Figure 3-89

Submit the revised database in the format specified by your instructor.

NOTES

NOTES

NOTES

NOTES

Appendix A

Project Planning Guidelines

Using Project Planning Guidelines

The process of communicating specific information to others is a learned, rational skill. Computers and software, especially Microsoft Office 2010, can help you develop ideas and present detailed information to a particular audience.

Using Microsoft Office 2010, you can create projects such as Word documents, PowerPoint presentations, Excel spreadsheets, and Access databases. Productivity software such as Microsoft Office 2010 minimizes much of the laborious work of drafting and revising projects. Some communicators handwrite ideas in notebooks, others compose directly on the computer, and others have developed unique strategies that work for their own particular thinking and writing styles.

No matter what method you use to plan a project, follow specific guidelines to arrive at a final product that presents information correctly and effectively (Figure A–1). Use some aspects of these guidelines every time you undertake a project, and others as needed in specific instances. For example, in determining content for a project, you may decide that a chart communicates trends more effectively than a paragraph of text. If so, you would create this graphical element and insert it in an Excel spreadsheet, a Word document, or a PowerPoint slide.

Determine the Project's Purpose

Begin by clearly defining why you are undertaking this assignment. For example, you may want to track monetary donations collected for your club's fund-raising drive. Alternatively, you may be urging students to vote for a particular candidate in the next election. Once you clearly understand the purpose of your task, begin to draft ideas of how best to communicate this information.

Analyze Your Audience

Learn about the people who will read, analyze, or view your work. Where are they employed? What are their educational backgrounds? What are their expectations? What questions do they have?

PROJECT PLANNING GUIDELINES

1. DETERMINE THE PROJECT'S PURPOSE
Why are you undertaking the project?

2. ANALYZE YOUR AUDIENCE
Who are the people who will use your work?

3. GATHER POSSIBLE CONTENT
What information exists, and in what forms?

4. DETERMINE WHAT CONTENT TO PRESENT TO YOUR AUDIENCE
What information will best communicate the project's purpose to your audience?

Figure A–1

Design experts suggest drawing a mental picture of these people or finding photos of people who fit this profile so that you can develop a project with the audience in mind.

By knowing your audience members, you can tailor a project to meet their interests and needs. You will not present them with information they already possess, and you will not omit the information they need to know.

Example: Your assignment is to raise the profile of your college's nursing program in the community. How much do they know about your college and the nursing curriculum? What are the admission requirements? How many of the applicants admitted complete the program? What percent pass the state board exams?

Gather Possible Content

Rarely are you in a position to develop all the material for a project. Typically, you would begin by gathering existing information that may reside in spreadsheets or databases. Web sites, pamphlets, magazine and newspaper articles, and books could provide insights of how others have approached your topic. Personal interviews often provide perspectives not available by any other means. Consider video and audio clips as potential sources for material that might complement or support the factual data you uncover.

Determine What Content to Present to Your Audience

Experienced designers recommend writing three or four major ideas you want an audience member to remember after reading or viewing your project. It also is helpful to envision your project's endpoint, the key fact you wish to emphasize. All project elements should lead to this ending point.

As you make content decisions, you also need to think about other factors. Presentation of the project content is an important consideration. For example, will your brochure be printed on thick, colored paper or posted on the Web? Will your PowerPoint presentation be viewed in a classroom with excellent lighting and a bright projector, or will it be viewed on a notebook computer monitor? Determine relevant time factors, such as the length of time to develop the project, how long readers will spend reviewing your project, or the amount of time allocated for your speaking engagement. Your project will need to accommodate all of these constraints.

Decide whether a graph, photo, or artistic element can express or emphasize a particular concept. The right hemisphere of the brain processes images by attaching an emotion to them, so audience members are more apt to recall these graphics long term rather than just reading text.

As you select content, be mindful of the order in which you plan to present information. Readers and audience members generally remember the first and last pieces of information they see and hear, so you should place the most important information at the top or bottom of the page.

Summary

When creating a project, it is beneficial to follow some basic guidelines from the outset. By taking some time at the beginning of the process to determine the project's purpose, analyze the audience, gather possible content, and determine what content to present to the audience, you can produce a project that is informative, relevant, and effective.

Appendix B

Publishing Office 2010 Web Pages Online

With Office 2010 programs, you use the Save As command in the Backstage view to save a Web page to a Web site, network location, or FTP site. **File Transfer Protocol** (**FTP**) is an Internet standard that allows computers to exchange files with other computers on the Internet.

You should contact your network system administrator or technical support staff at your Internet access provider to determine if their Web server supports Web folders, FTP, or both, and to obtain necessary permissions to access the Web server.

Using an Office Program to Publish Office 2010 Web Pages

When publishing online, someone first must assign the necessary permissions for you to publish the Web page. If you are granted access to publish online, you must obtain the Web address of the Web server, a user name, and possibly a password that allows you to connect to the Web server. The steps in this appendix assume that you have access to an online location to which you can publish a Web page.

To Connect to an Online Location

To publish a Web page online, you first must connect to the online location. To connect to an online location using Windows 7, you would perform the following steps.

1. Click the Start button on the Windows 7 taskbar to display the Start menu.
2. Click Computer in the right pane of the Start menu to open the Computer window.
3. Click the 'Map network drive' button on the toolbar to display the Map Network Drive dialog box. (If the 'Map network drive' button is not visible on the toolbar, click the 'Display additional commands' button on the toolbar and then click 'Map network drive' in the list to display the Map Network Drive dialog box.)
4. Click the 'Connect to a Web site that you can use to store your documents and pictures' link (Map Network Drive dialog box) to start the Add Network Location wizard.
5. Click the Next button (Add Network Location dialog box).
6. Click 'Choose a custom network location' and then click the Next button.
7. Type the Internet or network address specified by your network or system administrator in the text box and then click the Next button.
8. Click 'Log on anonymously' to deselect the check box, type your user name in the User name text box, and then click the Next button.
9. If necessary, enter the name you want to assign to this online location and then click the Next button.
10. Click to deselect the Open this network location when I click Finish check box, and then click the Finish button.

11. Click the Cancel button to close the Map Network Drive dialog box.

12. Close the Computer window.

TO SAVE A WEB PAGE TO AN ONLINE LOCATION

The online location now can be accessed easily from Windows programs, including Microsoft Office programs. After creating a Microsoft Office file you wish to save as a Web page, you must save the file to the online location to which you connected in the previous steps. To save a Microsoft Word document as a Web page, for example, and publish it to the online location, you would perform the following steps.

1. Click File on the Ribbon to display the Backstage view and then click Save As in the Backstage view to display the Save As dialog box.

2. Type the Web page file name in the File name text box (Save As dialog box). Do not press the ENTER key because you do not want to close the dialog box at this time.

3. Click the 'Save as type' box arrow and then click Web Page to select the Web Page format.

4. If necessary, scroll to display the name of the online location in the navigation pane.

5. Double-click the online location name in the navigation pane to select that location as the new save location and display its contents in the right pane.

6. If a dialog box appears prompting you for a user name and password, type the user name and password in the respective text boxes and then click the Log On button.

7. Click the Save button (Save As dialog box).

The Web page now has been published online. To view the Web page using a Web browser, contact your network or system administrator for the Web address you should use to connect to the Web page.

Index

Quick Reference Summary

Task	Page Number	Mouse	Ribbon	Shortcut Menu	Keyboard Shortcut
Advanced Filter/Sort, Use	AC 153		Advanced button (Home tab | Sort & Filter group), Advanced Filter/Sort		
All Fields in Query, Include	AC 79, AC 80	Double-click asterisk			
Alternate Row Colors, Change in Datasheet	AC 181, AC 182		Select table, Alternate Row Color button arrow (Home tab | Text Formatting group), select color OR Datasheet Formatting Dialog Box Launcher (Home tab | Text Formatting group)		
Append Query, Use	AC 164		Append button (Query Tools Design Tab | Query Type group)		
Ascending Button, Use to Order Records	AC 194		Select field, Ascending button (Home tab | Sort & Filter group)	Right-click field name, click Sort A to Z or Sort Z to A	
Calculated Field in Query, Use	AC 116			Right-click field row, Zoom	
Calculated Field, Create	AC 159	In Design view, create new field, click Data Type box arrow, click Calculated			
Caption, Change in Query	AC 118		Property Sheet button (Query Tools Design Tab | Show/Hide group), Caption box	Right-click field in design grid, click Properties on shortcut menu, Caption box	
Close Object	AC 23	Close button for object		Right-click item, Close	
Collection of Legal Values, Specify	AC 167	In Design view, enter criterion specifying legal values in Validation Rule property box in Field Properties pane			

Microsoft Access 2010 Quick Reference Summary *(continued)*

Task	Page Number	Mouse	Ribbon	Shortcut Menu	Keyboard Shortcut
Column Headings, Modify	AC 54			Right-click field name, Rename Field	
Column, Resize	AC 54, AC 55	Double-click right boundary of field selector in datasheet		Right-click field name, Field Width	
Common Filter, Use	AC 150			Click arrow for field, point to Text Filters	
Comparison Operator, Use	AC 91	Create query, enter comparison operator in criterion			
Compound Criterion Involving AND, Use	AC 92				Place criteria on same line
Compound Criterion Involving OR, Use	AC 93				Place criteria on separate lines
Criteria, Use in Calculating Statistics	AC 121		Totals button (Query Tools Design Tab | Show/Hide group), Total box arrow, click calculation		
Criterion, Use	AC 46	Right-click query, Design View, Criteria row			
Crosstab Query, Create	AC 124		Query Wizard button (Create tab | Queries group), Crosstab Query Wizard		
Data, Export to Excel	AC 111		Excel button (External Data tab | Export group)	Right-click object, click Excel on Export menu	
Data, Import	AC 38		Button for imported data format (External Data tab | Import & Link group)	Right-click object, click selected format on Import menu	
Data, Sort in Query	AC 96		Select field in design grid, click Sort row, click Sort row arrow, select order		
Database Properties, Change	AC 59		View and edit database properties link (File tab | Info tab)		
Database, Create	AC 13		Blank database button (File tab | New tab)		
Default Value, Specify	AC 167	In Design view, select field in upper pane, enter value in Default Value property box in Field Properties pane			
Delete Query, Use	AC 163		Delete button (Query Tools Design tab | Query Type group)	Right-click any open area in upper pane, point to Query Type on shortcut menu, click Delete Query on Query Type submenu	

Microsoft Access 2010 Quick Reference Summary *(continued)*

Task	Page Number	Mouse	Ribbon	Shortcut Menu	Keyboard Shortcut
Design Grid, Clear	AC 95	In Design view, select all columns, DELETE			
Duplicate Records, Find	AC 193		Query Wizard button (Create tab | Queries group), Find Duplicates Query Wizard		
Duplicates, Omit	AC 97		In Design view, click first empty field, Property Sheet button (Query Tools Design tab | Show/Hide group), click Yes in Unique Values property box	Right-click first empty field, click Properties on shortcut menu, click Yes in Unique Values property box	
Field, Add to Report	AC 175		In Layout view, Add Existing Fields button (Report Layout Tools Design tab | Tools group), drag field from field list to desired location		
Field Contents, Change	AC 146	In Datasheet view, click in field, enter data			
Field in Query, Add	AC 79	Double-click field in upper pane			
Field, Add New	AC 155		In Design view, Insert Rows button (Table Tools Design Tab | Tools group)		Design view, INSERT
Field, Delete	AC 155	In Design view, click row selector for field, DELETE	Delete Rows button (Table Tools Design tab | Tools group)		
Filter by Form, Use	AC 152		Advanced button (Home tab | Sort & Filter group), Clear All Filters, Advanced button, Filter by Form		
Filter by Selection, Use	AC 148		Selection button (Home tab | Sort & Filter group), select criterion		
Filter, Clear	AC 150		Advanced button (Home tab | Sort & Filter group), Clear All Filters		
Filter, Toggle	AC 150		Toggle Filter button (Home tab | Sort & Filter group)		
Font, Change in Datasheet	AC 181		Select table, Font box arrow (Home tab | Text Formatting group), select font		
Font Color, Change in Datasheet	AC 181		Select table, Font Color button arrow (Home tab | Text Formatting group), select color		
Font Size, Change in Datasheet	AC 181		Select table, Font Size box arrow (Home tab | Text Formatting group), select size		
Form for Query, Create	AC 109		Select query, Form button (Create tab | Forms group)		

Microsoft Access 2010 Quick Reference Summary *(continued)*

Task	Page Number	Mouse	Ribbon	Shortcut Menu	Keyboard Shortcut
Form, Create	AC 48		Form button (Create tab | Forms group)		
Format, Specify	AC 168	In Design view, select field, type format			
Gridlines, Change in Datasheet	AC 180		Gridlines button (Home tab | Text Formatting group)		
Grouping, Use	AC 122	Create query, select Group By in Total row, select field to group by			
Join Properties, Change	AC 105			In Design view, right-click join line	
Lookup Field, Create	AC 156	In Design view, click Data Type column for field, Data Type box arrow, Lookup Wizard			
Make-Table Query, Use	AC 165		Make Table button (Query Tools Design tab | Query Type group)		
Multiple Keys, Sort on	AC 98	Assign two sort keys in design grid			
Multivalued Field, Query Showing Multiple Values	AC 183	Create query with specified fields			
Multivalued Lookup Field, Use	AC 172	In Datasheet view, click field, click check boxes, OK			
Navigation Pane, Customize	AC 127	Navigation Pane arrow			
Number Criterion, Use	AC 90	Create query, select table, enter criterion in field grid			
Open Database	AC 27		Open button (File tab)		
Open Table	AC 24	Double-click table in Navigation Pane		Right-click table in Navigation Pane, click Open in shortcut menu	
Parameter Query, Create	AC 87		In Design view, type parameter in square brackets in criterion row of field grid, View button (Query Tools Design tab | Results group)		
Preview or Print Object	AC 31		Print or Print Preview button (File tab | Print tab)		CTRL+P, ENTER
Query, Create in Design View	AC 78		Query Design button (Create tab | Queries group)		
Query, Create using Simple Query Wizard	AC 43		Query Wizard button (Create tab | Queries group)		

Microsoft Access 2010 Quick Reference Summary *(continued)*

Task	Page Number	Mouse	Ribbon	Shortcut Menu	Keyboard Shortcut
Query, Export	AC 111, AC 113, AC 114		Select query in Navigation Pane, application button (External Data tab | Export group)	Right-click query in Navigation Pane, click Export	
Range, Specify	AC 166	In Design view, select field, enter criterion specifying range in Validation Rule property box in Field Properties pane			
Record, Add	AC 28	New (blank) record button in Navigation buttons	New button (Home tab | Records Group)		CTRL+PLUS SIGN (+)
Record, Delete	AC 147	In Datasheet view, click record selector, DELETE	Delete button (Home tab | Records group)		DELETE
Record, Search for	AC 144		Find button (Home tab | Find group)		CTRL+F
Record, Update	AC 146	In Form view, change desired data			In Datasheet, select field and edit
Records in a Join, Restrict	AC 115	In Design view, enter criterion for query			
Referential Integrity, Specify	AC 186		Relationships button (Database Tools tab | Relationships group)		
Remaining Fields in Table, Define	AC 19	In Datasheet view, click Click to Add field (Fields tab)			
Report, Create	AC 52		Report button (Create tab | Reports group)		
Report, Create Involving Join	AC 106		Select query, Report Wizard button (Create tab | Reports group)		
Required Field, Specify	AC 166	In Design view, select field, Required property box in Field Properties pane, down arrow, Yes			
Save Object	AC 21	Save button on Quick Access Toolbar	File tab, Save		CTRL+S
Single or Multivalued Lookup Fields, Modify	AC 161	In Design view, select field, click Lookup tab in Field Properties pane, change list in Row Source property to desired list			
Split Form, Create	AC 142		Select table, More Forms button (Create tab | Forms group), Split Form		
Statistics, Calculate	AC 119		Create query, Totals button (Query Tools Design tab | Show/Hide group), click Total row in design grid, click Total box arrow, select calculation		

Microsoft Access 2010 Quick Reference Summary *(continued)*

Task	Page Number	Mouse	Ribbon	Shortcut Menu	Keyboard Shortcut
Subdatasheet, Use	AC 191	In Datasheet view, click plus sign in front of row			
Table, Create in Design View	AC 33		Table Design button (Create tab | Tables group)		
Table, View in Design View	AC 21		View button arrow (Table Tools Fields tab | Views group), Design View		
Tables, Join	AC 102		Query Design button (Create tab | Queries group), add field lists for tables to join, add desired fields to design grid, view query		
Text Data Criterion, Use	AC 80	Enter text as criterion in Criteria row of design grid			
Top Values Query, Create	AC 99		In Design view, Return box arrow (Query Tools Design tab | Query Setup group)		
Totals, Add to a Report	AC 57		Totals button (Report Layout Tools Design tab | Grouping & Totals group)		
Totals, Include in a Datasheet	AC 177		In Datasheet view, Totals button (Home tab | Records group), click Total row, click arrow		
Totals, Remove from a Datasheet	AC 179		Totals button (Home tab | Records group)		
Unmatched Records, Find	AC 193		Query Wizard button (Create tab | Queries group), Find Unmatched Query Wizard		
Update Query, Use	AC 162		Create query, Update button (Query Tools Design tab | Query Type group), select field, click Update To row in design grid	Right-click any open area in upper pane, point to Query Type on shortcut menu, click Update Query on Query Type submenu	
Wildcard, Use	AC 83	In Design view, click Criteria row in design grid, type criterion including wildcard			